JÜRGEN HABERMAS

The most important intellectual in the Federal Republic of Germany for the past three decades, Habermas has been a seminal contributor to fields ranging from sociology and political science to philosophy and cultural studies. Although he has stood at the center of concern in his native land, he has been less readily accepted outside of Germany, particularly in the humanities. His theoretical work postulates the centrality of communication and understanding, and as such his strategy of debate is marked by a politically informed unity of theory and practice.

Holub's book is the first detailed account of the major debates in which Habermas has engaged since the early 1960s. It stems from the conviction that his critics have not understood the political strategy behind his various interventions, or the consistency that informs his intellectual activities.

Habermas is viewed in dialogue with important philosophical, sociological and political currents in West Germany. Holub demonstrates how Habermas pursues a course that incorporates various aspects of his opponents' positions, while simultaneously defending perceived threats to democracy and open discussion.

Robert C. Holub is professor in the German Department at the University of California at Berkeley. His publications include *Reflections of Realism* (1991), *Reception Theory* (1984), and *Heinrich Heine's Reception of German Grecophilia* (1981). He has edited two volumes of Heine's works in English as well as the collection *Teoria della ricezione* (1989).

CRITICS OF THE TWENTIETH CENTURY
General Editor: Christopher Norris,
University of Wales,
College of Cardiff

A. J. GREIMAS AND THE NATURE OF MEANING
Ronald Schleifer

CHRISTOPHER CAUDWELL
Robert Sullivan

FIGURING LACAN
CRITICISM AND THE CULTURAL UNCONSCIOUS
Juliet Flower MacCannell

HAROLD BLOOM
TOWARDS HISTORICAL RHETORICS
Peter de Bolla

F. R. LEAVIS
Michael Bell

POSTMODERN BRECHT
A RE-PRESENTATION
Elizabeth Wright

DELEUZE AND GUATTARI
Ronald Bogue

ECSTASIES OF ROLAND BARTHES
Mary Wiseman

JULIA KRISTEVA
John Lechte

GEOFFREY HARTMAN
CRITICISM AS ANSWERABLE STYLE
G. Douglas Atkins

EZRA POUND AS LITERARY CRITIC
K. K. Ruthven

PAUL RICOEUR
S. H. Clark

JÜRGEN HABERMAS

Critic in the Public Sphere

Robert C. Holub

R ROUTLEDGE

London and New York

First published 1991
by Routledge
11 New Fetter Lane, London EC4P 4EE

Simultaneously published in the USA and Canada
by Routledge
a division of Routledge, Chapman and Hall, Inc.
29 West 35th Street, New York, NY 10001

Phototypeset in 10/12pt Palatino by
Intype, London
Printed in Great Britain by
St. Ives plc, Bungay, Suffolk

British Library Cataloguing in Publication Data
Holub. Robert C.
Jürgen Habermas: critic in the public sphere. — (Critics
of the twentieth century).
1. German philosophy. Habermas, Jürgen   2. Social
sciences. Theories of Habermas, Jürgen
I. Title   II. Series
300.92

Library of Congress Cataloging in Publication Data
Holub, Robert C.
Jürgen Habermas: critic in the public sphere / Robert C. Holub.
p. cm. – (Critics of the twentieth century)
Includes bibliographical references and index.
1. Habermas, Jürgen. 2. Sociology – Germany (West) – History.
3. Critical theory. 4. Communication – Philosophy. I. Title.
II. Series: Critics of the twentieth century (London, England)
HM22.G3H335   1991
301′.0943-dc20
90–23443

ISBN 0–415–02208–8
0–415–06511–9 (pbk)

Contents

Editor's Foreword — vii
Preface — xi

1 Introduction: intervention in the public sphere — 1
  The rise and fall of the bourgeois public sphere — 2
  Universal pragmatics and communicative action — 8
  Debating in the public sphere — 16

2 Methodology in the social sciences: the positivist
  debate — 20
  Popper's critical rationalism — 22
  Adorno's dialectical alternative — 25
  Habermas's defense of the dialectical totality — 29
  Habermas on the question of value — 33
  Hans Albert and the defense of Popper — 38
  Habermas and comprehensive rationality — 41
  Consequences of the positivist dispute — 45

3 On ideology and interpretation: the debate with
  Hans-Georg Gadamer — 49
  The hermeneutic tradition — 50
  The ontological turn in the twentieth century — 51
  Gadamer's Truth and Method — 53
  The provocation of Truth and Method — 56
  Habermas's agreement with Gadamer — 60
  Habermas's critique of tradition and authority — 64
  The dispute over hermeneutic universality — 67
  Politics and ontology — 73

Contents

4   Democracy and the student movement: the debate
with the left   78
The charge of 'leftist Fascism'   81
The phantom revolution and its children   86
Countercharges from the new left   94
The reconstruction of historical materialism   98

5   Systems and society: the debate with Niklas
Luhmann   106
Systems theory and meaning   108
The logic of systems theory   114
Meaning, truth and ideology   118
Politics and progress   124
Postscript: On complexity and democracy   129

6   Modernity and postmodernity: the debate with
Jean-François Lyotard   133
The uncompleted project of modernity   134
*Jean-François Lyotard and the heterogeneity of language
    games*   139
The narrative of postmodernity   143
The aesthetics of postmodernity   149
The philosophy of modernity   152
The defects of postmodern discourse   157

7   National Socialism and the Holocaust: the debate
with the historians   162
Bitburg and the conservative agenda   162
Rewriting German Fascism   165
Ernst Nolte and the singularity of Auschwitz   170
The impoverished public debate   176
History, politics and postconventional identity   179
Epilogue to the debate   186

Notes   190
Index   205

Editor's foreword

The twentieth century has produced a remarkable number of gifted and innovative literary critics. Indeed it could be argued that some of the finest literary minds of the age have turned to criticism as the medium best adapted to their complex and speculative range of interests. This has sometimes given rise to regret among those who insist on a clear demarcation between 'creative' (primary) writing on the one hand, and 'critical' (secondary) texts on the other. Yet this distinction is far from self-evident. It is coming under strain at the moment as novelists and poets grow increasingly aware of the conventions that govern their writing and the challenge of consciously exploiting and subverting those conventions. And the critics for their part – some of them at least – are beginning to question their traditional role as humble servants of the literary text with no further claim upon the reader's interest or attention. Quite simply, there are texts of literary criticism and theory that, for various reasons – stylistic complexity, historical influence, range of intellectual command – cannot be counted a mere appendage to those other 'primary' texts.

Of course, there is a logical puzzle here, since (it will be argued) 'literary criticism' would never have come into being, and could hardly exist as such, were it not for the body of creative writing that provide its *raison d'être*. But this is not quite the kind of knock-down argument that it might appear at first glance. For one thing, it conflates some very different orders of priority, assuming that literature always comes first (in the sense that Greek tragedy had to exist before Aristotle could formulate its rules), so that literary texts are for that very reason possessed of superior value. And this argument would seem to find commonsense support in the difficulty of thinking what 'literary criticism' could *be* if it seriously renounced all sense of the distinction between literary and critical texts. Would it not then find itself in the unfortunate position of a discipline that had willed its own demise by declaring its subject non-existent?

But these objections would only hit their mark if there were indeed a special kind of writing called 'literature' whose difference from other kinds of writing was enough to put criticism firmly in its place. Otherwise there is nothing in the least self-defeating or paradoxical about a discourse, nominally that of literary criticism, that accrues such interest on its own account as to force some fairly drastic rethinking of its proper powers and limits. The act of crossing over from commentary to literature – or of simply denying the difference between them – becomes quite explicit in the writing of a critic like Geoffrey Hartman. But the signs are already there in such classics as William Empson's *Seven Types of Ambiguity* (1928), a text whose transformative influence on our habits of reading must surely be ranked with the great creative moments of literary modernism. Only on the most dogmatic view of the difference between 'literature' and 'criticism' could a work like *Seven Types* be counted generically an inferior, sub-literary species of production. And the same can be said for many of the critics whose writings and influence this series sets out to explore.

Some, like Empson, are conspicuous individuals who belong to no particular school or larger movements. Others, like the Russian Formalists, were part of a communal enterprise and are therefore best understood as representative figures in a complex and evolving dialogue. Then again there are cases of collective identity (like the so-called 'Yale deconstructors') where a mythical group image is invented for largely polemical purposes. (The volumes in this series on Hartman and Bloom should help to dispel the idea that 'Yale deconstruction' is anything more than a handy device for collapsing differences and avoiding serious debate.) So there is no question of a series format or house-style that would seek to reduce these differences to a blandly homogeneous treatment. One consequence of recent critical theory is the realization that literary texts have no self-sufficient or autonomous meaning, no existence apart from their after-life of changing interpretations and values. And the same applies to those *critical* texts whose meaning and significance are subject to constant shifts and realignments of interest. This is not to say that trends in criticism are just a matter of intellectual fashion or the merry-go-round of rising and falling reputations. But it is important to grasp how complex are the forces – the conjunctions of historical and cultural motive – that affect the first reception and the subsequent fortunes of a critical text. This point has been raised into a systematic programme by critics like Hans-Robert Jauss, practitioners of so-called 'reception theory' as a form of historical hermeneutics. The volumes in this series will therefore be concerned not only to expound what is of lasting significance but also to set these critics in the context of present-day argument and debate. In some cases (as with Walter Benjamin) this debate takes the form of a struggle for interpretative power among disciplines with sharply opposed ideological viewpoints. Such controversies cannot simply be ignored in the interests of achieving a clear and balanced account. They point to unresolved tensions and problems which are there in the critic's work as well as in the rival appropriative readings. In the end there is no way of drawing a neat methodological line between 'intrinsic' questions (what the critic really thought) and those other, supposedly 'extrinsic' concerns that have to do with influence and reception history.

The volumes will vary accordingly in their focus and range of coverage. They will also reflect the ways in which a speculative approach to questions of literary theory has proved to have striking consequences for the human sciences at large. This breaking-down of disciplinary bounds is among the most significant developments in recent critical thinking. As philosophers and historians, among others, come to recognize the rhetorical complexity of the texts they deal with, so literary theory takes takes on a new dimension of interest and relevance. It is scarcely appropriate to think of a writer like Derrida as practising 'literary criticism' in any conventional sense of the term. For one thing, he is as much concerned with 'philosophical' as with 'literary' texts, and has indeed actively sought to subvert (or deconstruct) such tidy distinctions. A principal object in planning this series was to take full stock of these shifts in the wider intellectual terrain (including the frequent boundary disputes) brought about by critical theory. And, of course, such changes are by no means confined to literary studies, philosophy and the so-called 'sciences of man'. It is equally the case in (say) nuclear physics and molecular biology that advances in the one field have decisive implications for the other, so that specialized research often tends (paradoxically) to break down existing divisions of intellectual labour. Such work is typically many years ahead of the academic disciplines and teaching institutions that have obvious reasons of their own for adopting a business-as-usual attitude. One important aspect of modern critical theory is the challenge it presents to these traditional ideas. And lest it be thought that this is merely a one-sided takeover bid by literary critics, the series will include a number of volumes by authors in those other disciplines, including, for instance, a study of Roland Barthes by an American analytical philosopher.

We shall not, however, cleave to theory as a matter of polemical or principled stance. The series will extend to figures like F. R. Leavis, whose widespread influence went along with an express aversion to literary theory; scholars like Erich Auerbach in the mainstream European tradition; and others who resist assimilation to any clear-cut line of descent. There will also be authoritative volumes on critics such as Northrop Frye and Lionel Trilling, figures who, for various reasons, occupy an ambivalent or essentially contested place in modern critical tradition. Above all the series will strive to resist that current polarization of attitudes that sees no common ground on interest between 'literary criticism' and 'critical theory'.

CHRISTOPHER NORRIS

Preface

Jürgen Habermas has been the most important intellectual in the Federal Republic of Germany for over three decades. In fields ranging from sociology and political science to philosophy he has contributed seminally to West German intellectual life. Most previous studies of his work, however, have taken little account of his frequent conflicts and debates. Thomas McCarthy's excellent study of his work through the late 1970s, David Ingram's monograph on his monumental *Theorie des kommunikativen Handelns* (1981) [*The Theory of Communicative Action*] and Stephen White's review of his most recent work have all treated important theoretical dimensions;[1] other important monographs and collections have dealt in exemplary fashion with specific aspects of his thought: historical materialism, his relationship to the Frankfurt School, his views of modernity.[2] But none of these books seems to appreciate the significance Habermas has obviously placed on engaging others in controversy. My thesis in this book is that Habermas's debates are significant both for his own self-understanding and for the defense of democratic principles in West Germany. By focusing on the content as well as the manner of intervention, I hope not only to present major stages in the development of Habermas's thought, but also to shed light on the intellectual and political life of the Federal Republic.

My decision to write this book and to concentrate on Habermas's debates stems from my convictions that Habermas has been too easily dismissed and too often misunderstood in recent years. This is particularly true for the United States in the academic realm which I know best: the humanities. In the

1980s Habermas has frequently functioned as a straw man representing simplistic notions of enlightenment and reason. Even worse his theories have been wrongfully portrayed as politically regressive, conservative, or even potentially fascist. To a large degree the responsibility for such absurd evaluations is attributable to the continued predominance of poststructuralist thought in academic circles purportedly concerned with 'critical theory'. I do not imagine that my book will do much to convince the true believers that their judgements have been hasty or faulty. But I do hope that it can at least clarify issues for those who have not been swept away by the global and facile 'critique of reason', and show them and others how Habermas has consistently followed a progressive political strategy. My goal, then, is not only to explain Habermas's position as an abstract theorist, but to situate him as a practical agent in the ideological maelstrom of the Federal Republic. In this sense I conceive of my work, like Habermas's, as a political and theoretical intervention whose goal is open and honest discussion of meaningful issues.

I would like to express thanks to the University of California at Berkeley for financial support while I was researching and writing this book. A Humanities Research Fellowship from the University in the fall of 1989 was particularly helpful. I am also grateful for the research assistance of three students in the German Department: Courtney Federle, Linda von Hoene and Wayne Miller. I appreciate the input from members of a seminar I gave on Habermas in the spring of 1990, as well as their patience in listening to and commenting on first drafts and fragments from the final manuscript. Thanks also go to Marty Jay, Russell Berman and Peter Hohendahl for their help with the formulation of my original project. Finally, my wife, Renate Wiesner Holub often took time from her own work to give me the intellectual and moral support so necessary for this type of work. The debt I owe to her cannot be expressed in words. I would like to dedicate this monograph to our son Alexei, who recently tried to convince me of the meaninglessness of all endeavor from the perspective of the cosmos. I hope that some day I will able to convince him that the only perspective that has meaning at all is one that values and affirms human existence.

1

Introduction:
intervention in the public sphere

This book is concerned chiefly with the debates in which Jürgen Habermas has engaged. For the vast majority of contemporary intellectuals a study of scholarly or political controversies would result in a limited monograph concerning one aspect or area of an entire *oeuvre*. The main features of Habermas's thought, however, can be developed fairly comprehensively by attention to his various interventions in academic and public disputes. The frequency and significance of debate during his intellectual career are remarkable when compared with other postwar thinkers. Why has Habermas over the past three and a half decades been so eager to enter into controversy? Why has he sought to challenge so many people in various disciplines, from philosophy and sociology to history and political science, in such a variety of forums, from academic conferences and seminars to speeches at mass demonstrations and newspaper articles? One answer to these question is surely that Habermas has advanced his own theory in a 'dialectical' fashion in the older sense of that word, namely, through pointing out and overcoming arguments that he finds in his opponents' thought. Often Habermas rejects an adversarial position, but simultaneously incorporates significant dimensions of that same position into his own theoretical outlook. On one level Habermas obviously enters debates in order to learn and expand his own horizons through the complex process of absorption, adaptation, critique and self-reflection.

There are two additional reasons why debate has played such a seminal role in Habermas's intellectual *vita*. The first has to do with the political goals implicit in his work. In almost all instances Habermas has intervened in an ongoing

1

controversy or initiated a conflict when he perceived an ideological threat to his own project or to the democratic principles
that his theory supports. This dimension of his debating practice is sometimes overt, but frequently political aspects are
derivative from more abstract theoretical positions. Portions of
the following chapters are devoted to clarifying what exactly
was at stake politically for Habermas and how his critique on a
theoretical level has implications for the realm of social praxis.
Perhaps the most important reason why debate has been such
an integral part of Habermas's way of being has to do with
a consistency he has maintained between his philosophical
positions and the putting into practice of these positions in his
various talks and writings. Unlike the theorists he would later
group under the rubric 'critics of reason', Habermas's project
is in harmony with his own philosophical presuppositions. He
presents a theory of argument and controversy by means of
argument and controversy. The 'performative consistency' that
Habermas exhibits throughout his writings enhances the political appeal of his theoretical position. Ranging over a spectrum
of disciplines in the social sciences and humanities, Habermas
does not have to proceed marginally, poetically or textually in
guerrilla attacks against a putatively repressive establishment,
but rather assaults frontally the central issues in contemporary
theory and in modern society.

THE RISE AND FALL OF THE BOURGEOIS PUBLIC SPHERE

It is no coincidence that the first topic Habermas tackled after
his dissertation was the place of public debate. Nor is it atypical
of his writings that *Strukturwandel der Öffentlichkeit* (1962),
which recently appeared in English as *The Structural Transformation of the Public Sphere* (1989),[1] was one of the most influential books for the incipient oppositional movement at German
universities and one of the most hotly debated works of the
1960s. Like almost everything that Habermas has written since
that time, it elicited numerous, sometimes persuasive, often
lively responses among contemporary readers. Several books
appeared as direct replies to this work, and scores of essays
augmented, corrected, or rejected his account of the public
sphere. Almost no one ignored it, however, and scarcely a

social scientist or humanist in Germany was unfamiliar with its central premises. When compared to his later work, however, *The Structural Transformation of the Public Sphere* is slightly unusual in Habermas's *œuvre*. No other work by Habermas is as accessible as this one. While most of his more theoretical endeavors include heavy doses of philosophical abstraction and specialized vocabulary drawn from a variety of fields, *The Structural Transformation of the Public Sphere* employs a less technical sociological jargon and includes much illustrative material. In this monograph the theoretical discourse is often interrupted by talk of coffee houses, newspaper circulation or literary salons. Although it employs an interdisciplinary approach and has interdisciplinary implications, it fits the paradigm for a sociological study more readily than the works Habermas has subsequently written.

Despite its slightly anomalous character in Habermas's writings, *The Structural Transformation of the Public Sphere* articulates concerns that are foundational for his general perspective and that have continued to be important for Habermas even in his most recent work. Indeed, as recently as June 1989 he published an essay in which he sketched a normative concept of the public sphere.[2] What attracted Habermas to the notion of a public sphere then and now is its potential as a foundation for a critique of society based on democractic principles. The public sphere is a realm in which individuals gather to participate in open discussions. Potentially everyone has access to it; no one enters into discourse in the public sphere with an advantage over another. These generic qualities of the public sphere are of course subject to particularization based both on historical context and on the topics that are admitted for discussion. The bourgeois public sphere in its classical form, which is the central focus for *The Structural Transformation*, originates in the private realm; it is constituted by private citizens who deliberate on issues of public conern. The literary public sphere, which Habermas considers a prefiguration of a political public sphere oriented towards matters of state policy, deals with issues of cultural, rather than governmental concern. As an institution mediating between private interests and public power, the public sphere in its bourgeois form and political variant is based on a fundamental ideological obfuscation: the fictional identity of the property owner (*bourgeois*)

3

and the human being pure and simple (*homme*). Yet in all of its manifestations the principles of equality and accessibility are indispensable ingredients. In contrast to institutions that are controlled from without or determined by power relations, the public sphere promises democratic control and participation.

Habermas's sociological examination of the rise of the public sphere (mainly in English society) is supplemented with an account of the public sphere in the tradition of political philosophy. Most important for him in this regard is German idealism, one of the chief sources for his early theory and the focus of his earlier dissertation on Friedrich Schelling. In central chapters Habermas examines previous theorizing on matters pertaining to the public sphere in the works of Immanuel Kant and Georg Friedrich Wilhelm Hegel. The former places the public sphere at the very center of his enlightenment project. Like most thinkers of the eighteenth century, Kant conceived of public debate as the business of philosophers, not of common people. But his conception of philosophy, unlike ours today, was that it is not an exclusively academic affair without practical consequences for the lives of all citizens. Debate on a variety of issues had to be submitted to the public, conceived of course as a 'reasoning public', for decisions. His claim is that 'the public use of one's reason must always be free, and it alone can bring about enlightenment among men. The private use of reason, on the other hand, may often be very narrowly restricted without particularly hindering the progress of enlightenment.'[3] Kant considered the rise of secret societies such as the Freemasons to be the result of the restriction of public debate; and he even went so far as to consider it a natural vocation of mankind to communicate with his fellow men, especially in matters affecting mankind as a whole. He did not, of course, admit the propertyless or those who are not their own master to the citizenry of the state. And like many in the age of Enlightenment, he felt that civil society would transform itself naturally and without force into an entity capable of guaranteeing a just functioning of the state. In other words he shares the optimistic enlightenment view which maintains that private vices become public virtues, that the *bourgeois* of the private realm becomes the *citoyen* whose

4

discourse takes place from the perspective of the *homme*, from the perspective of humanity as a whole.

This view was exploded by the French Revolution as well as by subsequent historical conflicts between the classes. In Habermas's view the most incisive theorist for this new stage of development was Hegel. Severing civil society from science, Hegel contends that subjective views and opinions have nothing to do with science. As Habermas summarized his thought on this issue: 'The public opinion of the private people assembled to form a public no longer retained a basis of unity and truth; it degenerated to the level of a subjective opinion of the many.'[4] So on the one hand, Hegel's writings signal the dissolution of the liberal model in which a private sphere is complemented by a public sphere. The opinions of the multitude are degraded to common knowledge, and like common knowledge in the *Phenomenology of the Spirit*, there is no necessary relationship between what the multitude thinks and what is true. Enlightenment and publicity are thus radically separated in Hegel's system. On the other hand, Hegel sees through the liberal ideology that trusted in civil society as a natural state of affairs and accepted uncritically the equation of *bourgeois* and *homme*. He thus sets the stage for Marx's further reflections on the problem by cutting through the delusions of enlightenment thought.

Marx starts by analyzing further the notion of civil society. In contrast to his predecessors, he finds that it should not be conceived as a unity, but rather as a contradictory entity composed of classes that are necessarily antagonistic to one another. Public opinion as it is manifested in the bourgeois public sphere therefore amounts to false consciousness. Like Hegel, Marx presupposes a radical separation of civil society from science; but unlike his idealist predecessor, he sees the public sphere as an arena of conflict. The notion of general accessibility and unconstrained dialogue is an obfuscation by and of bourgeois ideology, since it stands in contradiction to the empirical reality of the public sphere in capitalist societies. The question Marx leaves us with is the following: is the public sphere able to hold to its own premises without dissolving civil society? One key difference between Marx and Habermas is the way in which each answers this question. Marx cannot envision a public sphere that realizes the ideal conditions imputed to it by bourgeois ideology within bourgeois society. The satisfaction of the demands for true accessibility and total lack of constraint can only be achieved through the socialization of the means of production and thus the destruction of the category of bourgeois (and proletariat). This situation can only come about, Marx contends, through a violent revolution that removes all class antagonism. Habermas, although he never deals with the question directly, suggests that something like a public sphere can be realized without recourse to the violent overthrow of the existing social order. This does not mean that significant and drastic changes are unnecessary for unconstrained public debate to occur. But in general, Habermas places greater faith in those potentially democratic forms that have developed in bourgeois society.

None the less, the public sphere, at least its bourgeois prototype, began to decline during the course of the past century, and Habermas devotes the final third of his book to a discussion of its demise. The collapse occurs because of the intervention of the state into private affairs and the penetration of society into the state. Since the rise of the public sphere depended on a clear separation between the private realm and public power, their mutual interpenetration inevitably destroys it. The role that the public sphere had played in the intellectual life of society is then assumed by other institutions that reproduce the image of a public sphere in distorted guise. Parliament, for example, has its ideological origins in the same bourgeois ideology that promoted a public sphere, but its development gradually belies its ideal form. As we progress into the twentieth century, the free exchange of ideas among equals becomes transformed into less democratic communicative forms, for example public relations. Party politics and the manipulation of the mass media lead to what Habermas calls a 'refeudalization' of the public sphere, where representation and appearances outweigh rational debate. He analyzes this and kindred symptoms of modern society in some detail, although his basis for analysis appears more restricted than in his earlier discussion of the rise and constitution of the public sphere. Too often Habermas's remarks on modern society are too strongly tied to the postwar situation in the Federal Republic, which, because of its status as a European, a vanquished and a formerly Fascist nation, may be atypical of modern

6

societies. The inclusion of the United States or a country like Japan might have forced Habermas to rethink some of his conclusions, particularly as they relate to family structure and the welfare state.

This narrowing of scope is one of the chief weaknesses of the volume. But the work also evidences other problems of a more theoretical nature. Chief among these is the oscillation between normative concepts and historical accounts. At times it appears that Habermas wants to merge history and theory in the notion of the bourgeois public sphere. This appearance is fostered by the fact that the text is structured as a rise and fall, and it is reinforced by the talk of a 'refeudalization' of the public sphere in the final chapters. If the bourgeois variant does serve as the norm for the public sphere, then Habermas has opened a methodological conundrum. Marxist analysis of concepts, to which Habermas would subscribe at this stage of his development, has more often followed the remarks Marx himself made in the Introduction to the *Grundrisse* (1857–8).[5] Here Marx states that only the most fully developed form enables us to understand the history of a concept. The bourgeois norm for the public sphere, however, does not occur in fully developed bourgeois society, but rather in its early liberal phase; some critics have even suggested that if such a sphere existed at all it should be located in the incipient phases of bourgeois society when it began to assert itself against feudalism. No matter where we locate the public sphere historically, it seems certain that the bourgeois ideal must possess normative value for all notions of the public sphere. Habermas conceives of the bourgois public sphere as an ideological anticipatory form that, like ideology itself, 'transcends the status quo in utopian fashion'.[6] If he did not, the construct would forfeit all political relevance, and this work would amount to an antiquarian investigation of an obsolete institution.

At the basis of this vacillation between normative and historical description is a conceptual tension that originates in Habermas's indebtedness to two different traditions of political thought. To a large degree Habermas adheres to the critique of twentieth-century society developed by his predecessors in the Frankfurt School. Enunciated in its most drastic and pessimistic form in Adorno and Horkheimer's *Dialektik der Aufklärung* (1947) [*Dialectic of Enlightenment*], this critique suggests that mass culture and instrumental rationality have captured the political stage to such a degree that no leverage point exists for effective oppositional activity. The single qualification of this bleak picture, found in Adorno's valorization of certain types of esoteric art, provides scant hope for any genuine political change either. Habermas shares in this vision when he discusses the bureaucratization of society, the role of the mass media in manipulating or curtailing public discussion and the bourgeois system of political parties.

Yet frequent remarks demonstrate that he does not partake completely in the general pessimism of Adorno and Horkheimer, that he appreciates more than they did the positive aspects of the political thought of the Enlightenment. He recognizes that it is impossible to return to the liberal public sphere as it once existed – if in fact it ever existed – but he is unwilling to relinquish the conceptual underpinnings he has associated with it. This difference in attitude stems largely from Habermas's more differentiated analysis of the modern world. German Fascism and the American culture industry often appear equally pernicious in the writings of the first generation of the Frankfurt School. Habermas's more favourable, although hardly uncritical, views on the Western heritage cause him to find a ray of hope even in the stifling political climate of contemporary parliamentary democracies.

UNIVERSAL PRAGMATICS AND COMMUNICATIVE ACTION

This ray of hope becomes, so to speak, the sunbeam shining on communicative action in Habermas's later theory. Rational discourse that is free from both domination and linguistic pathology, and oriented towards intersubjective understanding and consensus is precisely the type of activity appropriate to the public sphere. Departing from a theory about the societal location for democratic discourse, Habermas proceeded in the next two decades to ground a critical theory of society in language itself. He chose this route, however, only after his initial foundational attempts had failed. The document of this failure is *Erkenntnis und Interesse* (1968) [*Knowledge and Human Interests*], the first volume in the most prestigious series published by Suhrkamp, the foremost publisher of theoretical works in Germany since the war. Habermas's thesis in this book should probably be read as an outgrowth of or a reflection on the positivist dispute, which is discussed in detail in the next chapter. Essentially he postulates three deep-seated interests that inform our preoccupation with various branches of knowledge. The technical interest is invoked to describe our relationship to nature. In the empirico-analytical sciences our endeavor to control and manipulate nature leads to what Habermas calls monological knowledge. Our practical interest is associated with intersubjectivity and communication. In the historical-hermeneutic sciences we encounter the interest in reaching mutual understanding and self-understanding in the conduct of our daily lives. Finally, and most controversially, Habermas posits an emancipatory interest that describes our ability to reflect critically on our own presuppositions. This interest is emancipatory because it allows us to free ourselves from constraints imposed on us by non-natural, i.e. human, causes. In this category Habermas includes both philosophical reflection and self-criticism in the spirit of Marx and of Freud.

The position developed in *Knowledge and Human Interests* elicited even more critical response than *Structural Transformation*. One of the central criticisms concerned the status of the three interests Habermas had defined. Habermas himself had called them 'quasi-transcendental', a description that was clearly meant to hedge his bets. In one sense they were obviously associated with Kantian transcendentals in that they were conditions of possibility for knowledge as such. But they were non-Kantian in that they originate in human history and develop with the progress of humankind. Such a half-way stance came to be intolerable even for Habermas, and he eventually abandons this description. Even more troublesome, however, was his postulation of an emancipatory interest and his linking of it to the notion of reflection. The problem was that reflection was made to do double duty. On the one hand, as consideration of the subjective conditions of possibility for knowledge in general, it is part of the mainstream philosophical tradition from Socrates through Kant. On the other hand, it refers more particularly to a subject's reflection on specific obfuscations that have developed in the course of human history and the resultant reorientation of action on the basis of ridding oneself of these obfuscations. The former does not necessarily involve anything emancipatory; the latter does. Habermas addresses this issue, but never resolves it, probably because he discarded interest as the basis for critical theory and turned instead, like so many twentieth-century philosophers, to the paradigm of language.

Habermas's linguistic turn is already evident in his afterword to *Knowledge and Human Interests*, where he admits that 'the paradigm of language has led to a reframing of the transcendental model'.[7] During the late 1960s and early 1970s, Habermas gradually abandons the model of cognition based on quasi-transcendental interests and concentrates his research project on what would later be called a 'Theory of Communicative Action'.[8] Some of the steps toward this theory are recapitulated later in discussion of the debates with Hans Albert, Hans-Georg Gadamer and Niklas Luhmann. The cornerstone of this turn towards language, and of Habermas's work since *Knowledge and Human Interests*, was the notion of universal pragmatics, which he developed in conjunction with the work of Karl-Otto Apel, a noted expert in the philosophy of language. Pragmatics is the branch of linguistics that deals with actual utterance. If we think of Ferdinand de Saussure's distinction between *langue* (language) and *parole* (speech), then pragmatics would be the study of the latter of these two terms. It is a relative late-comer to the field of linguistics; the traditional field of study has included phonetics and phonology, the areas dealing with the creation of sounds, morphology, which studies word units, syntax or grammar, which deals with the structure of phrases and sentences, and semantics, which examines meaning. Pragmatics, which studies the performative aspect of language, has been an accepted field of linguistic endeavor for only the past quarter of a century, and the boundary line between it and semantics is still not clear. Indeed, it can be persuasively argued that one should be subsumed under the other.

Habermas approaches the topic of pragmatics differently from most linguistic practitioners. In almost all definitions of pragmatics by linguists we note a dependence on what we might call the empirical as opposed to the universal, general, formal or theoretical. If we divide enquiry into language the way it is usually divided – into *langue* and *parole*, or competence and performance – then, as we have already seen, pragmatics is usually said to encompass the latter parts of these dichot-omies. Most linguistic analysis deals with sounds, words or sentences as abstract or generalized entities; pragmatics deals with the performance of these abstract entities or the concretiz-ation of general rules or laws in particular utterances. Haber-mas, however, is not interested in the empirical realm of actual statements or in categorizing statements or in actual speaker intention, motivation or context. Rather he is looking for prin-ciples that are active on a general or universal level whenever we use language pragmatically. This has been done only for the *langue* or competence side of the linguistic equation in the past. But Habermas wants to do the same for the *parole* or performance side of the dichotomy. He contends that the prag-matic dimension of language from which one usually abstracts is itself not beyond formal analysis, that speech also has a universal dimension. He further maintains that this universal dimension is accessible on a basis other than semiotics or a model of coding and decoding, since these options do not permit reflection on the conditions of possibility of utterances, which are Habermas's main concern. The field of study he proposes is thus called universal pragmatics because it exam-ines the performative aspect of language, not by taking an empirical (psycholinguistic and sociolinguistic) or behaviorist approach (associated with semiotics), but through the more Kantian investigation of the formal conditions of possibility for concrete utterances.

The immediate problem Habermas encounters is how to investigate the topic of universal pragmatics. Normally studies of pragmatics approach their topic with empirical methods, collecting data and making inferences from this data. Obvi-ously what Habermas has in mind is not a matter for empirical investigation, since he is not interested in the laws that actual utterances obey, nor in what speaking subjects report about their intentions or motivation for making specific utterances, but rather in the universal conditions that underlie the pro-duction of all utterances. Habermas therefore opts for what he terms a 'rational reconstruction'. Reconstructive procedures are non-nomological and formal, as opposed to empirical, and they are 'characteristic of *sciences that systematically reconstruct the intuitive knowledge of competent subjects*'.[9] Habermas clarifies the distinction between empirical and reconstructive sciences by postulating three levels of knowledge. The first entails direct observation of the objective world. Habermas is not naive enough to think that perception itself is unmediated, but this type of interaction can be called direct because it does not involve intersubjectivity and hence it is not mediated by language. This is what he means when he writes that 'sensory experience is related to sectors of reality immediately'.[10] This is the domain of the natural sciences and corresponds to the realm of the technical interest in *Knowledge and Human Interests*.

The second level, which involves statements made about reality, is what really interests Habermas. On this level, which corresponds somewhat to the realm of practical interests, we deal with reality mediately through language. This dichotomy between an investigation of nature and a preoccupation with the human sphere of action should be fairly familiar from the traditional separation of the natural from the human sciences. It is related to the distinction made by Giambattista Vico in the eighteenth century and to Wilhelm Dilthey's separation of a realm of explanation (*Erklären*) in the natural sciences from the realm of understanding (*Verstehen*) in the *Geisteswissenschaften*. Habermas also treats these two areas with sets of binary terms: perceptible reality versus symbolically prestructured reality; observation versus understanding; explanation of causal meaning versus explication of meaning; description and explication. Habermas, however, claims that this level contains two distinct applications. The first is directed to the semantic content of the symbolic formation, to the explication of meaning. A second level entails looking beyond the surface level of meaning to the very rules that inform the production of utterances or that inform linguistic interaction. This is the level of reconstruction. It examines 'the domains of pretheoretical knowledge' or 'intuitive foreknowledge'. With this Habermas does not mean merely unconscious assumptions or prejudices on the part of a particular speaking subject; this would be a worthwhile study and could conform to the projects of a critique of ideology or of Freudian analysis and would thus fall into the earlier category of reflection. What he means, by contrast, are the general rules by which every interaction is governed. He is aiming here at universal rules of pretheoretical knowledge or universal capabilities built into the human being for the production of utterances.

12

To carry out his rational reconstruction Habermas recruits two theoretical aids. The first is Popper's three-world theory. Like Popper, Habermas assumes that we exist simultaneously in (1) an external world of states of affairs and objects; (2) an internal world of ideas, thoughts, emotions; and (3) a normative world of intersubjectively determined norms and values. Every statement, according to Habermas, relates to these three worlds because implicit in all utterances is a relationship to (1) an external state of affairs; (2) an internal motivation or intention; and (3) a normative reality. In turn, these relationships imply validity claims that would not be present in the abstract world of conventional linguistic analysis, but only under pragmatic conditions. These validity claims are four in number: comprehensibility, truth, truthfulness and correctness or appropriateness. Comprehensibility is a claim fulfilled within language itself and thus does not belong to pragmatics. So the object domain of universal pragmatics is mapped out according to the remaining three validity claims. With regard to the first world: to study acts of reference and predication; with regard to the second world, to study linguistic expression of intention; and with regard to the third world, to study via illocutionary speech acts the way in which interpersonal relations are established.

Habermas concentrates his efforts in the last of these areas, calling on the theory of speech acts to assist him. Speech act theory is a branch of contemporary enquiry that was inspired by the later work of Ludwig Wittgenstein, and continued by his student J. L. Austin and by John Searle. Habermas believes that speech act theory can serve as a foundation for universal pragmatics since it postulates a general communicative competence and is concerned with 'the conditions for a happy employment of sentences in utterances'.[11] Most important for Habermas is Austin's discussion of 'illocutionary acts'. The performance of a locutionary act is simply the act of saying something; an illocutionary act refers to the act of doing a specific task with language: promising, wishing, commanding and so on.[12] Habermas redefines Austin's notions slightly to fit his tripartite scheme of worlds and the corresponding validity claims. He divides the locutionary act into a propositional component and a special class of illocutionary acts called 'constative speech acts'.[13] This division allows him to establish two levels for every speech act: a propositional level and an illocutionary level. Habermas maintains further that there are exactly three uses of language. The cognitive use of language is concerned with propositional content and employs constatives as the predominant speech act. The interactive mode of communication establishes interpersonal relations through regulatives (commands, promises, recommendations, etc.): these are speech acts that 'characterize a specific relation that speaker and hearer can adopt to norms of action or evaluation'.[14] Finally, in its expressive function, avowals are used to divulge the intentions of the speaker. These three modes of communication – cognitive, interactive and expressive – correlate with the validity claims of truth, appropriateness and truthfulness respectively. The following table summarizes these various relationships.[15]

Mode of communication	Type of speech action	Theme	Thematic validity claim
Cognitive	Constatives	Propositional content	Truth
Interactive	Regulatives	Interpersonal relation	Rightness appropriateness
Expressive	Avowals	Speaker's intention	Truthfulness

Finally Habermas wants to establish a rational basis for the validity claims he has postulated. Austin and Searle had sought the conditions of acceptability for speech acts by examining their institutional setting. If conventional preconditions are not fulfilled, then the speech act will not succeed or will be infelicitous. It is inappropriate for a lieutenant to utter a command to a general; a promise cannot be made successfully to someone who does not want the promised task to be done. Habermas, however, is examining conditions of a different and noninstitutional variety. He is interested in 'conditions for acceptability that lie within the institutionally unbound speech act itself'.[16] He argues that validity claims are precisely such conditions; every utterance necessarily includes an implicit reference to truth, appropriateness and truthfulness. Furthermore the guarantee of rationality is grounded in the potential testability and criticizability of all validity claims. The cognitive

14

use of language demands of us that we supply reasons for assertions, and these can be checked by the experience of the listener. The interactive use of language compels us to provide justification. If there is a dispute, the speaker and listener can proceed to the level of 'discourse' concerning the normative assumptions. The expressive use of language brings with it the obligation to demonstrate trustworthiness. This is checked by examining the consequence of the action and by the simple experience of consistency of behavior.

The rationality built into universal pragmatics informs Habermas's theory of communicative actions. In contrast to the instrumental rationality that depends on a subject-object relationship, Habermas posits communicative rationality as the basis for a critical social theory. In his later work he often contrasts a 'philosophy of consciousness', which proceeds from a solitary subject contemplating the world, to a notion of inter-subjectivity, where shared meanings, norms and values predominate. What Habermas finds confirmed in his dealings with language and in his analysis of universal pragmatics is the primacy of actions oriented towards reaching an understanding, as opposed to controlling or manipulating objects or other agents in the world. His theory thus has an analytical as well as a utopian dimension. A theory of communicative action grounded on the validity claims inherent in normal speech provides a vehicle for criticizing the distortions of communication that have characterized human history. But such a theory also envisions as its never-realizable *telos* a state in which unconstrained, perfectly free communication occurs. With the theory of communicative action, therefore, Habermas has come full circle and arrived back at his starting point in the public sphere. But now the entity that was portrayed in terms of a bourgeois institution that underwent a demise in the modern age is conceived as a state of affairs whose realization lies in the future. On the basis of his linguistically based model Habermas has been able to provide a substantive foundation for free debate as the rationale and goal of social existence.

DEBATING IN THE PUBLIC SPHERE

Habermas's theoretical emphasis on argument and public debate has a practical counterpart in his actual interventions at pivotal points in the intellectual and political life of the Federal Republic. Indeed, one of the very first essays he published initiated a small and politically significant controversy. At issue was the republication in 1953 of Martin Heidegger's 1935 lecture *Einführung in die Metaphysik* [*An Introduction to Metaphysics*]. In a critical review in the *Frankfurter Allgemeine Zeitung* Habermas used this publication as an opportunity to discuss the Fascist perversion of learning and the apologetic tendencies in the early Adenauer era that make the appearance of such texts possible. Heidegger's complicity with the National Socialists was well known in Germany in the early 1950s, and Habermas does not care to rehearse the details of his involvement. More upsetting is the total absence of repentance or understanding signaled by the republication of a text without commentary and without qualifying footnotes. Habermas has to assume that Heidegger still subscribes to his claim that 'the movement' (a term used during the Third Reich to refer to the National Socialist movement) contains an 'inner truth and greatness', and that his appeal to Germany as a land caught in the middle is still his current thinking on the geopolitical situation. In short, Habermas judges Heidegger's philosophical work to be in consonance with his political views from the 1930s. The lecture from 1935 evidences clearly the 'fascist coloration of the time'[17] and seeks, in the abstract language of ontology, to inculcate today's students with the identical values that led to catastrophe.

Habermas's review appeared on 25 July. On 13 August a defense of Heidegger penned by Christian E. Lewalter appeared in *Die Zeit*. Lewalter begins and ends his apology by casting political innuendoes from the cold war: he condemns the witch-hunt on Fascists, supposedly conducted in Frankfurt by the 'neo-Marxist' Theodor Adorno, and discredits Habermas as someone who takes from Marx alone 'his criteria for his critique of philosophers'.[18] In the body of the article Lewalter does admit that Heidegger had some involvement with National Socialism, but he asserts that the *Introduction to Metaphysics* demonstrates precisely Heidegger's distance from the politics he had momentarily embraced. Like most of Heidegger's apologists before and since, he produces a series of citations that purportedly show the philosopher's disapproval of and disdain for Hitler and his party. The sentence referring to the 'inner truth and greatness of the movement' is interpreted as a rejection of current National Socialist philosophy and politics. In a letter to *Die Zeit* of 24 September 1953 Heidegger himself supports Lewalter's interpretation and claims that he intentionally left the questionable sentence in the manuscript:

> It would have been very easy to strike the sentence from the printed version. . . . I did not do this and will keep it this way in the future. In the first place the sentences belong to the lecture historically, and, moreover, I am convinced that the lecture can tolerate these sentences for a reader who has learned the skill of thinking.

Heidegger closes by assuring readers of the newspaper that 'those who could hear among the auditors' [*die Hörenden unter den Hörern*] understood what he said very precisely.[19]

The debate broke off abruptly at this point and was taken up again only indirectly in the 1970s and 1980s. As far as we can tell, Heidegger came back to the issue of his involvement only once, in an interview with the news magazine *Der Spiegel* that he insisted be published posthumously.[20] In the 1953 book that Habermas had reviewed the following parenthetical comment appeared after the phrase referring to the 'internal truth and greatness of the movement': 'namely with the meeting of planetary specific technology and contemporary humanity'. Habermas did not question that this phrase was in the original manuscript, feeling evidently that no qualification exonerates Heidegger's praise of National Socialism. The interviewer from the *Spiegel* asked Heidegger, however, whether this parenthetical remark was actually in the manuscript and whether he actually included it in his 1935 lecture. Heidegger insisted that the printed version was taken directly from the original manuscript, but that he did not say those qualifying words in 1935. He had to avoid the suspicion of spies – Heidegger portrays himself as persecuted during the Third Reich; but most students understood what was meant.

The publication of the book *Heidegger et le nazisme* (1987)

[*Heidegger and Nazism*] by Victor Farias[21] cast new doubt on this and other apologies proffered by Heidegger and his friends. From Farias we learn in general that Heidegger's involvement with National Socialism was deeper and had a greater duration than we previously knew. The foreword to the German edition of Farias's book was written by Habermas, whose political agenda was slightly different in the second half of the 1980s than in the early 1950s. His later comments on Heidegger should be seen as part of his struggle with neo-Heideggerian currents in France and with neo-conservatism on the German political scene. In this foreword Habermas comes back to the disputed sentence and reveals that Heidegger had been candid neither in his 1953 publication of the *Introduction to Metaphysics*, nor in his letter to *Die Zeit*, nor in the *Spiegel* interview. One of the three persons who assisted in preparing the manuscript has stated that there was no parenthetical remark in the original manuscript. The three assistants, horrified by the remark, advised Heidegger to delete it entirely. Instead of following their advice, he decided to retain the sentence and include the parenthetical clarification cited above. Curiously, this manuscript page is now missing in Heidegger's archive.[22]

This minor skirmish from 1953 with Heidegger's disingenuousness and political prevarication would be inconsequential if it did not foreshadow Habermas's intellectual path. In the subsequent three and a half decades he has spoken out often against regressive tendencies in the Federal Republic and consistently supported democracy and a theoretical position that furthers democratic principles. The remainder of this volume treats six major confrontations in which Habermas was centrally involved. Sometimes these conflicts occurred within academic settings and involved theoretical matters. Chapter 2 deals with the methodological issues surrounding his debate with Hans Albert and 'positivism' in the social sciences. In Chapter 3 the topic is hermeneutics and its relationship to a reflective, critical theory. Chapter 5 takes up Habermas's debate with Niklas Luhmann's systems theory, the chief sociological challenge to Habermas's analysis of modern society, while the following chapter examines the philosophical dispute with poststructuralism. Despite the academic nature of these various controversies, Habermas's interventions aided in bringing them out of the narrow confines of the academy, and to a larger reading public. By contrast, the student movement and the historians' debate, dealt with in Chapters 4 and 7, were initiated as public issues. Common to all these debates is Habermas's refusal to separate philosophical positions and political implications or to admit a cleavage between theory and practice. Indeed, this is perhaps his major advantage over his various adversaries. No matter what the merits of his individual arguments may be, and no matter how they may strike the readers of this book, we must acknowledge to Habermas's credit that he consistently practices the theoretical positions that he preaches.

2

Methodology in the social sciences: the positivist debate

The first major debate in which Habermas was engaged became known by the name of the 'positivist dispute in German sociology', a controversy that initially attracted much attention in Germany and subsequently gained a certain notoriety in other parts of the world. Perhaps the most unusual part of this dispute was that its title was almost totally inappropriate to the issues being discussed. In the first place none of the participants sought to defend or to represent positivism. Although the advocates of a dialectical procedure, Habermas and Theodor Adorno, accused Karl Popper and his German disciple Hans Albert of positivist methodology, both of the accused denied the accuracy of this label, preferring instead the name of critical rationalist. Indeed, Popper's self-understanding of his methodological stance is that he was one of the first to firmly oppose positivism as a valid approach to research. If we conceive of positivism as it is customarily described in philosophical handbooks, then Popper would most definitely have to be excluded from the category.

In its original sense positivism is associated with Auguste Comte, the nineteenth-century sociologist who juxtaposed the investigation of positive facts, the observation of phenomena and the inductive development of laws to metaphysical speculation and theological dogma. It has come to be identified with empirical methods of investigation and in particular with a unified approach to research that claims universality for the methods of the natural sciences. Logical positivism, an early twentieth-century offshoot of certain empiricist positions, is perhaps best known for its efforts to separate the realm of logic and reason from the unverifiable speculation of metaphysics. The most celebrated philosophers of logical positivism were the members of the Vienna School in the late 1920s and 1930s. Popper had many connections with this Viennese group and shared common concerns, but his relationship was a critical one. Although in the postwar period he has sometimes been identified as a positivist, in his intellectual autobiography he feels compelled to 'admit responsibility' for killing logical positivism.[1] It is therefore understandable that in the English edition of the essays from the positivism dispute he strongly objects to his inclusion in a movement he had adamantly and repeatedly rejected.[2]

The location of the debate seems to be as vaguely defined as the topic about which the participants supposedly debated. Both the German book and the English translation give the impression that this controversy took place inside the confines of German sociology and therefore raise the expectations that the discussion revolves around sociological theory. But this is only superficially true. Although the initial contributions by Karl Popper and Theodor Adorno were presented as part of a conference held by the German Sociological Association in Tübingen in 1961, their concerns transcend what is traditionally conceived as sociology. Both Popper and Adorno, after all, are better known as philosophers, and Habermas, who joined the fray belatedly a few years later, is likewise not a sociologist by training or academic appointment. Indeed, the issues that were most important in this dispute concern the philosophy of science, differences between the natural and the social sciences, the appropriateness of traditional logic and the approach to social sciences in general. At one point Adorno even remarks ironically that he hopes René König, the editor of a leading sociology journal, will not be upset that the discussion is more about philosophy than sociology (p. 118). Sociology as a traditional academic discipline is not the focal point for any of the interlocutors; the central concerns are more accurately formulated in the title of Adorno's reply, which Habermas subsequently used for one of his books: *Zur Logik der Sozialwissenschaften* ['On the Logic of the Social Sciences'].

Finally, the appropriateness of the designation 'dispute' can itself be disputed. Considering that Popper and Adorno are two philosophers who hold such divergent opinions on politics, worldview and method, there was really very little obvious difference of opinion. The fault for this does not lie with Popper, who, as we shall see, expressed his views with his usual forcefulness and brashness, but with Adorno, who seemed content to articulate his objections under the cloak of apparent agreement. Ralf Dahrendorf, who was assigned the task of commenting on the dispute, expressed what was apparently a general feeling of disappointment at the 'lack of intensity' in the two presentations and the 'lack of tension' between them. 'At times', he continues, 'it could indeed have appeared, astonishingly enough, as if Popper and Adorno were in agreement' (pp. 123–4). The intellectual positions of Popper and Adorno may have been formulated with precision, as Dahrendorf maintained, but it was not until Habermas's contribution to the discussion in 1963 and Hans Albert's reply to him the following year that the two sides of this controversy were expounded with equal distinctness.

POPPER'S CRITICAL RATIONALISM

If in its initial phase the 'positivist dispute in German sociology' is neither about positivism, nor in German sociology, nor a confrontational dispute, we might want to enquire what the series of misnomers conceals. The best way to do this is to look at what the two sides apparently agreed about: the inadequacy of positivism as a methodology. The objections to positivism are best expressed by Popper, who prefers the term naturalism or scientism. In the seventh of the twenty-seven theses that comprise his initial presentation Popper first cites a familiar view of how most people believe scientists proceed with their work. According to this belief scientists begin with observations and measurements, collecting data carefully and compiling statistics from it. Perceiving patterns and regularities, they then advance by induction to general conclusions or laws that describe their data. This approach secures objectively since the scientist endeavors to eliminate all subjective prejudices. When applied to the social sciences such a procedure may then be termed 'value-free', meaning that the researcher brackets to the largest possible extent his/her own values and opinions.

Popper and Adorno concur that this description is a myth that has unfortunately gained currency in the social sciences.

They differ, however, on both their reason for rejecting this myth and the alternative they propose. Popper claims that naturalism or scientism is not only an inaccurate depiction of the way scientists actually go about their business, but also no guarantee for objectivity or value-freedom. Scientists do not start by collecting data, but rather from problems to which they formulate tentative solutions. These solutions must be open to criticism, which may be based on observation and the collection of data. If a solution is refuted, the scientist tries another solution until a solution is found that withstands criticism temporarily. This solution is then accepted until further criticism refutes it. Science thus proceeds not inductively from observation to generalized laws, but deductively. By the word 'deduction' Popper is not so much concerned with the transmission of truth from premises to conclusions, that is, the notion that if the premises are true, then the inferences from these true premises are also true. Rather he is concerned with the transmission of falsity from the conclusions to the premises. If we find that conclusions are false, then one or more of the initial assumptions must also be false. The procedure of the scientist therefore depends not on theories derived inductively from positive facts, but on the falsification of tentative solutions proposed to problems. The science of nature as well as the social sciences are conducted as never-ending trial-and-error experiments.

Popper must also dispute the purported objectivity of scientific procedures. In the mythical schema he outlines, the objectivity of science depends on the objectivity of the scientist. Only when the scientist as person eliminates all subjective presuppositions is an objective result secured. Popper, by contrast, shifts objectivity from the person to the critical method itself, claiming that objectivity is the social result of the mutual criticism of scientists. According to this view the natural scientist is neither more nor less partisan or 'subjective' than his social science counterpart. All science derives its objectivity from a critical tradition that allows and fosters the criticism of dominant theories. Objectivity in science is related directly to social and political circumstances, not to prejudices of the individual investigator. Ultimately it is explicable in terms of social ideas such as competition (both of individual scientists and of various schools); tradition (mainly the critical tradition); social institutions (for instance, publication in various competing journals and through various competing publishers; discussion at congresses); the power of the state (its tolerance of free discussion). (p. 96)

In describing objectivity in these terms, Popper has obviously severed it from its usual connections with a reality existing independent of the human mind. His point seems to be that speculation on such a reality is meaningless. If we want a functional notion of objectivity, the best we can do is to guarantee the conditions within which scientists can apply the critical-rationalist method to general nomological claims.

Popper's position on value is slightly different. He begins by asserting two different realms of values. One relates to the truth of an assertion and its relevance, interest, and significance to matters under investigation. We might conceive of this realm as inner-scientific. A second realm refers us to the relevance and interest for assertions outside the narrower field of scientific endeavor; this is the arena of extra-scientific problems. With regard to values, Popper summarizes as follows: 'in other words, there exist *purely* scientific values and disvalues and *extra*-scientific values and disvalues' (p. 97). The task of scientific criticism is then to maintain this separation, to assure that extra-scientific evaluations do not become confounded with 'questions of truth'. This ideal to which Popper subscribes is one of the 'enduring tasks of mutual scientific criticism' (p. 97). It can never be attained, but the integrity of science demands that we fight for it.

There are at least two problems with this distinction, and both are consequences of Popper's own argument. First, in his discussion of objectivity, the foundation of scientific procedure was deemed to be the extra-scientific, i.e. the social and the political. The values of the scientific community, the society, and the state must therefore be such that they permit the critical method to function. So it is difficult to see how purely scientific and extra-scientific values can be separated, or why it is necessary to isolate the former, when the latter serves as its basis. As Popper later states, our purely scientific ideals are anchored in the extra-scientific. Second, the affirmation of objectivity or value-freedom as desirable features of scientific procedure is itself the expression of a value. In short, value-freedom is itself a value. Popper thinks that this insight is of little significance and advocates instead of value-freedom the separation of values internal and external to science. But this will not do. For the affirmation of the necessity to separate purely scientific and extra-scientific as something desirable for or essential to scientific method is also a value rooted in the realm Popper has labeled extra-scientific. No matter how he twists his argument, Popper is unable to maintain the initial distinction in values that he posits. Not only is there no neat or eternal distinction between purely scientific and extra-scientific values, reference to the latter realm always undermines any attempt to distill scientific purity from the contamination of the non-scientific world.

ADORNO'S DIALECTICAL ALTERNATIVE

Adorno's agreement with Popper extends only to the rejection of the erroneous naturalist paradigm and its extension to social scientific research. When Adorno refers to 'positivism' it seems that, depending on the context, he means both more and less than Popper's brief description of scientism. He means more in that he extends the category to cover all procedures that isolate objects without reference to the totality of relations in which they are necessarily embedded. In his specific discussions of sociology, however, he means less since he tends to reduce positivism to empirical survey studies. These studies are not without a place in research. The Frankfurt School often undertook empirical studies in examining the authoritarian personality, and Adorno himself points to the importance of these investigations. Although they only reflect the subjective and reified opinions of the subjects interviewed or surveyed, and therefore represent ideology or false consciousness, Adorno, relying on Hegel, recognizes that even false consciousness is a part of social reality. Empirical research may not deliver the essence of any given question, but 'appearance is always also an appearance of essence and not mere illusion' (p. 84). For Adorno 'positivism' in sociological research is not illicit as long as it is accompanied by a realization of what its results represent.

Paradoxically, then, Adorno appears to be more tolerant of positivism than the philosopher whom he accuses of adhering to this doctrine. But this tolerance is strictly limited by a distinction that Adorno draws and Popper does not. From Popper's talk it is evident that he conceives of critical rationalism as a method applicable to both natural and social science. He draws no distinction between problems that arise in the course of our interaction with nature and those that pertain to society and history. Adorno, by contrast, insists on separating the method for achieving genuine knowledge in social sciences from other approaches to knowledge. The line Adorno draws is not quite the traditional one between the natural and the social sciences found in the works of Vico, Herder, Dilthey and Rickert. As we have just seen, research in the social sciences may even involve survey-style, positivist techniques if used appropriately. Rather, Adorno's distinction resembles what Horkheimer proposed in positing a critical theory that opposes a traditional theory.

In an essay considered to be a founding document of the Frankfurt School, Horkheimer describes a traditional epistemology and method that encompasses such diverse philosophical directions as the rationalism in Descartes, the empiricist heritage of the British and the phenomenology of Husserl. Common to all these schools is the tendency to isolate knowledge for practical purposes and to accept as fixed the relations between subject and object, theory and fact. 'Theory in the traditional sense established by Descartes and everywhere practised in the pursuit of the specialized sciences organizes experiences in the light of questions which arise out of life in present-day society.' The resulting knowledge is useful inside an already established context and therefore not unimportant for humankind. But the procedures involved in traditional theory exclude reflection on the social presuppositions of knowledge, on the unreflected background against which scientists conduct normal business. It is therefore the job of critical theory to examine the conditions of possibility for knowledge, 'to reflect upon the actual process of cognition' (p. 111), not in a Kantian or transcendental sense, but as an actual activity and as a potentiality of human beings acting in this

26

world. Critical theory thus seeks to examine those areas that science brackets: 'the social genesis of problems, the real situations in which science is put to use, and the purposes which it is made to serve'.[3] To some extent Horkheimer is positing a distinction not unlike the one Popper suggests between pure science and the extra-scientific, except that he does not seek to validate the former at the expense of the latter. For Horkheimer and Adorno, the error of 'pure' science is to imagine the desirability or even the possibility of its purity.

Put another way, critical theory is that type of theory which has society as a totality for its object. Adorno's specific reference to Horkheimer and to the impetus behind Kant's critical philosophy makes it obvious that he has something like this in mind when he distinguishes his brand of critical theory from Popper's (p. 114). A crucial point in the controversy therefore entails the dialectical relationship between isolated facts and the social totality. Adorno's criticism of positivism is that it isolates the particular from the general and thereby never gets to its real object of study: society. This criticism can be extended to Popper's methodological arguments in that he does not understand the nature of a dialectical contradiction. For Popper if facts contradict a given theory or 'solution', then another theory or solution must be found. This anti-dialectical notion of logic, which Popper developed more explicitly in 'What is dialectic?' from 1940,[4] sees contradictions as confrontations that need to be resolved, rather than as manifestations of a social totality. Popper reduces contradiction to logical or cognitive moments that must be eliminated; Adorno sees them as structural and necessary conditions of a society based on class hegemony. For Popper science is productive when it seeks the state of non-contradiction; for Adorno, grasping the contradiction as necessary and 'extending rationality to it' (p. 109) is the guarantee for knowledge.

Because neither positivism nor Popper's critical rationalism with its tendency toward pure science understands the contradictory nature of the social totality, neither can achieve objectivity. Survey-style positivism, in fact, despite its claims to objectivity, merely regurgitates subjective views. Adorno's critique of the false notion of objectivity in census-like procedures, however, can be extended to Popper's methodological suggestions as well. Common to both is the claim that objectivity does not reside in the individual researcher, but in the method that the researcher applies. For Adorno neither the objectivity of the researcher nor the method is important, but rather the objectivity of the object. By this Adorno means that the (critical) theorist must try to grasp the thing itself, human society, rather than collecting the distorted reflections of society in the minds of individuals or applying a reified method that fetishizes facts. Although Adorno can provide no methodological recipe for objectivity, nor any procedure to verify its attainment, his is not an empty notion devoid of methodological significance, as Popper would claim. For if we accept as valid only those procedures or concepts that can be confirmed through recourse to data, we would already be operating within the confined methodological universe that is the very object of Adorno's critique. Since the dialectical approach aims at an objective knowledge of society as a contradictory totality, it is not subject to contradiction at the level of facts, but rather at the level of theory.

By locating objectivity outside both the researcher and the procedure, Adorno does not encounter the same problems with value-freedom that Popper does. Although Popper clearly recognizes that objectivity and value-freedom are themselves values and that therefore the attainment of value-free science is impossible (and for other reasons undesirable), his affirmation of 'pure' science suggests a realm in which non-scientific values hold sway. For Adorno value and value-freedom are part of a dialectical unity, two sides of one problem whose separation is both erroneous and necessary: 'The separation of evaluative and value-free behaviour is false in so far as value, and thus value freedom, are reifications; correct in so far as the behaviour of the mind cannot extricate itself at will from the state of reification' (p. 117). Adorno continues by associating this separation with a situation in which means and ends have been 'torn asunder' for the purpose of dominating nature. Value arises, according to Adorno, in the exchange relationship and entails a 'being-for-the-other'. Reification occurs when this 'being-for-the-other' is transformed into a being-in-itself. Henceforth values appear as substantialized entities that can theoretically be eliminated during 'scientific' procedures. But reality cannot be conceived as merely existing, as an arena of being that can be separated from ethics or the 'ought' (*Sollen*).

'The dichotomy of what is (*Sein*) and what should be (*Sollen*) is as false as it is historically compelling, and for this reason it cannot be ignored. It only achieves an insight into its own inevitability through social critique' (p. 118). Value-freedom, conceived as a realm of existence without ethics, is impossible for sociology because its object, society 'can only crystallize at all around a conception of the just society [*von richtiger Gesellschaft*]' (p. 118). What Adorno seems to mean by this is that society in its very essence is composed of human values. An investigation of society by researchers who are necessarily social beings themselves falsifies the object if it pretends that it can locate a realm in which the choice between knowledge distorted by values and knowledge freed from values exists. A focus on society, for Adorno the object itself of social research, always presupposes an interest arising from criticism itself and entailing an awareness of both the contradictions in society and their necessity.[5]

HABERMAS'S DEFENSE OF THE DIALECTICAL TOTALITY

Habermas's first contribution to the positivist controversy has the appearance of a defense of the position developed by Adorno. It was first published in a Festschrift for Adorno on the occasion of his sixtieth birthday and is structured around citations from Adorno's response to Popper and from an earlier essay 'Sociology and empirical research' (pp. 68–86 in *The Positivist Dispute*).[6] By placing quotations from Adorno at the beginning and the end of several sections of the essay, Habermas gives the impression that he is perhaps doing nothing more than explicating the thought of his mentor. But this appearance is deceptive to a certain extent. From the discussion Habermas offers it soon becomes evident that he is both more thoroughly acquainted with Popper's works and better able to deal with the issues relating to methodology in the natural sciences. If we consider Habermas's other writings from this period, it is also obvious that this putative defense of Adorno outlines some of the central considerations that would later surface in *Zur Logik der Sozialwissenschaften* (1967) ['On the Logic of the Social Sciences'] and in *Knowledge and Human Interests*. None the less, Habermas was probably more concerned with a defense of Adorno and more indebted to a Hegelianized Marxism in this essay than he was in his later reply to Hans Albert. Here he uses the opportunity to begin to expound his own theoretical position, one that assimilates much of the Frankfurt School, but which also incorporates portions of the pragmatist and hermeneutic heritage.

Habermas begins his discussion by reasserting the category of totality. Citing Adorno's use of this concept, he reasserts the fundamental proposition that the research process in which human beings are engaged when they investigate society is part of the object to be examined. Totality therefore entails the notion of self-reflection: if the researcher works dialectically, he/she must reflect upon his/her own research as part of the social totality. In a dialectical totality the parts are not related to the whole in an additive fashion; nor is there a mutual implication of parts and whole. Rather, it appears that 'totality' in the sense that Adorno and Habermas use the word is something to be intuited. Habermas distinguishes this intuited notion of a dialectical totality from 'system', a designation referring to a social totality whose parts are related to the whole in 'the deductive connections of mathematical functions' (p. 132), and outlines in some detail four characteristic distinctions between the functionalist concept of system and the dialectical concept of totality:

Relationship of theory to object

Habermas points to the generally precarious notion of the theory–object fit. At times we may assume that a theory is isomorphic to the object is apprehends, but there is in fact very little we can say about the ontological correspondence of categories and reality. Theories for Habermas are nothing more than 'ordering schema' that can be applied and utilized. The natural sciences are able to utilize theories to produce a kind of knowledge that results in a technical control of nature. By employing knowledge derived from empirically controlled experimentation, human beings have learned to manipulate and to dominate nature. When this same procedure is transferred to the social sphere, however, the result is a distortion of the object. Systemic conceptions of social science research, by neglecting the fact that the researchers themselves are part of the total process and by refusing to reflect on methodological presuppositions, inevitably fail to grasp society. A dialectical approach to research understands the 'societal life-context as a totality which determines even research itself'. Such an approach, Habermas claims, entails a circular rather than an analytical logic. 'The scientific apparatus reveals an object whose structure must nevertheless previously be understood to some degree, if the categories chosen are not to remain external to it' (p. 134). In short, the relationship of theory to object is a hermeneutical one, in which the attempt to grasp the presuppositions of knowledge involves employing intuitively those very presuppositions.

Relationship of theory to experience

The analytical-empirical mode associated primarily with the natural sciences only allows for a single type of experience based on controlled observation of physical behaviour under reproducible conditions. This dramatic limitation of experience has the advantage of producing a highly reliable, intersubjectively verifiable perception. But however adequate such experience is for experimentation in the natural sciences, it is totally inappropriate for examining society. The 'fund of prescientifically accumulated experience' that makes up the lifeworld is inaccessible to analytical-empirical procedures and not expressible in the 'formal language of a hypothetico-deductive connection'. In contrast to these methods Habermas again suggests that a dialectical theory have recourse to hermeneutics. The limited validity of results associated with analytical-empirical methods is contrasted to a hermeneutic adequacy to the object of study: society as a totality. Dialectical theory must accord with experience also; but this experience is not synonymous with the restricted experience of controlled observation.

Relationship of theory to history

Habermas argues again that analytical-empirical procedures have only limited application outside natural science. Referring back to a distinction that runs from Vico to Dilthey, he claims that the achievement of the natural sciences and their concomi-

31

tant methods lies in explanation (*Erklären*), while historical or human sciences must rely on a hermeneutically informed understanding. For this reason he takes exception to Popper's rejection of historical laws. In *The Open Society and its Enemies* Popper had contended that institutional analysis, no matter how excellent and how empirically secure, cannot lead to nomological statements. The 'poverty of historicism' stems from the fact that tendencies observed today can have an altogether different appearance tomorrow.[7] Habermas considers this an illicit confounding of natural and historical laws. The latter cannot be determined by analytical-empirical methods, but only by a dialectical theory of society. Their validity is both less and more comprehensive than natural laws: less comprehensive in that they do not refer to any givens or constants in either the anthropological or historical realm, but rather to 'a particular concrete area of application, defined in terms of a process of development both unique *in toto* and irreversible in its stages' (p. 138). It is more comprehensive, however, in that it encompasses the social lifeworld as a totality. Proceeding hermeneutically, a dialectical theory must elude the objectivism inherent in considering interhuman relationships to be the same as lawlike relations between things while simultaneously avoiding the dangers of subjectivism resulting from regarding consciousness as transparently reflected in individual utterances. It must combine and transcend both the procedures of a causal science and the methods of hermeneutic understanding.

Relationship of theory to practice

Habermas's initial claim that empirical procedures produce explanations that have only 'retrospective value' is difficult to understand, especially since the determination of laws for natural or social phenomena is usually undertaken for predictive purposes. His clarification makes more sense. Lawlike hypotheses, he maintains, have only limited prognostic value since they relate only to technical aspects of our existence. The application of empirical methods to social phenomena can result at most in an 'auxiliary science for rational administration'. But such methods depend on the isolation of phenomena from each other and from the social totality. Indeed, the social system itself stands in a historical life-context that cannot be comprehended by empirical-scientific procedures. With Adorno, Habermas insists on thinking together the realms of existence and ethics or being (*Sein*) and ought (*Sollen*). For both men the objective meaning inherent in the social order cannot be separated from the demand for social emancipation. In this view practical questions are not juxtaposed to technical tasks, but are rather mutually implicated in the object: society as totality. Critical science 'allows its problems to be posed by its object' (pp. 141–3). So the call for an immanent critique, shared by Adorno and Habermas, entails a unity of theory and practice.

HABERMAS ON THE QUESTION OF VALUE

The remainder of Habermas's defense of Adorno's position is devoted to a detailed and important examination of the notion of value-freedom. Popper's views on this problem, we will recall, were equivocal. While he correctly recognizes that value-freedom is itself a value and therefore not realizable, his insistence on the separation of the scientific from an extra-scientific realm suggests that purely scientific values are at least possible in theory. Habermas, following and expounding on Adorno's reply, argues that the postulate of value-freedom rests upon a series of dualisms that stem from a 'systemic' or analytical-empirical perspective. Among these dichotomies are facts (*Tatsachen*) and decisions (*Entscheidungen*), natural laws and social norms, existence and ethics, and cognition and evaluation. The valorization of the first half of these binary pairs results in a reduction of acceptable knowledge to that produced by empirical sciences, and excludes questions of practice, ethics, and the lifeworld from the purview of scientific enquiry. The consequences for the realm of values, norms, and decisions are the equally inadequate alternatives of *objective value ethics* or *subjective value philosophy*. The former locates values in a transcendental realm, and while it accords them an 'ontological dignity', they are accessible only intuitively. Subjective value philosophy, accepting the same fact-decision distinction, ultimately reduces norms to decisions that are not grounded on any rational comprehension. Whether one considers the existential-personal decisionism of a Jean-Paul Sartre, the public-political decisionism of a Carl Schmitt or the anthropologically based decisionism of an Arnold Gehlen, the common denominator remains that the choice of life decisions can never be rationalized through scientific procedures. The dangerous implications of such a pure decisionism are obvious. The sphere of rationality, reduced to its analytical-empirical form, is sealed off from an ethical realm that is subject to non-rational procedures. As Adorno and Horkheimer demonstrated in the *Dialectic of Enlightenment* the complement to purposive-rational knowledge is a realm of values and norms based on a mythological order, for example, under Fascism.[8]

Popper seeks to avoid both objective value ethics and subjective value philosophy, but since his initial starting point also advocates a separation between facts and decisions, he is left with a rather unattractive alternative. Since he can conceive of a rational attitude only in the mode of empirical science, he is forced to conclude that there can be no comprehensive rationalism. If the rational attitude is characterized by experience and argument, there can be no rational justification for preferring rationalism to irrationalism. A rational justification of rationalism would entail the prior acceptance of a rational attitude. Thus Popper concludes that our choice of rationalism over the alternative must be described as an 'irrational *faith in reason*'.[9] He admits that a choice of a 'comprehensive irrationalism' would be just as logically tenable, that there are no logical reasons for opting for his critical-rationalist attitude. Ultimately for him the choice is a 'moral decision', and this is precisely Habermas's point. By separating reason from morality, Popper affirms a rationality in the moral realm only to the extent to which it can be employed to manipulate or administer over human beings, but he denies a rational basis for norms and values. So Habermas's question for Popper is the following: is knowledge as Popper conceives it only possible in the realm of empirical science that is released from all normative bonds?

To answer this Habermas turns to Popper's discussion of the so-called basis problem in Popper's *Logic of Scientific Discovery*.[10] He credits Popper first with his justified criticism of the logical positivism of Carnap and Neurath, who had unproblematically assumed a definite relationship between statements and experience. Observational or protocol statements are needed in their philosophies to confirm hypotheses and prove their empirical validity. Thus the connection between experience as observation and statement is basic to their theoretical project. In contrast to their theory of verification, Popper, as we have seen, posits a general theory of falsification. Lawlike hypotheses can never be verified, he asserts; at most they can be accepted tentatively if they are criticizable and if they withstand contradiction by statements derived from observation. But Habermas points out that statements resulting from observation are themselves no more susceptible to verification than the lawlike hypotheses they are supposed to contradict. Every basic statement contains universal terms that have the same status as hypotheses. 'The simple assertion that "here is a glass of water" could not be proved by a finite series of observations, because the meaning of such general terms as "glass" or "water" consists of assumptions about the law-like behaviour of bodies' (p. 150). Popper is not unaware of this difficulty, nor is he the first to recognize this difficulty. His logical objections to an unmediated relationship between experience and basic statements is anticipated by Charles Sanders Peirce's pragmatic views and by Hegel's critique of sense certainty in the *Phenomenology*. But his solution to this problem involves neither the dialectical transcending of experience that we find in Hegel, nor the examination of a realm of pre-understanding such as we might find in Husserl's phenomenology. Instead Popper insists that the acceptance of basic statements must depend on 'a provisional consensus that can be refuted at any time' (p. 151). In short, it is based on a decision that cannot be logically or empirically proved or refuted.

Habermas points out that Popper's solution entails conclusions that are unwelcome to him, but not at all unexpected if we have considered the matter dialectically. The key term for Habermas is consensus and the dependence of the scientific research process on intersubjective agreement. For this agreement can only be based on norms drawn from the lifeworld, that 'extra-scientific' arena that Popper endeavors to bracket from pure science. When Popper compares the process by which a basic statement is accepted to a legal process, Habermas contends that he has tacitly admitted the hermeneutic substructure of scientific thought. In the legal analogy one cannot apply laws unless one is certain of the facts to which they are supposed to be applied. The establishment of the facts, however, presupposes an advance determination of the laws. This circle is evidence of the hermeneutic prestructuring of the legal process and, by extension, of an identical foundation for cognitive sciences. The purely scientific realm conceived by Popper is therefore a fiction. Research is above all a social institution based on communication and consensus, and the demand for controlled observation 'presupposes a pre-understanding of certain social norms' (p. 152).

The question Habermas next poses concerns why we normally do not call into question the validity of basic statements. This question can be answered by referring to the nature of most universals found in every basic statement. Habermas has shown that the degree of generality in statements of perceptual judgement always exceeds the particularity of what is perceived. When we state 'here is a glass of water', we are asserting very little in the way of specific content and a great deal about various properties of matter that have yet to be proved. Indeed, every basic statement threatens to unravel into an infinite series of statements, none of which would ever be unequivocally confirmed. Yet we are rarely in doubt about the assumptions behind the universals in these statements. The reason for this faith is not irrational decisionism, but rather the fact that such universals form an unquestioned background to our enquiry. They are the 'unproblematic convictions' and 'pragmatically proven ideas' that make up our lifeworld. They become thematic for us only when they are called into question. Ultimately, then, the validity of basic statements and the scientific theories that they falsify (Popper) or validate (positivists) rests on the intersubjective agreement of the communities out of which they arise. Concealed by the analytical theory of science is an enabling realm of pre-understanding accessible only through hermeneutic procedures.

What remains for Habermas to show is how and when this concealment occurred in the history of humankind. He begins this explanation by positing certain interests that are anthropologically constant. Although he would develop this reasoning more extensively in *Knowledge and Human Interests*, as we saw in Chapter 1, he already states in 1963 that the interest humans have had in the domination of nature, an interest that is intimately connected with the survival of human communities, has been constant throughout history. Because of the centrality of this interest, consensus was easily reached on the meaning of technical domination. As a result the intersubjective validity of statements concerning purposive action, which ultimately extends to the validity of the analytical-empirical sciences, was secured. Indeed, the high level of intersubjectivity, as compared to other areas of communal living, causes the interest guiding such actions to recede into the background and to become forgotten. Positivism, which Habermas characterizes broadly in *Knowledge and Human Interests* as a lack of reflection,[11] may be considered that mode of thought and theory which continues to propagate the concealedness of the technical interest in modern times. Dialectics, by contrast, is for Habermas the theoretical movement that locates the technical interest in the intersubjective arena of social labor by reflecting on its unconscious presuppositions.

Historically the concealment of the theoretical interest is connected in particular with the rise of the empirical sciences in the seventeenth century and the simultaneous advent of the bourgeoisie. Until that point the ruling classes had exerted a monopoly on the acquisition of knowledge, while the lower classes produced the material goods necessary for the reproduction of life. Theory and labor were distinct realms. This separation ends in the framework of modern bourgeois society, where the spheres of theory and labor interpenetrate. Modern physics as expounded from Galileo to Newton and the rationalization of manufacturing are part of a historical process that begins to define knowledge as the mechanistic control of nature. Gradually knowledge becomes reduced to technical domination and instrumental action. The intersubjective world out of which it arose and over which it begins to exert an unmistakable hegemony recedes into an unproblematic background and is dissociated from knowledge. At this moment in historical development the question of value-freedom emerges as the reified expression of this exclusionary process. Having forgotten or repressed the interest guiding empirical sciences, we adopt a disinterested approach to knowledge or a 'theoretical attitude'. But the very postulate of value-freedom, as Popper inadvertently shows, 'testifies that the analytical-empirical procedures cannot ensure for themselves the life-reference (*Lebensbezug*) within which they themselves objectively stand' (p. 158). The separation of value and value-freedom, like the dichotomies of descriptive and normative content, facts and decisions, existence and ethics, theory and practice, are the reified products of the concealed interest in technical knowledge.

Habermas's concern in disclosing this concealed interest is not to discredit the methods of the natural sciences. He concedes that the pursuit of knowledge through empirical methods has been successful and has led to progress in our ability to manipulate nature. Although the ecological consciousness that has arisen in recent years may now want to question exactly how unproblematic means-ends relations are in the technical domination of nature, Habermas's objection stems primarily from the transfer of empirical methods to the social sciences. He argues that the prerequisites for scientific practice – the ability to distinguish between an initial starting point, alternative means and ultimate ends – are not applicable to social processes, since none of these terms can be isolated. In the realm of practical life technical parameters acquire meaning through life references. The social embeddedness of knowledge in the lifeworld does not disqualify empirical methods in social sciences, and Habermas, like Adorno, admits their usefulness. If such methods are employed, however, they must relinquish their claim to universal knowledge, incorporate 'situationally-bound experiences' at the outset and reflect upon their own situatedness in the social totality. This can only be accomplished by recourse to dialectical thought, whose immediate goal is to dispel the illusion that emancipation in history can be secured by the same method that has resulted in the emancipation from natural constraint (p. 162).

HANS ALBERT AND THE DEFENSE OF POPPER

Although Habermas's comments were addressed mainly to Popper's arguments, he received no reply. In fact, Popper apparently has made only one additional comment in the context of this debate, and this is the short note included in the English version of *The Positivist Dispute*. It was left to one of Popper's German disciples, the sociologist Hans Albert, to construct a defense against Habermas's critique. No one can accuse him of not being energetic on behalf of Popper and the theory of critical rationalism. In several essays and books written over the next few years Albert argued against the objections of the 'dialecticians'; and does not hesitate to employ every means at his disposal to discredit this direction. The last section in his essay directed against Habermas contains, for example, accusations of obscurity and illicit argumentative strategies. According to Albert, Habermas resorts to 'insinuation, allusion and metaphor' in order to affirm 'the dialectical cult of total reason' (p. 197). In another part of the polemical attack Albert tries to discredit his adversary politically by connecting dialectics with their perversion by Eastern European regimes. In this connection he asserts that 'dialectical attempts to interpret reality, in contrast to the "positivism" which Habermas criticizes, are frequently quite popular in totalitarian societies' (p. 189). It is impossible to determine whether Albert considers these to be serious and persuasive arguments, but it is none the less interesting to note that their force has little to do with the spirit of critical rationalism that he upholds.

Despite red-baiting and other questionable debating tactics, Albert does raise major issues of content. Chief among these is Habermas's understanding of empirical procedures. Albert contends that Habermas accepts an instrumentalist view of the empirical sciences that is specifically rejected by Popper. Repeating Popper's plea for a critical rationalism in the social sciences, Albert maintains that 'we can learn from our mistakes by exposing the theories in question to the risks of destruction at the hands of the facts' (p. 171). Habermas's 'denunciation' of empirical procedures as purely technical presumably misunderstands this potential. What is worse, the alternative that Habermas proposes would subject the social scientist to arbitrary categories and models. Albert points out that the notion of 'totality' is ill defined and subject to methodological abuse. He is particularly concerned at the contention that dialectical theory cannot be converted into a suitable form for testing. Inadvertently proving Habermas's point, Albert appears to assume that only the ability to be criticized by empirical procedures is a guarantee of validity. Albert is equally distressed at Habermas's recourse to hermeneutics and pragmatism. Misinterpreting Habermas's references to 'the hermeneutics of everyday life' as an exclusive reliance on common sense and everyday knowledge, Albert argues that Habermas's proposals wind up being more conservative than Popper's because they adhere to tradition instead of subjecting tentative solutions to critical tests. Albert correctly identifies a danger of hermeneutics in this criticism, but, as we shall see in the next chapter, his criticism is anticipated by Habermas as well. If the hermeneutic approach is conceived as a passive acceptance of tradition then it will indeed have a conservative bent, but Habermas insists that it must be complemented by the dimension of ideological critique.

The other major point in Albert's diffuse polemic deals with the issue of value-freedom. He approaches this issue first from a more global perspective. Albert recognizes that Habermas's general project is the production of 'a scientifically organized philosophy of history with practical intent' (p. 179), a project that he, following Popper, considers impossible. Indeed, he correctly notes that Popper's purpose in writing *The Open Society and its Enemies* was precisely to criticize historical-philosophical theories that assert a hidden meaning in history. In the second volume of this influential work Popper examines perhaps the two most important nineteenth-century philosophers of history who found meaning and a *telos* in history: Hegel and Marx. The gist of this portion of Albert's criticism is that Habermas, like his two illustrious predecessors, is guilty of assigning a meaning to an essentially neutral historical process. The recourse to hermeneutics is nothing more than a *deus ex machina* to infuse history with something foreign to it.

Albert's second objection has to do with Habermas's specific formulation of the problem of value-freedom. Albert contends that modern advocates of value-freedom do not neglect knowledge-guiding interests; rather, they propose more detailed solutions to account for various aspects of the problem. This misses the point of Habermas's critique entirely, for Albert never even attempts to explain how these more refined models avoid recourse to what Habermas has described as positivistically informed procedures. Instead of broaching this issue, he proceeds to attack the notion, held by both Adorno and Habermas, that the issue of evaluation and value-freedom is a reification. But he never tackles the historical or the logical analysis Habermas provided in his initial discussion and winds up with little more than the assertion that scientific method demands a bracketing of the totality in order to reach solutions.

He seems not to understand that Habermas would agree that solutions can be reached in this fashion, but that the bracketing of totality and the pretense that this procedure allows the scientist to embrace a neutrality with regard to values are themselves the unreflected 'positivist' assumption that Habermas has critiqued.

HABERMAS AND COMPREHENSIVE RATIONALITY

Habermas recognized that Albert's response consists largely of misapprehensions spiced with preposterous accusations of obscurantism and irrationality. The latter objections he treats rather summarily in the last few paragraphs of his reply. The substantive misunderstandings are accorded more extensive discussion, although Habermas is much more aware that his real debating partner is Popper and not his German disciple. Accordingly most of what Habermas addresses has its foundation in Popper's works as much as in Albert's critique. He sets the stage for his discussion by stating that his earlier paper did not take issue with research practices in the social sciences but, rather, with 'the positivistic interpretation of such research processes' (p. 198). His objection to positivistic interpretation is that it excludes areas of human activity and experience that are susceptible to rational discussion, even though they cannot be formulated as a 'solution' to a 'problem' that can be criticized with empirical data. Habermas proposes as an alternative to the 'bisected' or limited rationalism of positivism a 'comprehensive rationality' based on the 'old-fashioned' notion of self-reflection. Admitting that Popper attains a first level of self-reflection in his objections to the logical positivists, Habermas contends that his failure to reflect upon the technical-cognitive interest of empirical science opens the door to positivist contamination of critical rationalism.

To discuss this larger issue in more detail and to make explicit Albert's misunderstandings, Habermas divides his discussion into four interrelated areas. The first concerns the role of experience in empirical studies. Habermas's original contribution claimed that positivism allows only a limited range of experience. He clarifies this statement by admitting that a wider range of experience is permitted in the formation of theories or solutions, but maintains that the insistence on test-

41

able hypotheses narrows unnecessarily the type of experience that can verify or falsify a given theory. Habermas feels that the positivists are caught in a circle. The experience they rely on is dependent on the standards of the experiment; but the standards of these sciences are supposed to be based on experience. There is thus a mutual dependence of experience and positivist science that tends to exclude other types of experience and validation.

The question of the experimental basis for positivist testing is particularly interesting because, as Habermas admits, Popper shares in the general philosophical tendency that 'challenges the thesis of the manifest self-givenness of the existent in sense experience' (p. 201). The reliance on the senses as an immediate and reliable source of knowledge was challenged not only by German idealism (Kant's categories and Hegel's critique of sense certainty) but also by such diverse modern philosophical schools as pragmatism (Peirce), phenomenology (Husserl) and Critical Theory (Adorno and Horkheimer). Popper's criticism of the logical positivists is consistent with this anti-empirical tradition: by maintaining that 'all observations are theory-impregnated' (p. 299), he 'strips the origins of knowledge, enlisted in empiricist studies, of their false authority'. His problem, however, is that he does not go far enough with his critique. By having recourse to testing as a method of falsification he retains 'a deep-seated positivistic prejudice' that postulates an autonomy of experience from the testing situation. For Popper, 'tests examine theories against "independent" facts. This thesis is the pivot of the residual positivistic problematic in Popper' (p. 203). Thus Popper gets it half right. He correctly identifies the interdependence of facts and theories when it comes to criticizing positivism, but he maintains their independence when it is a question of checking and refuting theories.[12]

In connection with the place of positivism in the research arsenal, Habermas argues that there are other deficiencies in Popper's notion of falsification. Indeed, in this regard Habermas is willing to concede more validity to positivist procedures than Popper. The reason for this difference has to do with their respective demands on research models. Whereas Popper must refute positivism because it cannot supply a universally valid procedure for all sciences, Habermas, by limiting the competence of empirical-analytical research to a particular type of knowledge derived from a particular interest, can affirm its significance for one aspect of human endeavor. Empiricism, Habermas argues, establishes an area of validity by making assumptions concerning experience, testing and facts. If we step outside these assumptions and criticize them then we will see their limitations, but if we work inside them they retain a restricted validity. Habermas claims that a 'pragmatic' view of empirical theories shows them to be based on 'the structure of feedback-regulated action, which always allows itself to be guided by anticipations of behavioural regularity' (p. 207). If we assume this pragmatic stance then there is no need to resort to a theory of falsification, since both verification and falsification are ultimately based on the false assumption of a correspondence between statements and states of affairs. Operating inside the empirical-analytical framework and under its technical interest (Habermas conceives of technique in its widest sense as 'a socially institutionalized regulatory system which . . . is designed to be technically utilizable'), we can verify theories pragmatically, positively and positivistically. In doing so, however, we must always remember what positivism represses: 'all the answers which the empirical sciences can supply are relative to the methodical significance of the questions they raise and nothing else' (pp. 208–9). Habermas thus validates positivist procedures on a limited basis. Far from denouncing such methods, as Albert claims, he critiques them in the Kantian sense of exploring their inherent limitations.

The third point in Habermas's rejoinder concerns the nature of proof in critical procedures. He is particularly interested in how arguments for empirical procedures can be validated. This is not accomplished through criticism, even in Popper's sense of the word. The reason for this is that criticism is not the testing itself but, rather, the 'test itself as discussion'. Defined by Habermas as 'the unreserved discussion of propositions', criticism employs testing as well as other available techniques to refute or prove a proposition (p. 210). What Habermas means is really quite simple if we take Popper's argumentative practice as seriously as his notion of critical rationalism. In criticizing positivist positions and developing his own alternative, Popper has to have recourse to means that fall outside the very method he suggests. He supports his position against logical positivism and for critical rationalism not with arguments, whether verificationist or falsificationist, founded on deductive logic, but on a 'hermeneutical form of argumentation' that eschews 'the rigid monologues of deductive systems of propositions' (p. 211). Popper, as we have seen, feels that ultimately the decision to opt for critical rationalism is an act of faith. But Habermas counters that Popper sets the stakes for justification too rigidly when he admits only deduction. Although it is true that there will never be a proof for adopting the critical attitude, it is only 'unscientific in comparison with logical deduction'. It we consider that all methods, including analytical-empirical ones, are grounded on supporting arguments and not on tests, then Popper need not have recourse to faith, and, indeed, in his practice he does not. The problem with his theoretical position is simply that he does not recognize that he himself continually has recourse to non-deductive principles that are as legitimate as any other method for validating his theory.

Whereas Popper's own arguments contradict his narrow notion of scientific procedure, they also suggest the untenability of the distinction between facts and decisions. This distinction, we will recall, forms the basis of the demand for value-freedom and is thus at the very center of the debate. Habermas claims that Popper cuts off reflection on this matter by accepting the correspondence theory of truth. According to this theory facts and relationships between facts exist independent of our discussions of them, and our propositions correspond to them. In his argument for the autonomy of facts, however, Popper has recourse to a notion of truth that he cannot ground. He argues that knowing truth and establishing a standard for truth are two different things, that the former is simply 'understood' in an intuitive manner. Habermas agrees and finds that Popper here 'makes use of the hermeneutic insight that we understand the meaning of statements from the context even before we can define individual terms and apply a general standard' (p. 217). What Popper has inadvertently conceded, then, is that the distinction he wishes to make breaks down. We never have access to an independent realm of facts uncontaminated by values or decisions. Although their separation is a prerequisite for empirical methods and for their effective performance in producing nomological knowledge, a hermeneutically informed approach demonstrates their mutuality.

Habermas concludes that Popper himself does not manage to uphold the distinctions that he needs for his theory. Instead he unwittingly confirms a more encompassing notion of rationality. Habermas employs the term 'comprehensive rationality' to refer to this rationality of argument that underlies Popper's procedures, and it appears that he is using this synonymously with the notion of dialectics, which plays a less prominent role in this rejoinder than it did in the original comment, and with the theory of a hermeneutics of argumentation. Habermas notes three interconnected types of statement that play a part in rational argumentation: the descriptive, the postulatory and the critical:

> A critical discussion, regardless of whether it concerns the acceptance of proposals or propositions, includes a threefold usage of language: the descriptive, in order to describe states of affairs; the postulatory, in order to establish rules of procedure; and the critical, in order to justify such decisions. (p. 218)

These three types of statement or uses of language correspond roughly to the three types of science Habermas discusses in his inaugural lecture at Frankfurt and in *Knowledge and Human Interests*. The descriptive evokes the empirical-analytical sciences with their technical interest and resultant nomological knowledge; the postulatory in its concern for norms comes close to the historico-hermeneutical sciences, which are based on practical interests and produce an interpretive understanding of meaningful structures; the critical statement, which here includes language-transcendent outlooks, corresponds to the critical sciences with their emancipatory interest and reflexive knowledge. Indeed, it is criticism as an encompassing and self-reflexive activity that enables us to see that the descriptive and the postulatory, facts and norms, science and ethics, are ultimately inseparable.

CONSEQUENCES OF THE POSITIVIST DISPUTE

In the context of German sociology the positivist dispute marked a significant turning point. For the first time in the postwar period considerable attention was given to the problems of methodology in the social sciences. That this occurred at the beginning of the 1960s is probably not coincidental, for this was the same period in which a deeper questioning of the values and norms of West German society could be encountered in various cultural and intellectual circles. As Agnes Heller has pointed out, prior to 1960 three modes of sociological study predominated in Germany. The first, propagated by disciples of the inner exiles Heidegger and Gehlen, was somewhat contaminated by its association with dubious politics. The sociology of the Frankfurt School thus saw the importation of American empirical models, represented in the Cologne School, as its chief threat. On the part of Adorno the dispute can therefore be understood as an effort to assert a dominance of critical theory over the incursion of empirical procedures.[13] The early stages of the dispute also had its roots in Popper's and Adorno's respective views of mass democracy. The former embraced Western democratic governance despite its imperfections; the latter was always more critical of what he felt was government by surveillance and control of the contents of reified consciousness.

Although the debate created widespread discussion in Germany, particularly after the publication of the seminal essays and responses, its importance for Habermas lies less in his superiority over Albert than in the gradual clarification of his position. In an important sense this debate was not Habermas's affair. It was started by Adorno; it spoke centrally to concerns that touched the raw nerve at the root of critical theory as discussed by Horkheimer and Marcuse in the mid-1930s; and in its initial stage at least it related much more to Adorno's experiences in the United States and his Hegelian-based Marxism than to Habermas's incipient concerns. In addition Habermas was never able to debate with the person whose theories were most interesting to him. Albert indefatigably represented Popper in a stream of articles and books – whose discussion has not been included here because they add little to the substantive issues already addressed – but Popper's only response to Habermas was the dismissive afterword referred to above. Since it is clear that Habermas had a better grasp and a more sympathetic understanding of Popper's project than Adorno,[14] and since Albert showed such a poor understanding of Habermas's position even when it was honestly engaged with Popper's, we can reaffirm the contention made at the outset that the 'dispute' – or at least the most seminal confrontation in the dispute – never really occurred.

Perhaps because this was less an intervention and a debate than a defense and a rejoinder, the political dimensions of the controversy were never at the center of Habermas's concerns. In contrast to the controversies discussed in the next chapters, Habermas does not appear to be overly distressed at the political implications of positivist research or of their Popperian variation. Indeed, it is Adorno who consistently points to the dangers of a positivistically conceived research program. Not only does he cite the false notion of democracy that lies behind survey-style research and, by extension, the electoral process in capitalist societies, he also argues that empirical methods have something inherently conservative in them. Because they do not reflect upon their own presuppositions, they support the status quo: 'In that moment in which one hypostatizes that state which research methods both grasp and express as the immanent reason of science, instead of making it the object of one's thought, one contributes intentionally to its perpetuation' (p. 74). Whereas Habermas credits the empirical-analytical research method with gains in technical knowledge, Adorno tends to dismiss it as false consciousness and ideology. The only other overtly political tone struck in the debate comes from Albert, whose contentions, as we saw earlier, are based on either a false notion of hermeneutics as inherently conservative or an illicit identification of dialectics with its perversion. Habermas, by contrast, appears to avoid direct political confrontation, relegating even his reply to Albert's red-baiting tactics to a brief footnote.

The reason for this is perhaps that Habermas was not quite in control of his philosophical foundations at this point, or, more accurately, that they underwent a change from the essay in which he defended Adorno to the rejoinder to Albert. Albert may then be correct when he notes in a later essay[15] that Habermas has shifted his arguments in the two pieces discussed earlier. In the first he remains a more or less faithful student of Adorno. Although his indebtedness to pragmatism and hermeneutics is already evident there, the repeated references to totality and to the dialectic of the particular and the general reveal the strong influence of Adorno's Hegelianism. In the response to Albert, Habermas sets a somewhat different tone. Although one of Albert's chief objections concerns the vagueness of the category of totality, Habermas does not bother to clarify. Moreover, his notion of dialectics in this piece is both an expansion on and a reduction of the earlier, more Hegelian notion. Habermas asserts that dialectics 'only expresses the fact that we think and are able to think when, according to the traditional rules of logical inference, we really should not be able to do so' (p. 223). In becoming all thought that escapes traditional logic, dialectics loses its specificity as logic and method. Habermas is already operating within the framework of *Knowledge and Human Interests*, where critical science becomes what dialectical thought once was. There is also a hint of what lies beyond *Knowledge and Human Interests*, however, when Habermas alludes to notions that will later become the focus of his *Theory of Communicative Action*. In the context of the critical use of language, Habermas states, 'As soon as we discuss a problem with the aim of reaching a consensus rationally and without constraint, we find ourselves in a dimension of comprehensive rationality which embraces as its moments language and action, statements and attitudes' (p. 219). In his *magnum opus* this comprehensive rationality is identified as communicative. But before Habermas developed this notion, he first confronted the linguistic turn in the tradition he had so prominently employed to critique positivism: philosophical hermeneutics.

3

On ideology and interpretation: the debate with Hans-Georg Gadamer

We have just seen that Habermas has repeated recourse to hermeneutics in his dispute with positivism. Indeed, the reliance on hermeneutics is one of the key features that separates his arguments from Adorno's. The precise meaning of hermeneutics that Habermas employed in these essays, however, is difficult to ascertain. Although it is clearly used as a counterweight to empirico-analytical methods, its use in several contexts allows it to cover a wide range of senses, from dialectical logic to life references. Three different fields of meaning for hermeneutics are none the less discernible in Habermas's discussion. In some cases it recalls the standard Vico-Dilthey tradition in which understanding (*Verstehen*) in the human science is juxtaposed to explanation (*Erklären*) in the natural sciences. In other instances it appears to be related to all structures of pre-understanding, that is, to all those things that we normally do not thematize as knowledge, but that nevertheless form the background or horizon that enables us to have successful communication. At other points in his arguments it seems to possess a sociological bent, and we can easily see how his notion of hermeneutics in the positivist dispute is related to the concept of the lifeworld developed in the phenomenological sociology of Alfred Schütz and later appropriated by Habermas himself as a key term in his *Theory of Communicative Action*.[1] What is missing at this point in Habermas's discussion is how he sees hermeneutics fitting into a tradition of critical science with an emancipatory interest. This question became more urgent for Habermas in the 1960s because of the appearance and success of Hans-Georg Gadamer's *Truth and Method*, and it is in a confrontation with

Gadamer's book in the early 1970s that Habermas clarifies for himself the role of hermeneutics in his project.[2]

THE HERMENEUTIC TRADITION

Without exaggeration one can state that Gadamer's work is the most important development in twentieth-century hermeneutics, but to comprehend its importance we must view it against the theories of his predecessors. Up until the nineteenth century, hermeneutics had been associated primarily with the exegesis of the Bible and the interpretation of laws, that is, with specific applications. During the eighteenth century a general hermeneutics arose that attempted to formulate broad rules for the understanding of all texts, but it was not until the advent of romantic hermeneutics at the beginning of the nineteenth century that we find an intensive occupation with universal rules for interpretation. Although the classical philologist Friedrich Ast was primarily concerned with the mediation of the classical authors, he developed a notion of 'spirit' (*Geist*) that has wider implications for the hermeneutic enterprise. According to Ast the task for all understanding is to find the spirit of the whole in the individual occurrence and to comprehend the individual through the whole. We thus encounter a hermeneutic circle in Ast's work that should remind us of remarks Habermas makes about the dialectic of individual phenomena within the social totality.

The philologically based model of hermeneutics found in Ast's work was broadened by the theologian Friedrich Schleiermacher, who is generally regarded as the founder of the modern hermeneutic tradition. Schleiermacher was the first to universalize the question of understanding: his hermeneutics is tantamount to an epistemology of objects from historical and intellectual life. It consists of two levels. The first is grammatical and has to do with understanding the text as part of a linguistic universe. The interpreter is called upon to understand the supra-individual aspects of language use as well as their particular application by the individual author. The second level he called psychological or technical and entails the individual contribution of the author as psychological subject. The interpreter's task on this level is to understand the author better than he understood himself. Again we are dealing with a circle involving a particular and a general, and Schleiermacher introduces the notion of the 'divinatory' to explain how we might productively enter into this circle. Understood as a fundamental willingness to confront otherness on unfamiliar terms, the divinatory is a necessary first moment in a process of understanding that is in principle infinite.

The hermeneutic theory of Wilhelm Dilthey represents a continuation of and a regression from Schleiermacher's work. Because key works were not at his disposal, Dilthey developed only the psychological side of his predecessor's theory, ignoring the linguistic dimension that became so central for twentieth-century hermeneutics. For Dilthey, then, understanding was based primarily on recovering the psychology of the author, on approximating his or her experience through sympathetic reactions to textual evidence. He therefore advocates working backward through texts that are authentic life expressions to arrive at the original experience of their author. Dilthey's major contribution to hermeneutic theory, however, was probably his separation of knowledge into two spheres, one for the natural sciences and one for the social or human sciences (*Geisteswissenschaften*). Affirming a methodology based on a subject-object distinction for scientific explanations, Dilthey proposes that historical knowledge, by contrast, is acquired hermeneutically through empathetic understanding. Although this separation did not originate with him – he had predecessors in Giambattista Vico and Johann Gottfried Herder – Dilthey none the less was its most influential advocate in the modern era. Under the pressure of nineteenth-century positivism and the success of natural science, hermeneutics in his works retreats slightly from the universality it had achieved with Schleiermacher, but it becomes the only valid method for scholarship dealing with the historical past.

THE ONTOLOGICAL TURN IN THE TWENTIETH CENTURY

In the twentieth century the central innovation in hermeneutics is associated with the work of Martin Heidegger and his student Hans-Georg Gadamer. The general shift they advocated can be summarized in three areas. (1) In contrast to the tradition since at least the Enlightenment, hermeneutics no longer concerns itself exclusively with the understanding and interpretation of written documents or speech. (2) Unlike romantic hermeneutic theory from Schleiermacher to Dilthey, the aim of understanding is not focused on communication with, or the psychology of, another person. (3) The hermeneutics of Heidegger and Gadamer explores a realm that exists prior to or more fundamental than Dilthey's separation of the natural sciences from the human sciences. Twentieth-century hermeneutics takes leave of the epistemological arena in which previous theories of understanding had operated and moves into the area of 'fundamental ontology', to use Heidegger's phrase. This means that understanding is not to be conceived transitively; we are not concerned with understanding something. Rather, understanding is grasped as our way of being-in-the-world, as the fundamental way we exist prior to any cognition or intellectual activity. Ontological hermeneutics thus replaces the question of understanding as knowledge about the world with the question of being-in-the-world.

Heidegger's discussion of 'the existential constitution of the There' (*Die existentiale Konstitution des Da*) in the fifth chapter of *Sein und Zeit* (1927) [*Being and Time*][3] is largely responsible for this decisive shift in the history of hermeneutic thought. Heidegger had already alluded to the central place of hermeneutics in his philosophy early in this work, when he labeled his task the phenomenology of *Dasein*, a hermeneutic undertaking in the original sense of the word. In contrast to his teacher Edmund Husserl, who tried to introduce a rigorous 'scientific' method into philosophy, Heidegger's equation of phenomenology and hermeneutics announces an abandonment of this methodological path for 'non-scientific' truth. Later in the work, however, he is concerned more with clarifying the actual relationship between *Dasein* and *Verstehen* (understanding). Although for convenience *Dasein* may be thought of as human existence, it should not be confused with the Cartesian or the Kantian subject. It is that particular type of being for whom the question of Being arises, rather than the subject of cognition.

Heidegger makes clear that by understanding he does not mean a mode of cognition opposed to explanation, as Dilthey had defined the term. For him understanding is something prior to cognition, a primordial state or power of Being. The essence of understanding does not entail grasping the present situation, but rather projection (*Entwurf*) into the future. It has to do with the grasping of *Dasein*'s own potentiality-for-Being, the Being-possible that is essential for the structure of *Dasein*. Thus understanding has two aspects in Heidegger's thought: it designates both the existentially prior order of *Dasein* and the possibility of Being belonging to *Dasein*. This latter aspect Heidegger associates with interpretation (*Auslegung*), which is always grounded in understanding. For Heidegger interpretation is actually what we have already understood or the working out of possibilities projected in understanding. This conception of understanding and interpretation has enormous ramifications for textual criticism. To understand a text in Heidegger's sense does not involve ferreting out some meaning placed there by the author, but the unfolding of the possibility of Being indicated by the text. And interpretation does not entail imposing a 'signification' on a text or placing a value on it, but clarifying the involvement that is disclosed by the text in our always prior understanding of the world.

GADAMER'S *TRUTH AND METHOD*

Gadamer's magnum opus *Wahrheit und Methode* (1960) [*Truth and Method*] can be considered an explanation and expansion of the most important passages on hermeneutics in *Being and Time*. Indeed the title reiterates Heidegger's basic position concerning the nature of understanding in human endeavor. Unlike Heidegger's own use of 'and' in the title of his book, Gadamer's conjunction should not be read in its connective but in its disjunctive sense. Rejecting Husserl's notion of consciousness, Heidegger sought a new basis for phenomenology by investigating temporality, thus connecting Being with time. Gadamer's title, by contrast, must be read as an implicit dissociation of 'truth' from 'method'. Like Heidegger, the question of truth for Gadamer is prior to or outside of methodological considerations. The main target of the book in this regard is the experimental method of the natural sciences, which has too often been associated with truth in everyday consciousness. Much of what Gadamer opposes, of course, is a stereotypical picture of nineteenth-century methods rather than actual scientific practice; his criticism does not take into consideration more recent theorizing on scientific method by writers such as Popper, Kuhn, Feyerabend or Lakatos. None the less, his criticism is a valid refutation of traditional conceptions of our approach to natural phenomena. Method for Gadamer is something that a subject applies to an object to yield a specified result, which then in turn is labeled true. Gadamer's continuation of Heidegger's hermeneutic project is meant to counter the pernicious association of truth and method. Against the tendency of natural science to ignore the primordial scope of understanding, Gadamer proposes hermeneutics as both a corrective and a metacritical orientation that would oversee the whole field of methodology. Gadamer, unlike Dilthey and like Heidegger, thus claims for hermeneutics a universal status. He is interested in explaining understanding as such, not in its relationship to a particular discipline, but conceived as the essence of our being-in-the-world. In this sense his book is best viewed as an attempt to mediate between philosophy and natural science by going beyond the narrow horizon of scientific enquiry.

Gadamer's concerns, like Heidegger's, are thus philosophical and ontological in nature; *Truth and Method* introduces hermeneutics not to provide a new and better method, but to question methodology and its relationship to truth. To accomplish this task Gadamer constructs two philosophical narratives in his book. The first, heavily indebted to Heidegger, tells the story of the Western philosophical tradition in the form of a fall from grace and a possible future redemption from this fallen state. In some pre-Cartesian time – Heidegger specifies pre-Socratic Greece, but Gadamer remains evasive on this point – the scientific method had not yet come to dominate the notion of truth. Subject and object, being and thinking, were not radically severed from each other as they became later. But with the advent of Cartesian dualism the alienation of Western human beings, which had presumably been detectable long before Descartes, became the cornerstone of Western philosophy. According to this view of the history of philosophy the unstated task of speculative activity from the seventeenth to the twentieth century has been to conceal and to justify the alienation of mind and matter, subject and object, by constructing a philosophical basis for the scientific method. Kant's *Critique of Pure Reason* is the most important philosophical document in this tradition, since he supplies the most ingenious epistemological apology for the natural sciences.[4] Only in the twentieth century, with the work of Heidegger and Gadamer, is the forgotten notion of truth partly rehabilitated.

The second narrative embedded in *Truth and Method*, the history of hermeneutics, has similar concluding chapters, but a slightly different plot, since the hermeneutic tradition is generally associated by Gadamer with an opposition to the dominant scientific mode of thought. The beginning of this story lies in the pre-romantic era with the tradition of biblical exegesis and humanism. For Gadamer the origins of hermeneutics are intimately linked with the concern for discovering the correct sense of texts; hermeneutics seeks to reveal original meaning, whether the texts it treats are from the religious or the secular tradition. If the activity of legal interpretation is added to these two traditions, then we can see why preromantic hermeneutics is presented in terms of a threefold power: *subtilitas intelligendi* (understanding), *subtilitas explicandi* (explication) and *subtilitas applicandi* (application).

Once again this narrative is concerned primarily with the loss of an original state of existence. Gadamer's thesis is that hermeneutics in the course of its rather uneven development forgets its threefold power and is stripped eventually of its explicatory and applicative functions. Schleiermacher's writings represent a turning point in this development since he reduces hermeneutics to its power of understanding. Like Dilthey, Gadamer tends to associate his romantic predecessor with a psychologized version of hermeneutics, ignoring for the sake of his narrative the linguistic element in his work. The historians of the nineteenth century, especially Leopold von Ranke and Johann Gustav Droysen, added to hermeneutic reflection by considering the question of how tradition is mediated, and Gadamer credits Droysen in particular with debunking the notion of objectivity in historiography. But as heirs to the romantic tradition Gadamer considers their work to be deficient as well: they considered history as a text that is understood in much the same fashion as the work of an individual author is understood by Schleiermacher. Dilthey, according to Gadamer, has the distinction of recognizing the problem clearly. He saw the conflict between the psychology of understanding and the philosophy of history and sought to overcome the dichotomy by providing the human sciences with a new epistemological base. But Dilthey, like his predecessors, is unable to extricate himself from methodological thinking. He, too, sought objectivity and objective knowledge. His conception of the human sciences retains the subject-object duality inherent in the 'rival' scientific method.

The resolution to the hermeneutic dilemma, like the resuscitation of Western philosophy, involves Heidegger's overcoming of one final metaphysical obstacle: Husserl's phenomenology. Heidegger's thesis in *Being and Time*, as restated by Gadamer in an abbreviated and simplified form, is that 'Being itself is time'.[5] This radical rethinking of the historicity of *Dasein* has the effect of negating precisely the transcendental reduction that made Husserl's phenomenology possible. If the essence of *Dasein* lies in its finitude and temporality, being-in-the-world rather than transcendental ego, then the lifeworld (*Lebenswelt*) could not be reduced or bracketed as Husserl demanded. Nor could reflection set aside the facticity or situatedness of *Dasein* for a proto-I or transcendental subject. The ramifications of the historicity of *Dasein* for hermeneutics are enormous. Whereas for modern science and even for Dilthey historicity had been an obstacle to the ideal of objective knowledge, it was now transformed into a universal philosophical concept that enabled knowledge. As we have already seen, in *Being and Time* understanding becomes the way in which the historicity of *Dasein* is itself carried out. Dilthey's conflict between the psychology of understanding and the philosophy of history is thus dissolved by reformulating the question of Being and the role of hermeneutic reflection.[6]

THE PROVOCATION OF *TRUTH AND METHOD*

Gadamer understands his contribution to hermeneutics as a continuation of Heidegger's rethinking of Being. Especially important for him is his predecessor's affirmation of the pre-structured nature of understanding. While previous theory had advocated purging preconceptions to arrive at unbiased, objective knowledge about the world, Heidegger claims that it is precisely our being-in-the-world with its prejudices and presuppositions that makes understanding possible. This is made clear in his discussion of interpretation. For Heidegger interpretation is always grounded in something we have in advance, in a fore-having (*Vorhabe*), in something we see in advance, in a fore-sight (*Vorsicht*), and in something we grasp in advance, in a fore-conception (*Vorgriff*). This is another way of saying that we do not come to any object or text innocent of all presuppositions; we are always already filled with the primordial understanding Heidegger assigns to all *Dasein*. Analogously the meaning we derive from an object or a text must be conceived as the result of our presuppositions. Heidegger thus defines meaning as 'the "upon-which" (*Woraufhin*) of a projection in terms of which something becomes intelligible as something; it gets its structure from a fore-having, a fore-sight, and a fore-conception.'[7]

Gadamer takes up this issue most directly in his discussion of prejudice (*Vorurteil*). The German word, like its English equivalent, although etymologically related to prejudging or merely forming a judgement about something beforehand, has come to mean a negative bias or a quality that excludes accurate judgement. The Enlightenment, Gadamer claims, is responsible for discrediting the notion of prejudice. But this discrediting, he continues, is itself the result of a prejudice that is linked to the methodological claims to truth proposed by the natural sciences. Prejudice, because it belongs to historical reality itself, is not a hindrance to understanding but a condition for the possibility of understanding. Gadamer proposes a fundamental rehabilitation of this notion to do justice to the finitude of human existence and the necessarily historical mode of being-in-the-world. When Gadamer clarifies his use of 'prejudice' in this fashion, the reader can see that he is merely affirming with a different word the Heideggerian principles of fore-having, fore-sight and fore-conception. That he selects the word 'prejudice' instead of some less innocuous word can perhaps be explained by his desire to achieve a shock effect.[8]

Nevertheless, the notion that one's prejudices and preconceptions are a fundamental part of the hermeneutic situation has been extremely suggestive. In contrast to previous hermeneutic theory, which often incorporated an unwitting objectivist standpoint, the historicity of the interpreter is not a barrier to understanding. A truly hermeneutic thinking must take account of its own historicity (*die eigene Geschichtlichkeit mitdenken*). It is only a 'proper hermeneutics' when it demonstrates the effectivity (*Wirkung*) of history within understanding itself. Accordingly Gadamer calls this type of hermeneutics effective history (*Wirkungsgeschichte*). He is quick to caution that he is not trying to promote research to develop a new method that would take into account factors of effect and influence. He is not making a plea for a new and independent discipline ancillary to the human sciences. Instead he calls for a new type of consciousness – what he terms, somewhat awkwardly, 'effective-historical consciousness' (*wirkungsgeschichtliches Bewußtsein*) – which would recognize what is already occurring when we encounter documents from the past. Whether we approve of effective history or not, it is, according to Gadamer, intimately intertwined with our understanding, and effective historical consciousness simply makes us aware of this reality. It is consciousness of the inevitability of the hermeneutic situation.

To clarify further what this hermeneutic situation entails, Gadamer introduces the notion of 'horizon'. It is a term that he borrows from Husserl and the phenomenological tradition; in the phrase 'horizon of expectation' it later became a central concept of Hans Robert Jauss's aesthetics of reception.[9] In Gadamer's usage it designates 'a standpoint that limits the possibility of vision'[10] and is thus an essential part of the concept of situation. Horizon describes and defines our situatedness in the world. It should not be conceived in terms of a fixed or closed standpoint; it is 'something into which we move and which moves with us'.[11] It may also be defined with reference to the prejudices that we bring with us at any given time, since these represent a horizon beyond which we cannot see. The act of understanding is then described in one of Gadamer's most notorious metaphors as a fusion of one's own horizon with the historical horizon (*Horizontverschmelzung*). Gadamer concedes that the very idea of a separate horizon is illusory. There is no line that divides past from present horizon. The world of the past is not alien to us since it has contributed to the formation of our own horizon. Indeed, Gadamer claims at one point that in reality there is really only one horizon that 'embraces everything contained in historical consciousness'.[12] Nevertheless the illusion of a separate horizon, the necessary projection of a historical horizon, is a requisite phase in the process of understanding. It is immediately followed by historical consciousness recombining what it had distinguished in order to fuse and become one again. The fusing of horizons actually takes place, Gadamer maintains, but it means that the historical horizon is projected and then cancelled or eliminated as a separate entity. In an almost Hegelian manner it seems that understanding is historical consciousness becoming aware of itself.

This activity of consciousness is connected with what is possibly Gadamer's most original contribution to modern hermeneutics. Relying on legal hermeneutics as a paradigm, Gadamer insists that every interpretation is simultaneously an application (*Anwendung*). Restoring the *subtilitas applicandi* to hermeneutics, however, is not a mere gesture towards recapturing the original function of the interpretive enterprise. It is an affirmation and a logical consequence of principles developed in connection with effective-historical consciousness. Understanding means application for the present; tradition affects the present as the mediation of historical understanding. Legal hermeneutics is not a special case for Gadamer, but a paradigm for all hermeneutic activity. As in his usage of the term 'prejudice', he employs a provocative wording to elucidate an idea that is actually much less controversial. Application is not to be understood as a praxis in the Marxist sense, or as the performance of a physical deed. It does not entail a perceptible taking from the text and putting into activity in the real world. It is more akin to what Roman Ingarden has called 'concretion', an actualizing or making present for the interpreter.[13] In this sense a comparison could be drawn between a theater director interpreting a script and realizing it in performance, and the activity of a reader in understanding a text. Both include application in Gadamer's sense of the word. But we might also think of application within the frame of Gadamer's central analogy between the process of understanding and the dialogue. According to this model, when we encounter a text we enter into an open conversation with the past in which the give and take, the questioning and answering, leads to understanding. Application, then, can be described as a mediation between the then of the text and the now of the reader, as a conversation between the 'thou' of the past and the 'I' of the present. Seen as concretion or mediation, the concept of application loses some of its provocative appeal, and Gadamer's revival of the lost unity of legal hermeneutics is less radical than it appears at first glance.

It would be false, on the other hand, to go to the other extreme and to think of Gadamer's hermeneutics as a conservative enterprise, even though his plea for a rehabilitation of the notions of 'authority', the 'classical' and 'tradition' suggests a retrograde direction. Again the problem is largely, although not exclusively, one of provocative terminology. Gadamer accuses the Enlightenment of setting up an illicit opposition between authority and reason or freedom, and he points out in contrast to this view that authority as embodied in individuals is not the consequence of subjugation, but of a recognition that the person in authority has superior insight and judgement. Submission to authority is therefore grounded in reason and freedom, not power and arbitrariness. Tradition is seen as a form of authority, and it is also allied with reason and freedom in Gadamer's thought. For tradition is merely what generations have sought to preserve against the ravages of time. The act of preservation, Gadamer states, is no less a moment of freedom than that of rebellion or innovation. Rather than trying to cancel or avoid tradition, Gadamer feels that we have to recognize it as a part of historical relations and take account of its hermeneutic productivity. Much the same holds true for the classical (*das Klassische*). This notion should not be exclusively identified with antiquity or works of German classicism. It designates that which has distinguished itself over the years, works that persevered in the face of variable tastes and changing times. In a certain sense such works are timeless, but Gadamer emphasizes that their timelessness lies precisely in their historical being, in their ability to continue to speak to successive generations. Classical in the Gadamerian usage thus affirms both the appeal and the fundamentally limitless interpretability of a work. Classical works are simultaneously a testimony to the variability of human consciousness and the greatness of the finest products of human culture.

HABERMAS'S AGREEMENT WITH GADAMER

Since Habermas's first discussion of Gadamer's hermeneutics appears in the context of his book *Zur Logik der Sozialwissenschaften* ['On the Logic of the Social Sciences'], it is not surprising that he is initially enlisted as an ally.[14] A good portion of that work is meant to provide a foundation for the social sciences that would distinguish their methods from those of the natural sciences. Thus the book can be conceived in general as a continuation of basic propositions first developed in the positivist dispute. In their opposition to the hegemony of method over truth Habermas and Gadamer are part of a united front.

At first, however, Habermas discusses Gadamer in the context of the theory of language, particularly with regard to the language games postulated in the late works of Ludwig Wittgenstein. His main point is that the grammar of ordinary language supplies us with the ability to transcend the language that it defines and thus gives us the ability to translate from one language into another. When we learn a language we do not merely learn a language game that simply enables us to function in one particular language, as Wittgenstein suggests, but also what one might call a 'universal grammar' that allows us to go between languages. Among the plurality of languages Habermas postulates a unity of reason that transcends the particularity of an individual language. Wittgenstein can conceive of translation only as a transformation according to general rules, but he cannot admit these general rules into our practice of language learning. For Habermas, who uses Gadamer liberally to support his argument, the possibility of translation is founded upon ordinary language usage, and translation itself is only an extension of what occurs in normal conversation. In ordinary conversation the interlocutors must apply hermeneutic principles to understand what the speaker means. The assimilation of what has been said into something comprehensible is accomplished quickly and unconsciously in most cases; only when understanding becomes problematic are we aware of the process of 'translation' that underlies communication. For this reason the process of rendering an utterance in another language may be viewed as an extreme illustration of the hermeneutic process.

What unites Gadamer and Habermas against Wittgenstein therefore is the notion of language as dialogical and capable of reflecting upon its own preconditions, as opposed to the conception of language as a set of 'games' that competent speakers learn to perform and repeat. Habermas criticizes Wittgenstein precisely for conflating the primary process of language learning with the hermeneutic application of language. 'Wittgenstein failed to appreciate that the same rules also include the conditions of possibility of their interpretation.'[15] Learning a language the child learns not only the fundamental rules for accomplishing speech acts, but also the conditions for the potential interpretation of these rules. Although Wittgenstein recognized the societal origins of language and analyzed it accordingly as a life form, he unnecessarily limited the notion of language when he conceived linguistic practice as the reproduction of fixed patterns. Indeed, Habermas detects in this 'foreshortening of perspective' (p. 339) a residual positivism in Wittgenstein's work. Wittgenstein correctly saw that grammatical rules cannot be deduced from general rules, but failed to understand that the link between language and activity is not immutable, but subject to interpretation and development. Ultimately, Habermas detects in this rigid connection of ordinary language communication and grammatical rules a furtive adherence to the model of formalized languages he apparently abandoned. By contrast, for Habermas – and for Habermas's positive evaluation of Gadamer – language is characterized by its ability to thematize and question precisely the structures upon which Wittgenstein's theory depends. For hermeneutics language remains an open structure that allows native speakers both to interpret the rules that govern linguistic utterance and to distance themselves from these rules.

Habermas's alliance with Gadamer in opposing the formalist and 'positivist' residues in Wittgenstein point to two wider areas of agreement. The first of these is their mutual opposition to various forms of objectivism. For Gadamer objectivism was related in general to method, particularly to that of natural science. Habermas is more specific in his designations. In the first instance hermeneutic self-reflection opposes positivism, but it also furnishes a critique of phenomenological and linguistic foundations of the human sciences that retain objectivist vestiges. What Habermas finds especially useful in Gadamer is the notion of the always already situated nature of the interpreter. This notion argues against the claims of non-reflexive impartiality and scientific accuracy propounded by some brands of human science. Ultimately all forms of objectivism are incompatible with historicity as Gadamer conceives it.

Effective history supplies an antidote not only for historicist reductions, but also for positivist, neo-positivist and quasi-positivist ahistorical thought.

Habermas supports his (and Gadamer's) position with reflections on historiography. We may recall that the psychological tradition of hermeneutics identified with Schleiermacher and Dilthey assigned hermeneutics the task of approximating the experience of the original author. Gadamer and, following him, Habermas contend by contrast that the meaning of a text always exceeds that of the original author. For them meaning is not something that can be reconstructed by empathy or by the historicist method of recreating the original context. Meaning is conceived as a sedimentation of significations that continually emerge and change in the course of tradition. To illustrate this principle Habermas cites the case of historical statements. At the time that they are made historical accounts may be authentic descriptions of events, but because they are situated in a historical flux, their meaning changes with the course of history and our reading of history. A simple statement about the Thirty Years War, for example, acquires meaning according to developments that may occur many centuries later. From the perspective of the twentieth century it cannot be isolated from the delay in the development of German capitalism, or from the issue of German national unity, and it thus acquires a place in a narrative that progresses through to the events of the Third Reich. Eyewitness accounts, although they may be empirically accurate, are inevitably poorer than the historical description of events in the course of time. This is so simply because the later observer partakes in a more complete and richer narrative by being able to grasp cause and outcome more fully.

These observations on history lead Habermas to a second area of agreement with Gadamer: the reintroduction of application into hermeneutic reflection. We should recall that one of Habermas's chief objections to positivist thought was the separation of fact and decision or existence and ethics. In Gadamer's hermeneutic rehabilitation of application he believes that he finds a confirmation of his own insistence that these concepts be conceived as a unity. Comprehending events historically means for Habermas that we understand them in a scheme of possible action or life practice. Like Gadamer,

Habermas finds that theological and juridical hermeneutics are exemplary for their practical dimensions and the foundation for all interpretative understanding. Both agree that hermeneutics partakes in the Aristotelian notion of practical knowledge. It not only contributes to self-understanding and to the socialization process; it also affirms that goals and the means for attaining them share the same life form. Hermeneutics thus plays an important role in what Habermas would later develop in his theory of 'communicative action'. By mediating understanding from the past as well as between present cultures and groups, it proves itself essential for assisting in the formation of consensus. In this regard we can see the attraction for Habermas in a theory of hermeneutic understanding conceived as 'structurally oriented toward eliciting from tradition a possible action-orienting self-understanding of social groups' (p. 353).

HABERMAS'S CRITIQUE OF TRADITION AND AUTHORITY

Despite Habermas's recruitment of Gadamer for his battles with protean positivist tendencies, he feels that Gadamer is fundamentally mistaken in his rigid dichotomy of truth and method. For in separating hermeneutic reflection from the natural sciences, Gadamer unwittingly confirms the devaluation of hermeneutics made by its opponents. In contrast to this view Habermas contends first that hermeneutics cannot afford to remain metacritical. It must also partake in methodology if it is to be of any value to the human sciences. Like his colleague Karl-Otto Apel, Habermas seems uncomfortable with the total lack of objective standards in Gadamer's theory. If we are to be able to distinguish between understanding and misunderstanding then we must have some criteria on which to base this distinction. In short, we cannot be concerned solely with the structure of understanding or the possibility of understanding, we must also take into account the validity of understanding.[16] In order to accomplish this we cannot pretend that methodology is simply false. We must oppose the universalist claims of method, particularly as they have been represented by empirico-analytical sciences. But this opposition 'brings no dispensation from the business of methodology in general' (p. 356). With this Habermas suggests that his notion of hermeneutics should be situated at a different level to Gadamer's. Whereas ontological hermeneutics wishes to sever all connections with epistemology, Habermas wants to recruit hermeneutics for the methodology of the social sciences.

Second, Habermas points out that developments in the natural sciences have drastically altered the philosophical tradition and thus our present situation. To pretend that we can exclude the natural sciences is to ignore the horizon of our own age and to deny the historicity of knowledge. Method, including the method Gadamer associates with the natural sciences, is an integral part of our heritage. Gadamer violates his own notion of effective-historical consciousness by juxtaposing method and truth in an abstract schema. In general, then, Habermas wants to link the empirical and the analytical methods of natural sciences with hermeneutic procedures, to incorporate into his hermeneutic reflections the methodological consciousness of the natural sciences. But he is not completely consistent in this demand. At times he too appears to separate these realms, particularly in his discussion of technical knowledge and practical knowledge in his early writings, or in the dichotomy of instrumental reason and communicative reason in his more recent works. In his debate with Gadamer, however, he rejects a theory that would dissociate these two realms and thereby eliminate hermeneutic experience from methodological concerns, isolating it as the abstract bearer of truth.

Habermas's more serious objections concern the implications of Gadamer's work for an emancipatory political practice. At the center of his critique are Gadamer's anti-Enlightenment polemics on prejudice, authority and tradition. He accuses him of accepting the incomplete and undialectical view of the Enlightenment propagated by Edmund Burke and by German romanticism. At issue in particular is the role of authority. For Gadamer authority, as we have seen, is not necessarily authoritarian; true authority does not survive because of blind obedience to a superior force, but because of insight into superior knowledge. Habermas points out that such a view reveals 'a basic philosophical conviction that is not covered by hermeneutics but at most by its absolutization' (p. 357). In contradistinction to the ontologizing of tradition undertaken by Gadamer in Heidegger's footsteps, he introduces the notion of reflection. According to Habermas, Gadamer's championing of the prejudices handed down by tradition denies our ability to reflect upon these prejudices and to reject them. Agents appear as passive recipients caught in the endless stream of their heritage. What Habermas wants is a critical dimension in hermeneutic thought, one that would enable us to carry out a critique of ideology (*Ideologiekritik*). Ultimately Habermas's conception of knowledge is not rooted in tradition and the authority that emanates from tradition, but in 'rational insight and decision' (p. 358) that have the possibility to defy what has been handed down. What is at stake philosophically for Habermas is an adherence to the Enlightenment as mediated by German idealism. In his one-sided reception of the Enlightenment Gadamer aligns himself with a nineteenth-century provincialism in German thought that maintained 'a dangerous pretension to superiority' (p. 358) over the power of reason and rational argument.

But Habermas recognizes that the problem is not that simple. If he is going to argue for a critique of ideology that could oversee and correct appropriations of tradition, then he is called upon to legitimate this critique of ideology in something other than the very tradition from which it emerges. He locates this legitimation through an analysis of the role of language in Gadamer's thought. Gadamer has recourse to language to separate his hermeneutic theory from those of his predecessors. Indeed, Habermas correctly sees Gadamer as part of the 'linguistic turn' in twentieth-century philosophy: Wittgenstein's transcendental and socio-linguistic perspectives are superseded by Gadamer's hermeneutics, 'a third stage of reflection' on language, which incorporates history into linguistic analysis. With Gadamer the interpreter and the object are conceived as part of the same process, and tradition is conceived not as a body of knowledge that we master, but as a 'transmitted language in which we live' (p. 359).

Habermas agrees with this conception of our linguistic determination, but with significant limitations. The difference between Gadamer and Habermas with regard to ideology and emancipation can be seen as a function of the role of language in social action. For Gadamer language appears to be a pure system of exchange not subject to distortion by power or social processes. Thus Habermas objects to Gadamer's idealized meta-institution of language, reminding us that 'language is *also* a medium of domination and social power; it serves to legitimate relations of organized force' (p. 360). For Habermas 'the objective framework of social action is not exhausted by the dimension of subjectively intended and symbolically transmitted meaning' (p. 361). He insists that non-linguistic constraints on our outer and inner nature – he names them 'labor' and 'domination' – must be considered in an analysis of social process. Only a self-sufficient and idealized hermeneutics can exist in a pristine linguistic universe; if such a hermeneutics is to be of value for an emancipatory social science, it must address 'in the objective framework constituted conjointly by language, labor, and domination' (p. 361), the ideological distortions and oppression that are transmitted through our common heritage.

THE DISPUTE OVER HERMENEUTIC UNIVERSALITY

Gadamer correctly understood Habermas's objections as a challenge to his thesis of hermeneutic universality. When Habermas calls on reflection to correct false ideology or when he includes labor and domination in a triad with language, he is in effect asserting that we can call on some non-hermeneutic power to determine meaning or have recourse to a non-hermeneutic realm to analyze social action. Accordingly Gadamer's defense centers on a reaffirmation of our embeddedness in linguistic understanding. With regard to reflection and the critique of ideology that derives from it Gadamer detects only a furtive dogmatism. The separation between the ongoing tradition and a reflection on this tradition suggests that we can attain some vantage point outside the process from which to judge and evaluate. If the point from which we reflect is inside tradition, then we have no need for a non-hermeneutic assumption. If it is outside the heritage, or if it conceives of itself as a privileged perspective inside the heritage, then we are simply breaking off hermeneutic reflection in the face of dogmatically asserted truths. In Gadamer's view the critique of ideology, because it is itself a linguistic act of reflection, is already included in the universal concept of hermeneutics. Similarly, Gadamer does not challenge the notions of labor and domination, or 'work' and 'politics', as he renames them, but conceives of them as implicated in a linguistically mediated universe. He does not claim that language determines the material world, as the idealists did, but only that 'there is no societal reality, with all its concrete forces, that does not bring itself to representation in a consciousness that is linguistically articulated'.[17] Language is not determinate for reality and human action, but merely for an understanding of reality and of human action.[18]

Gadamer is somewhat less successful in countering Habermas's ideological objections. Although he tries to turn the tables on his adversary, imputing dogmatism and romanticism to his reliance on reflection, his defense of 'authority' leaves him open to renewed political attack. Habermas had not asserted that authority is always wrong or that authority and reason are antitheses, as Gadamer maintains. He had advocated reflection as a means of stripping away from authority those elements that are simply the results of domination. Gadamer, by contrast, defends his anti-Enlightenment stance by shifting the discussion from the propagation of authority to the acceptance of authority. Acceptance or acknowledgement of authority are the keys to its survival, he claims, and the fact that authority persists from one generation to the next is the result of 'dogmatic acceptance' not 'dogmatic power'.[19] The onus of rejecting authority is thus placed on those who are subjected to it. 'Authority can rule only because it is "freely" recognized and accepted. The obedience that belongs to it is neither blind nor slavish.'[20]

The manner in which Gadamer phrases his arguments demonstrates that once he ventures out of his ontological enclave into the field of social and political thought he is ill prepared for conflict. We might concur that there is nothing wrong with 'freely recognized' authority, but Habermas's point was that authority is not transmitted and institutionalized 'freely'. Freely accepted authority suggests that coercion is eliminated and that subjects can 'freely' situate themselves outside the tradition that validates authority. Habermas suggested something similar in his introduction of the critique of ideology, which would function as an independent check on coercive and oppressive traditions. Gadamer, of course, recognizes the precariousness of his argument when he places the key word 'freely' (frei) in quotation marks. But the use of quotation marks does not relieve him of the necessity to counter Habermas's objections to the power of oppressive and authoritative traditions. At critical points in his political defense, therefore, Gadamer indirectly supports Habermas's position by implying that there exists a 'freely' chosen perspective from which to evaluate tradition or independent criteria for judging 'authority'.

In his rebuttal Habermas does not exploit these slips in Gadamer's logic, but rather seeks to demonstrate the limits of hermeneutic competence.[21] He credits hermeneutics with achievements in four specific areas. In the social sciences and humanities it has contributed to a recognition that the objectivist models of the natural sciences are inadequate and distorting. With respect to methods in the *Geisteswissenschaften* hermeneutics reminds us of the symbolic prestructuring of the object that underlies all social enquiry and testing. In the natural sciences it has taught us that research decisions are never made on exclusively scientific principles, but on the basis of metatheoretical discussions in a scientific community. And finally hermeneutics provides the theoretical foundation for translating scientific knowledge into the normal language of the lifeworld.

As important as hermeneutics may be, Habermas notes several limitations on its claim to universality. He first hints at something external to hermeneutics when he discusses rhetorical persuasion. Rhetoric, like hermeneutics, manifests an element of force that cannot be entirely reconciled with Gadamer's dialogical notion of transmission. Although Habermas does not develop the argument here, he is obviously suggesting that the linguistically inherited tradition is not innocent of power relations that escape ontological hermeneutics. Habermas also sees a limit to hermeneutics in the methods of the natural sciences. In contrast to the dialogical model at the heart of hermeneutics, the interactive mode of the natural sciences can be conceived as a monologue of a subject about an object. Although 'monologically generated knowledge' must be translatable into everyday language and thus comprehensible for a human community, Habermas insists that we can detect a prelinguistic basis for purposive-rational action. Relying on the developmental psychology of Jean Piaget, Habermas posits a non-linguistic root for operative thought. The ramifications of such a postulate for the universality of hermeneutics are devastating:

> If it is the case that operative intelligence goes back to pre-linguistic, cognitive schemes, and is therefore able to use language in an instrumental way, then the hermeneutic claim to universality would find its limit in the linguistic systems of science and the theories of rational choice. (p. 189)

Habermas does not explore the monological use of language and its non-linguistic basis, but turns instead to another possible limit. Hermeneutics, he argues, depends on everyday or natural language as the last metalanguage. In principle everything must be translatable into a common idiom for understanding to occur. If, however, there exists a theory of retrieving meaning that is not dependent on hermeneutical presuppositions, which are always *ad hoc*, but is based on methodological premises, then hermeneutics must forfeit its claim to universality. Habermas believes that he has found two non-trivial examples of the limits of hermeneutics: psychoanalysis and the critique of ideology. In both cases the subject is not aware of or in control of the meaning of his/her utterances. This would appear to pose no problem for Gadamer's theory, since he does not rely on individual consciousness for the transmission of meaning. But Habermas's point seems to be that both psychoanalysis and the critique of ideology are illustrations of the collective, rather than the individual, transmission of meaning, and that, furthermore, the meaning of utterances in both cases is 'systematically distorted', and thus inappropriate for the sort of dialogue that Gadamer envisions. What Habermas is suggesting is that before a conversation can occur, a non-hermeneutical process of translation must be applied that will 'beat a path through to the pathologically blocked meaning-context' (p. 189). An ideologically informed statement cannot be taken at face value; it first has to be rendered capable of dialogue through a process of disclosing how it results from distortion.

Habermas does not choose the critique of ideology for further clarification, but examines instead the psychoanalytic claim to decipher a deeper level of meaning. In contrast to ideologically distorted statements, which may be viewed as

the consequence of false consciousness, psychoanalysis establishes the limits of normal hermeneutics by looking at distortions resulting from the layering of consciousness. Drawing
on the work of Alfred Lorenzer, Habermas outlines a depth
hermeneutics that is guided by specific theoretical assumptions
rather than by adherence to tradition. These theoretical
assumptions take account of the fact that language is no longer
employed in a public fashion and that there is no necessary
congruence between the intentions, actions and speech of the
patient. Depth hermeneutics also presupposes an organization
of symbols at a prelinguistic level; the logical and public use
of symbols we expect in everyday communication is not operative, for example, in dreams, as Freud had pointed out at the
beginning of the century. Thus instead of 'elementary hermeneutic understanding' (*einfaches hermeneutisches Sinnver-
stehen*) we must turn to what Lorenzer calls 'scenic understanding' (*das szenische Verstehen*) (p. 194), which makes clear the
meaning of utterances and symbols by clarifying the original
scene. Apparent nonsense at the level of consciousness is
explained by causes from unconscious sources. Meaning is not
determined by a content, by answering the question, 'what?',
but by reference to an initial situation, by answering the question 'why?'

Depth hermeneutics is therefore something of a misnomer,
since it is an explanatory rather than a hermeneutic procedure.
It is no longer based on the model of translation that is the
foundation of hermeneutic doctrine, but on systematic and
methodological principles. The distinction Habermas is trying
to draw can perhaps best be understood with regard to language. Depth hermeneutics requires a pre-understanding that
reflects upon language; it sets up assumptions about the way
in which the human mind functions and the way in which
symbols are produced and subjected to distortion. Regular
hermeneutics presupposes a placement within language; it
assumes that the interpreter or interlocutor is always located
within a tradition and denies methodological presuppositions.
Perhaps more important is that depth hermeneutics proceeds
from the notion of a distorted communication that needs analysis and correction. It thus takes upon itself the meta-hermeneu-
tical task of overseeing the dialogue that is the foundation of

normal hermeneutics. In terms of communicative competence Habermas formulates the difference as follows:

> explanatory understanding, in the sense of the depth-hermeneutical decoding of specifically inadequate expressions, does not only necessitate the skilled application of naturally acquired communicative competence, as is the case with elementary hermeneutical understanding, but also pre-supposes a theory of communicative competence (p. 202)

Only a theory of communicative competence can explain the deformations in the normal dialogical situation caused by the unconscious on an individual level or by power and ideology at the level of a society.

The objections that Habermas presents to Gadamer's claim to hermeneutic universality do not invalidate Gadamer's project and his enthusiasm for it. Habermas continues to subscribe to hermeneutic principles, but he senses a political danger in Gadamer's blind adherence to tradition and authority. In essence Habermas is uncomfortable with a theory that overturns the Enlightenment appeal to reason in favor of a potentially coercive or biased heritage. The differences between the two can be fruitfully understood in relation to the question of consensus and to the point at which they idealize the dialogical situation. Gadamer, according to Habermas, feels that interpretation and understanding take place against a background of a consensus that is reliable because it is part of the tradition. Habermas, by contrast, wants to guard against the possibility that such a consensus was achieved through 'pseudo-communication', that is, through communication that appears to be free, but is not. Two of the checks he suggests against 'false consensus' are psychoanalysis, which would identify distortions caused by repressions, and the critique of ideology, which would decipher utterances informed by oppression. Gadamer, in short, works with an always already achieved consensus; Habermas projects his consensus into the future when a distortion-free dialogue can occur.

The identical temporal discrepancy can be observed in their respective idealization of the hermeneutic dialogue. For Gadamer idealization appears to be built into the normal interchange. Language is conceived as a pure system of exchange not subject to distortion by power or social processes. Habermas's own idealization of dialogue occurs as a kind of utopian projection that informs actual interchanges. 'The anticipation of possible truth and true life is constitutive for every linguistic communication which is not monological' (p. 206), and only this anticipation enables us to posit a regulative principle of understanding. Gadamer's idealization is incorporated into our conversation with the other; Habermas's is the condition for the possibility of our entering into an understanding with the other.

POLITICS AND ONTOLOGY

For Habermas hermeneutics is clearly part of an emancipatory political project for the social sciences. Originally posited in the positivist dispute as an alternative to empirical methods, it first functions in a vaguely defined sense as a synonym for dialectics. By the time he takes up Gadamer's hermeneutics it has already developed in the direction of what would later become the foundation of a theory of 'communicative reason'. But the change in focus that has occurred between the two debates involves something more than clarification of direction and definition. At stake for Habermas in his debate with Gadamer are more than just theoretical issues of language or the methods of the natural sciences. The political integrity of his project depends on the possibility of combining critical reflection with hermeneutic understanding. The dispute with Gadamer is thus more imminently political than the controversy with Albert and Popper. Whereas Habermas acted in his first major public debate as a disciple of the Frankfurt School's concern for dialectical theory and concentrated on the rather technical issues of value-freedom and the limitations of analytical-empirical research methods, in his objections to Gadamer he is concerned with preserving a realm outside of an ontological hermeneutic understanding that will enable him to reflect critically and politically on tradition. Hermeneutics serves as an alternative to a politically retrograde positivism in the first debate, but in the second debate it is itself in need of a political corrective.

Obviously both Gadamer and Habermas understood that politics was the central issue in their dispute, and this is reflected in their last direct comments on one another's positions. Gadamer's response occurs at the end of a collection entitled *Hermeneutik und Ideologiekritik* (1971) ['Hermeneutics and the Critique of Ideology'] which includes the major contributions in the Habermas-Gadamer encounter plus additional essays by Karl-Otto Apel, Claus von Bormann, Rüdiger Bubner and Hans-Joachim Giegel.[22] In essence Gadamer reasserts the universality of hermeneutics by re-emphasizing its ontological status. If understanding defines our manner of being-in-the-world, then there is no outside point from which to reflect upon it unless one posits an idealist notion of transcendence. By postulating the ubiquity of tradition Gadamer effectively cancels an external challenge to the heritage. Everything, including revolutionary positions, are included in his all-encompassing notion of hermeneutics. 'Alteration of the existing conditions is no less a form of connection to tradition than is a defense of existing conditions.'[23] In a move resembling Hegel's dialectics, Gadamer's hermeneutics swallows up all opposition, including Habermas's critique of ideology and psychoanalysis. Indeed, Gadamer even recruits the latter to defend his notion of authority. In his version of the psychoanalytic process, the patient willingly submits him/herself to the authority of the therapist. Far from providing a counter-example to the hermeneutic project, Habermas's exemplary case, as Gadamer reworks it, serves as a paradigm for the hegemony of tradition.

Habermas ignored these remarks, but nearly a decade later in his *Theory of Communicative Action* he returns to Gadamer's hermeneutics in a slightly altered context. For Habermas what remains important in hermeneutical theory is its dialogical presupposition and hence its relation to communicative models, not its status as a foundation for the social sciences. Habermas's critique focuses on the one-sided conception of dialogue in Gadamer's work. Claiming that Gadamer draws his model from the interpretation of sacred scriptures, Habermas objects first to the passivity of the interpreter in the face of tradition. Although Gadamer's notion of a fusion of horizons emphasizes the mutuality of reader and text, Habermas argues that 'the knowledge embodied in the text is, Gadamer believes, fundamentally superior to the interpreter's'.[24] Opposed to this unequal relationship is an anthropological model that posits a process of reconstructing the history of rationality as a paradigm for understanding. Gadamer's theory is further criticized for its deficient notion of application. What Habermas detects here is the danger of an identification of understanding and agreement. 'To understand a symbolic expression means to know under what conditions its validity claim would have to be accepted; but it does *not* mean assenting to its validity claim without regard to content.'[25] Although Habermas no longer insists on an external check to hermeneutics – his check is internally derived from formal pragmatic considerations – his objection resembles his earlier criticism of hermeneutic universality. Understanding the other, whether as written text or as oral dialogical partner, may be achieved by hermeneutic insights, but reaching agreement demands an active and free participation that can reject and modify, as well as accept, tradition and authority.

Up until now we have related the differences between Gadamer and Habermas to a distinction between hermeneutics and the critique of ideology. But if we take a lead from the work of Paul Ricoeur, the leading French hermeneutic theorist in the twentieth century, we could also conceive of their differences in terms of their adherence to two different hermeneutic traditions.[26] In his book on Freud, Ricoeur outlines two types of hermeneutics that have been operative in the West. The first type attributes to hermeneutics the function of recapturing or 'recollecting' meaning. Although this variety of hermeneutics is associated primarily with the theological works of Rudolf Bultmann, it has definite affinities with Gadamer's theory as well. The hermeneutics of faith or hermeneutics of the sacred seeks to make manifest or to restore a meaning, understood as a message, a proclamation, or a *kerygma*. It tries to make sense of what was once understood, but has become obscure because of distantiation. Bultmann's demythologizing illustrates such a hermeneutic endeavor because it emphasizes an original and sacred meaning in the symbols of the New Testament. Demythologizing is not meant to discredit symbols, but to recover original meaning. Ricoeur associates this brand of hermeneutics with the phenomenology of religion. It presupposes a confidence in the power of language, but not necessarily as a medium of communication between individuals. Rather, the ability to interpret symbols stems from the fact that humans are born into language, 'into the light of the logos'. Despite its insistence on dialogue and the fusion of horizons, the reliance on tradition and on the omnipresence of language brings Gadamer's hermeneutics into the proximity of the hermeneutics of the sacred.[27]

Opposed to this religiously tinged hermeneutics of the sacred is a 'hermeneutics of suspicion'. Ricoeur identifies this type of interpretation specifically with three of the most seminal thinkers of the twentieth century: Marx, Nietzsche and Freud. Like Habermas, who draws from all three in his depth hermeneutics, each distrusted the word and sought to go below the surface to some more authentic realm of meaning. Implicit in this approach to interpretation is the belief that surface phenomena are concealing an essential reality, and that to arrive at truth one must penetrate to a totally different realm of existence. The hermeneutics of suspicion is not concerned with recovering the object, but with tearing away masks, with disclosing disguises, with revealing false consciousness. In relation to the philosophical tradition, this branch of hermeneutics casts doubt upon the last realm of certainty for modern thought since Descartes: human consciousness. In contrast to Bultmann's demythologizing, the hermeneutics of suspicion advocates the most radical demystification.[28] The Gadamer–Habermas debate is obviously a particular version of the larger conflict between these two hermeneutics. Habermas's call for a critique of ideology depends on insights developed in the hermeneutics of suspicion. Gadamer's ontological theory of understanding, like the hermeneutics of faith, aims to mediate tradition, disclosing some earlier meaning in light of present concerns. Ricoeur tries to reconcile these differences by a general strategy of mutual implication. As regards Habermas and Gadamer he shows how a true hermeneutic theory must include critical elements and how any critique of ideology cannot do without some notion of hermeneutic understanding.[29]

Despite the valiant mediating strategy of Ricoeur, the fundamental distinctions between Gadamer and Habermas cannot be solved quite so easily. It would be possible, of course, to dismiss their differences on the basis of an incongruity on the level of philosophical discourse. According to this view Gadamer is writing about ontology, a fundamental realm of Being, and his hermeneutics describes a non-negotiable condition of existence. This is certainly the way Heidegger conceived his philosophy in *Being and Time*, and Gadamer's indebtedness to his teacher has been documented earlier. Habermas, by contrast, would appear to be addressing concerns of the social sciences. When he posits the critique of ideology or psychoanalysis as a corrective for hermeneutic hegemony he is already operating within epistemological parameters, trying to ascertain the meaning of utterances and their function inside of a theory of social science. Gadamer, in short, can be seen as exploring the condition of possibility for meaningful dialogue, whereas Habermas's interventions relate to the actual methods of interpretation.

This separation of levels is open to two criticisms. In the first place, Gadamer, in contrast to Heidegger, does not rigorously distinguish the ontological from the epistemological. His formulations often suggest that he is concerned with a method that would underlie both the social and natural sciences. More important for Habermas's political critique, however, is the very legitimacy of setting up a hierarchy of levels that credits ontology with the most primary relationship to existence. Indeed, although it is never formulated in these terms, Habermas's assault on Gadamer's work can be conceived as a challenge to the ontological premises informing both Gadamer's and Heidegger's writings on hermeneutics. What is implicitly questioned in Habermas's objections is the legitimacy of carving out a privileged ontological realm that controls and oversees understanding. In this regard Habermas continues a critical tradition that rejects first philosophies for socially situated and pragmatically informed theory.

4

Democracy and the student movement: the debate with the left

Habermas's initial objections to Gadamer's hermeneutics were first published in the *Philosophische Rundschau* in 1967; his second contribution to this debate occurred in 1970 in a Festschrift for Gadamer.[1] This was not the only controversy Habermas was involved with during these years. More important, more immediate, and more sensational was his confrontation with the student movement. As in other Western nations, the student movement in Germany is a product of the 1960s. Associated with the maturation of the first generation of the postwar baby boom, the German movement exhibited many of the same causes and concerns that emerged in other industrialized countries. The general discontent with material accumulation and the lack of political commitment in the 1950s, as well as the first signs of economic instability in Western capitalism, are common sources for this widespread student unrest.

Specifically German, however, were two factors. First and foremost was the weight of the National Socialist past. Throughout the years of miraculous economic recovery, known as the *Wirtschaftswunder*, the deeds of National Socialism were repressed by a good portion of the population. With the Eichmann trial in 1961, the Auschwitz trial in 1963 and the production of several popular plays about the Third Reich, including Rolf Hochhuth's controversial drama *Der Stellvertreter* [*The Deputy*], the Fascist past began to enter into the consciousness of the new generation. Quite naturally they sought answers from their parents, and when these answers proved to be inadequate, conflict ensued. The generation conflict in the Federal Republic was more than the mere repetition of primeval struggles between fathers and sons, mothers and daughters. In Germany it assumed an overtly political dimension. Second, the student movement belonged to a larger oppositional tendency known as the extra-parliamentary opposition (APO). Perhaps the two most important factors in the emergence of the APO were the party congress of the SPD (Social Democratic Party of Germany) in 1959, at which certain socialist principles were revised, and the so-called Great Coalition between the two largest parties, the Social Democrats and the Christian Democrats, in 1966. The message that these events delivered to progressives was that they had no voice in the German parliament and that the only authentic opposition had to locate itself outside official governmental structures.[2]

Habermas sympathized with both of these larger concerns of the German APO. His opposition must be conceived more accurately as a disagreement with certain elements or with certain tactics in the student movement. Indeed, he has consistently maintained that he supported the general goals and aims of the students, that he had never placed himself 'outside the framework of the student movement', as some maintained.[3] Habermas has good reason to depict himself as an advocate of student concerns. Almost all observers of the West German political scene in the 1960s, whether conservative or leftist, have considered his works to be one of the inspirations of the student movement. As the most noted member of the second generation of critical theorists, Habermas himself was viewed throughout much of the 1960s as an important representative of a non-orthodox Marxist tradition. His first major work, *Structural Transformations of the Public Sphere*, which, as we saw in Chapter 1, was widely read and discussed among leftists, was conceived as a contribution to an oppositional political theory. In an interview from 1979 Habermas discusses events surrounding the composition of the book, including the expulsion of the SDS (Socialist German Students) from the SPD. To counter this exclusionary tactic of the SPD, Habermas, together with a small number of progressive colleagues, founded the Socialist League, and although he states that he did not write *Structural Transformations* to recruit students for the SDS, he did consider it part of a political project that analyzed the 'inherent weaknesses' in the Federal Republic that could become 'dangerous'.[4]

Not coincidentally, *Structural Transformations* thematizes one of the three central targets of the student movement. Habermas's discussion of the demise of authentic democratic discussion and of the role that the monopolized mass media play in keeping the general population uninformed and uncritical continued a critique that Adorno and Horkheimer had developed in their *Dialectic of Enlightenment*. The reception of this discussion by the students during the late 1960s led to the notorious anti-Springer campaign: the mass demonstrations against the Springer publishing house, one of the largest and most conservative in the Federal Republic and the publisher of the *Bildzeitung*, a sensationalist newspaper with the widest circulation in the country. This newspaper was particularly harsh in its criticism of the students, and no doubt its inflammatory rhetoric contributed to the violence and repression that occurred in 1967 and 1968.

A second important focus of the student movement was the university and university reform. West Germans shared this concern with most other student uprisings in the 1960s, but in some ways this issue was of greater consequence in Germany than elsewhere. The oppressive and hierarchical university system that had existed in Germany in the late nineteenth and earlier twentieth centuries had been only partly dismantled by reforms in the postwar period. Basically undemocratic and elitist, the German postwar university threatened to prolong, rather than eliminate the social and educational inequities that existed in the Federal Republic. Moreover, at many German universities the Fascist past still cast a long and pernicious shadow over many faculties. While the German Democratic Republic had virtually eliminated all former Fascists from teaching positions in higher education, in the West former National Socialists often retained their professorships, altering their pedagogical practices and their university politics only when they could not avoid doing so. For the leftist students of the 1960s the result was a tremendous amount of resentment against a generation of conservative and recalcitrant professors. To his credit, Habermas had pushed for university reforms since the late 1950s, and he continued to support actively and publicly democratic and education reforms throughout the 1960s.[5]

THE CHARGE OF 'LEFTIST FASCISM'

An event from the third area of concern for the student movement, oppression in the Third World, precipitated the initial
confrontation between Habermas and some factions of activists. This occurred in West Berlin, one of the centers of student
opposition throughout the 1960s. In 1964 demonstrations had
already taken place to call public attention to the injustices of
right-wing dictatorships in Third World countries. In December
1964 the visit of Moïse Tshombé, the Congolese head of state
deemed responsible for the assassination of the leftist leader
Patrice Lamumba, and in March 1965 a recruitment campaign
by officials of the South African government had been greeted
with student protests. In the following two years the Vietnam
war took center stage in foreign affairs, and Berlin witnessed
a series of angry street demonstrations against American
imperialism in South-East Asia. So the atmosphere in Berlin
was already charged when, on the occasion of a visit by the
Shah of Iran on 2 June 1967, students again organized a mass
protest. In the confrontation that ensued between supporters
of the Shah and opponents, one of the students, Benno Ohnesorg, was fatally wounded by a policeman. He was apparently
shot while fleeing the scene of the demonstration.[6]

The death of Ohnesorg unleashed a series of student activities throughout universities in the Federal Republic. Because
Ohnesorg was buried in Hanover, a special congress entitled
'University and Democracy' (*Hochschule und Demokratie*) was
scheduled at the local university, and Habermas was one of
the seven invited speakers. His talk began with a harsh con-
demnation of the role of the press and the political parties in
the Federal Republic. The former had fostered an anti-intellec-
tual campaign, while the latter, by distancing themselves from
the students, had promoted intolerance and an authoritarian
attitude. Habermas also expressed alarm at the events that had
taken place the week before in Berlin. The reaction of the
authorities to the demonstration evidenced a quality 'that we
recognize again for the first time since the days of Fascism in
Berlin and in the Federal Republic' (p. 138). The rest of the talk
is devoted to the role students can play in extra-parliamentary
opposition. Habermas credits the students with being an
important vehicle of political enlightenment. Because they are

81

not directly affected by economic interest groups they can perform the important function of compensating for the suppression of criticism by the press, political parties and the government:

> The task of the student opposition in the Federal Republic has been and continues to be to compensate for the lack of a theoretical perspective, for the lack of sensibility with regard to obfuscations and denunciations, for the lack of radicalism in the interpretation and practice of our legally binding and democratic constitution, for the lack of the ability to anticipate the future and to possess an imaginative fantasy, in short, for our omissions. (p. 141)

Yet Habermas feels that there are definite limits to student activities, and although he does not go into detail, he does discuss briefly a few 'objective and subjective dangers' of the movement. The objective dangers are all related to the structure of the university as a social institution. Universities are faced with a difficult dilemma. Either they can increase their productivity and thus integrate themselves into a system of social labor and remove themselves simultaneously from the political public sphere, or they can assert their position in the democracy by democratizing themselves. In opting for the second tendency, Habermas feels the students must insist on the integration of political questions into the educational process and their equal participation in the governance of the university, while struggling against the instrumentalization of education into a training ground for a social elite. The subjective dangers result from a series of tensions that operate in the consciousness of students. The tension between theory and practice can lead to the opposite poles of indifference or to an arbitrarily conceived 'actionism'. The tension between political engagement and preparation for a career can lead to the equally abhorrent alternatives of over-accommodation for the sake of career choices or to a rejection of intellectual exploration in the material studied. Finally, the tension between the need for a practical general orientation and more narrow scholarly pursuits can lead to the dichotomy of positivistic reduction of problems or theoretical oversimplification. Above all students must remember that in the present non-revolutionary situation the primary goal is enlightenment through reason and argumentation, not the provocation of violence.

Habermas's talk at the Hanover commemoration was hardly directed against the student movement. Yet the limitations he felt to be inherent in their struggle within an emancipatory process were perceived as a challenge to the activities that had been undertaken and that were being planned. This view is evident in the talk given by Rudi Dutschke, one of the leaders of the student movement, at the Hanover symposium on 9 June. Dutschke begins with a brief economic analysis that asserts a new dynamics of the class struggle and of the relationship between theory and practice as capitalism seeks to overcome barriers to accumulation. The material conditions are at hand, according to Dutschke, for the solution to problems of need, but human beings must take matters into their own hands.

> Everything depends on the conscious will of humankind, finally to become conscious of its history as something made by humankind, to control it, to tame it, that is, Professor Habermas, your conceptually deficient objectivism is destroying the subject that has to be emancipated.[7]

Dutschke sees the student movement as a response to the economically determined restructuring of the educational system in capitalist countries. The terrorist actions of the establishment against the students demonstrate the centrality of the anti-authoritarian, democratic movement. What is needed now, above all, Dutschke contends, is action. Enlightenment without action, he continues in an obvious allusion to Habermas's arguments, degenerates into meaningless consumption. He therefore calls upon the students of the Federal Republic to form action centers for the co-ordination of demonstrations and mass protest against the emergency laws, the right-wing nationalist party (NPD) and the Vietnam war.[8]

In several respects Dutschke's brief talk was a response to Habermas's analysis. What was most upsetting for Habermas, however, was not the criticism of his historical evaluation of the student movement, but the suggestion that voluntaristic action must supplant insight into objective social processes. Habermas's reply to Dutschke unfortunately occurred in the latter's absence since Dutschke had to hurry back to Berlin.

Otherwise, as he himself states, he would have formulated it even more sharply. Habermas was obviously concerned with the tendency towards anarchic actions. He distinguishes between two types of provocation, one a 'demonstrative provocation' that serves to direct attention to the justified rational arguments of the students, and the other a provocation whose purpose it is to turn the sublime power of the institution into a manifest power. The latter provocation is likened to playing with terror and is therefore viewed as illegitimate for the student movement. Just as Habermas does not condone all anti-authoritarian provocations, so too he is against some tactics undertaken by students with regard to the functioning of the university. The call for a 'destruction of the bourgeois educational process', mentioned by one of the radical students, is necessary in so far as it means subjecting the courses and programs to criticism or writing student guides to courses and professors. But the control of course offerings by plebiscites of students is a dangerous and troubling suggestion since it threatens academic freedom. In essence, here as elsewhere, Habermas seeks to preserve and extend the democratic possibilities that already exist.

What Habermas believes he has heard in Dutschke's talk is a call to action that would provoke a violent reaction from the establishment and thus not allow the students to accomplish their immanent political task of enlightenment. At one point Dutschke had obviously suggested a sit-in strike, that is, a form of non-violent demonstration that Habermas condones. He wonders, however, why Dutschke needed three-quarters of an hour to develop a 'voluntarist ideology' if he was only proposing a sit-in and why he did not declare his allegiance to non-violent principles. 'In 1848 one would have named this utopian socialism', Habermas continues, 'but under current circumstances – in any case I believe that I have reasons to suggest the following terminology – one has to call it "leftist Fascism" ' (p. 148).

The comparisons implied in this statement, which became the most controversial remark of the student movement, are (to say the least) unexpected. On one level Habermas is likening the student movement to the social reform movements that Marx and Engels labeled 'the critical-utopian socialists and communists' in the *Communist Manifesto* (1848). Specifically mentioned in that text are Saint-Simon, Fourier and Owen, but Marx and Engels include in this category any attempt to revolutionize society that does not have a solid connection with the proletariat. That these utopian socialists appear in pre-revolutionary situations, and that their main function is enlightenment are additional features that connect them with the students. But Marx and Engels also emphasize that the utopians endeavor to change society exclusively by peaceful means, that they shun political and revolutionary action. The motives Habermas imputes to Dutschke's suggestions run directly counter to this description; the voluntarism that Habermas questions is contained only in the second term, leftist Fascism, which recalls various right-wing youth movements of the 1930s. Perhaps the only thing that is clear from Habermas's remarks is that he condemns what he saw as the intensification of protest from a stage of demonstrative to a stage of violent provocation (pp. 146–9).

Unfortunately the central issues raised by Habermas in his talk and in his reply to Dutschke could be more easily ignored because of the infelicitous comparison of the student movement with Fascism. Habermas's clarification and partial retraction of his remark in two private letters, which he published along with his collected writings on student protests and university reforms in 1969, assist us in making sense of the seemingly misplaced comparison. In a letter to Erich Fried, a noted West German poet, Habermas explains that he perceived similarities between Dutschke's tactics and those of early Italian Fascism, and that he was particularly concerned about the absence of definite political goals. He feared that action was being proposed for the sake of action, that student activity would turn into a happening that could be channeled into right-wing causes. Although he recognizes that the use of the particular phrase 'leftist Fascism' is not justifiable, he feels that it has had a beneficial function in compelling student leaders to consider the question of violence (pp. 149–51). In a letter to C. Grossner, Habermas is a bit more charitable towards Dutschke and the students. At the Hanover conference he did not realize that new forms of provocation were necessary in order to force discussion of issues that were being suppressed. But even though he partly concedes validity to the movement's tactics and regrets his unfortunate slogan, he still rejects the

Jürgen Habermas

general and undifferentiated violation of rules, as recommended by some student leaders, and renounces the use of violence in the current non-revolutionary situation (pp. 151–2).

THE PHANTOM REVOLUTION AND ITS CHILDREN

During the following year Habermas's public pronouncements continued to support the goals of the student movement. In a speech delivered in New York in November of 1967 he even takes a further step towards revising his hasty formulation 'leftist Fascism'. What had once appeared to him as a tactic of the political right wing now seems just as plausibly related to strategies of resistance developed in the Third World to combat imperialism (pp. 153–77). At a podium discussion in Frankfurt in February of the following year Habermas once again praises the student movement and counters the charges of utopianism and Third World romanticism. Those who would seek to alter an industrialized society in a democratic fashion are hardly utopians, Habermas remarks, and the personal identification with the suffering in the Third World indicates a highly developed moral sensibility that is the prerequisite for understanding repression in general. Although he is not uncritical, his remarks certainly place him squarely in the camp of the opposition to the status quo (pp. 178–84). Events during the spring and summer of 1968 appear to have reawakened Habermas's misgivings from the Hanover conference. The nearly fatal shooting of Rudi Dutschke in April and the unruly protests it unleashed seem to have confirmed Habermas's earlier assessment of the proper limits to student activism. In May 1968 the student protests in Paris captured the attention of the entire world. And in Frankfurt, where Habermas taught, matters took an unexpectedly radical turn at the end of May, when students occupied the university, renamed it 'Karl Marx University', and organized seminars. After a group of protesters broke into official university records, the police intervened.

These were the events that immediately preceded Habermas's second confrontation with the student movement. At a conference of the Union of German Students (VDS) on 1 June Habermas developed five theses concerning the direction and aims of the movement; he added a sixth for a written version of his talk that appeared in the *Frankfurter Rundschau*, a liberal Frankfurt newspaper, a few days later. In the preface to the newspaper article, Habermas again makes it clear that he considers the student movement an important and progressive development in postwar German society. The perspectives that have been opened by the movement are 'new and serious'; they indicate possibilities for change in industrial societies; they contain the foundations for a socialist organization of production free of bureaucratic deformation. But Habermas also points to dangers, and he locates their origins in the adherence to a tradition – obviously the Marxist tradition – that has been too readily accepted and too rigidly followed by student leaders. The dogmatism that Habermas senses in the movement threatens to discredit its goals and to eliminate chances for successful political intervention. Although Habermas, therefore, maintains that his theses are meant as a response to the most recent occurrences, they are simultaneously a continuation and expansion of his remarks from the previous year in Hanover. They are, of course, not fully developed thoughts even in June 1968, and Habermas would comment in an interview that there is a story behind every sentence.[9] But they do provide us with a better idea of how the student movement fits into Habermas's analysis of postwar society and into his own theoretical concerns.

Habermas's first thesis is that 'the immediate goal of the student protest is the politicization of the public sphere' (p. 189).[10] The arguments supporting this thesis are drawn mainly from analyses contained in *Structural Transformations of the Public Sphere* and developed more extensively later in *Legitimation Crisis* (1973).[11] As we saw in Chapter 1, in the former work Habermas had shown how the liberal public sphere in which ideas were freely discussed had degenerated under the conditions of modern capitalism. Drawing on the analyses of Horkheimer, Adorno and Marcuse, he shows how the collapse of the public and private realms leads to deformations that are exploited by the mass media, advertising and parliamentary governance. In the latter work he contends that the potential for crisis in advanced capitalist societies has shifted from the sphere of economics and administration to the legitimation system. In its simplest form Habermas's argument can be restated as follows: the central conflict in capitalist society continues to be the unequal distribution of wealth across the population. With the growing interference of the state in regulating the market and the simultaneous political enfranchisement of almost the entire adult population, the possibility for conflict about legitimacy increases. The reason is simple: the representatives of the state, although elected by the entire population, have to legitimize their activity in securing more economic rewards for an increasingly smaller sector of society.

Legitimation is secured through a variety of mechanisms, including the adherence to formal democracy without mass participation, the propagation of ideologies that elicit mass loyalty, and the compensation for allegiance to the system paid in money and time. The student movement is of central importance, according to Habermas, because it calls into question the legitimacy of capitalist society at its weakest points. It unmasks the ideological obfuscations, critiques the attempts at diversion and opens discussion on fundamental issues of economics and politics. It does not accept the pretext that only experts can decide on matters of economic and political concern. Instead it removes the aura of expertise from state decision-making and subjects policy in general to public discussion. In this fashion it challenges a system that seeks to patronize its citizens and confine their demands to an exclusively private realm. The student movement is essential, in short, because it repoliticizes the depoliticized public sphere. This explains why many of the central targets of the student movement are those organs that regulate public discussion. When Habermas refers specifically to publishing conglomerates (*publizitische Großunternehmen*), he obviously has in mind the Springer press, against which student demonstrations increased in the wake of the shooting of Rudi Dutschke. A press such as Springer's has the double function of excluding the public from real issue-oriented discussions and of mobilizing the public against those who, like the protesters, try to engender public debate. In this respect Habermas approves of the campaign against Springer, the major initiative in the year preceding his theses, since it attacks the system at a vulnerable and central point.

Habermas's second thesis involves the historical significance of the student movement. The success of its activities, he claims, is due to its invention of new techniques of demonstration. He identifies three dimensions of these techniques.

1 The first is the non-violent resistance developed in particular in the United States during the civil rights movement. This type of protest is especially effective because it maximizes publicity with a minimum of risk and effort.

2 Habermas notes the proximity of student protest to the symbolic critique in popular culture. Here he seems to have in mind street theater or guerrilla theater, that is, those forms of popular culture that call into question matters that are usually taken for granted. Drawing its inspiration from general tendencies in modernism, in particular politicized forms of modernism like Brecht's alienation effect, these political forms of cultural activity produce a shock that forces the viewer to see through routines and conventions. They have an impact because they are playful, yet at the same time serious; Habermas feels that they are a forceful weapon in the struggle precisely because they are not lethal.

3 Habermas contends that the techniques of the student movement are specific to an age group and related to a psychological and ritualized form of rejection of the parent generation. Appeals by the students for members of other age groups to join their protest are therefore in vain; only those people who misunderstand their actions or who have been fixated at an earlier stage of development could comply with these appeals.

The three dimensions that Habermas outlines – non-violence, symbolic action and generation-specific behavior – are well suited to the purpose of attacking the established system, because they counter the depoliticization necessary to maintain legitimation in an advanced capitalist society.

Habermas's third thesis locates the source of student protest in a social-psychological, rather than in an economic realm. In stating this, Habermas differs from many of the prominent student leaders who, like Dutschke, derive the student unrest directly from economic factors. According to these theories, the educational system inside a capitalist society has become a vulnerable spot for an economy that seeks to solve its systemic crisis by internal regulations and repression and by external exploitation in the Third World. Students therefore are at one of the focal points of repression, the other focal points being the Third World and, to a lesser degree, the proletariat. Habermas contends, by contrast, that students still form a privileged group in society. Unlike anti-authoritarian struggles in the past, the student movement is not fighting for a larger share of the wealth, but is protesting against the very notion of rewards and achievement under capitalism. Students do this precisely because they have been raised in the absence of economic necessity and therefore see no function for the bourgeois and petty-bourgeois morality that had socialized previous generations. Because of this emancipation from immediate need, the students have developed 'a new sensibility' that questions the exclusion of fundamental moral norms from discussion. Habermas sees one area in particular where this new sensibility can function effectively. In advanced capitalist societies the actual acquisition of social wealth begins to belie the ethical postulate that achievement is rewarded with wealth. With regard to the realm of legitimation Habermas believes that the protest movement can exacerbate this contradiction between the reality and the ideology of rewards under capitalism.

Whereas the first three theses outline the goals, techniques and potentials of the student movement, the next two theses point to shortcomings in ideology and actions. In his fourth thesis Habermas claims that the students have been adhering to an interpretation of society that is either dubious or false, and that they have therefore not been able to develop coherent strategies from it. He points to three areas of Marxist dogma that have been uncritically accepted as the foundation of social analyses.

1 The student movement has adopted a crisis theory that is predicated on the labor theory of value. In his analysis of commodities in *Das Kapital* [*Capital*], Marx had contended that value is measured by the amount of abstract labor objectified in a commodity. The amount of abstract labor is measured in turn in units of time. The longer it takes to produce a commodity, the more value it contains. An increase in productivity across producers (technical advances, more efficient use of the workforce etc.) will mean a decrease in the value of the commodity. Crises in capitalist

society, according to Marx, are related to the tendency for profits to fall as capitalists are forced to compete with each other. The only way for the capitalist to make profits, however, is to extract surplus value from the workers; the capitalist pays the worker for only a portion of the value objectified in the commodity, the rest being 'surplus' value taken by the capitalist. The falling rate of profit is thus tied to the labor theory of value and is thought to lead to crises in capital accumulation, to stagnation, and to mass unemployment.

These theories and tendencies, Habermas maintains, although they may have a limited application for the nineteenth century, are of questionable validity today. There are no contemporary empirical studies of the economy, Habermas asserts, that adhere to a labor theory of value. Furthermore, state intervention has lent capitalism a stability that appears to invalidate the crisis theory of orthodox Marxism. At the very least one can say that the long-term survival and stability of capitalist economies no longer appears to be threatened by the types of crises Marx imagined.

2 Habermas maintains that the student movement has accepted a superannuated Marxist notion of class struggle. Classes are traditionally defined in terms of their relationship to the means of production. Marx's analysis of capitalist society led him to believe that the conflict between the proletariat, the class that has no effective control over the means of production and must hire itself out to capitalists for wages, and the bourgeoisie, the class that has secured effective control or ownership of the means of production, was the key to understanding revolutionary change. In his theory the proletariat is the only class capable of overthrowing capitalism and accomplishing a socialist revolution.

Habermas does not directly dispute Marx's class analysis, but he does argue that capitalism in the twentieth century has found ingenious ways of nullifying political conflict between the proletariat and the bourgeoisie. All the means at society's disposal, from the distribution of rewards to the development of propaganda, are mobilized to keep class conflict latent. Marginal conflicts – and Habermas probably includes the student movement here – by the very fact that they are tolerated are less threatening to the capitalist system. Groups that are underprivileged, for example the blacks in the United States, cannot threaten the system by refusing to co-operate; those that can threaten the system are loyal because no longer underprivileged.

3 The students also adhere to a theory that correlates the relative stability of the First World with the exploitation of the Third World. We have already seen that Dutschke posited a causal connection between prosperity in advanced Western countries and poverty in underdeveloped nations. Indeed, the protest against Vietnam and against the visit of oppressive foreign leaders was justified not on the basis of West German involvement – since the Federal Republic played at most an indirect role in these matters – but on the assumption of a general exploitative relationship between capitalism and the Third World.

Habermas disputes the nature of this relationship. He agrees that historically imperialism is responsible for the conditions created in Third World countries. But he maintains that the former economic exploitation is being replaced by different sorts of dependencies between these nations. With the absence of direct colonial ties, what remains is a moral outrage directed against the First World. This outrage has been appropriated by the students, and although it may be justified, it should not be attributed to a form of exploitation that no longer exists.

The acceptance of these three theoretical positions contributes to two basic misunderstandings in the student movement. The first is the notion that the protests are part of a revolutionary moment. Habermas claims that there are absolutely no indications that this is the case. Lacking, above all, is the subjective impression of an unbearable situation. Those who imagine that the revolution is imminent are deceiving themselves. Second, the students mistakenly believe that they are united in struggle with anti-imperialist and revolutionary movements in the Third World. Habermas points out that the respective conditions, methods and presuppositions are not at all comparable.

The fifth thesis draws the unfortunate consequences from the fourth. The false analysis of the situation has led to strategies that have isolated the students and weakened the powers that support democratic change. Student leaders have confused symbols with reality. Hoisting a red flag at the right moment can engender a new thought process, but it should not deceive students into thinking they are storming the barricades. The occupation of a university as a demonstration should not be confused with a *coup d'état*. This confusion of reality and wish has led to what Habermas terms a 'phantom revolution' (*Scheinrevolution*), in which the appropriate tactics of enlightenment have given way to senseless confrontation. This has resulted in a tactics of polarization at all costs. Alliances with groups or factions that are more moderate or that appreciate the constitutionally guaranteed freedoms that already exist are rejected; instead an illusory unity of workers and students is propagated that has no foundation in reality. The real institutional limits on activity are ignored. Three figures have therefore been allowed to assume center stage in this revolutionary farce. The first is the agitator, who lives narcissistically by placing himself at the center of mass action, but who has lost all contact with reality. The second is the mentor, the learned onlooker with little practical experience, who rationalizes through obscure arguments the actions of his cohorts. Finally, Habermas labels the 'harlequins' of the revolution those who have made themselves the poets of the phantom revolution by borrowing radical phrases from earlier times, but who remain unconcerned about the real consequences of their words.

Habermas's final thesis, added for the newspaper article, returns to a more positive theme. The 'phantom revolution' must change its long-term tactics and reassert its mission in the realm of mass enlightenment. The student movement has been guilty of two deceptions. It has confused the reactions of a state trying to maintain order based on accepted norms with the repressive actions of a Fascist regime. It has overestimated its own power in beginning to exert real force where only symbolic action is appropriate. Habermas calls for the movement to return to its laudable and emancipatory goal of a debureaucratization of power by orienting itself on tactics that correspond to the real situation. Demonstrators should first recognize that they are not acting in a revolutionary situation. They should assess more accurately the legal position of a democratic opposition inside German society and understand their constitutionally guaranteed rights. They should also differentiate more precisely with regard to postwar German history and exploit the gains that have been made even in the restoration of capitalist hegemony. They should learn to form alliances with those in the mass media who can assist them in getting their message across and with the unions, which can support their political strikes. Finally, students should reflect upon the relationship between theory and practice, and not act precipitously for a cause that they presume will have the endorsement of the masses at some future time.

COUNTERCHARGES FROM THE NEW LEFT

In the charged political atmosphere of 1968 Habermas's theses were understood less as an internal disagreement with strategies and policies of the left than as a fundamental challenge to working propositions. Parts of the radical student movement considered Habermas to be a traitor to the cause, an establishment intellectual of the left-liberal ilk, who retreats from the implications of his own position when presented with a radical praxis. Slightly more generous were the contributors to a volume entitled *Die Linke antwortet Jürgen Habermas* (1968) ['The Left Answers Jürgen Habermas'], many of whom were associates or students of Habermas. The book starts with a reprint of Habermas's six theses, followed by an introduction and fourteen responses, mostly written by activists in the student movement. In Oskar Negt's introductory remarks the reader learns that Habermas was supposed to close the volume with a rebuttal, but it seems that he was so disturbed by the harsh comments that he did not do so. In his final paragraph Negt tries to mitigate some of the bitterness directed against Habermas. Here he states that those familiar with Habermas's thought will recognize the extent to which individual contributions are indebted to him, and that the book as a whole really represents the public discussion of a controversy internal to the German new left. 'It is not anti-Habermas', he emphatically maintains; the volume should more properly be conceived as an attempt to protect Habermas against false friends on the right rather than as an assault on him from the left.[12] The tenor and maliciousness of some of the essays, however, belie this benevolent interpretation.

The objections to Habermas can be divided into three categories. Almost all respondents take exception to the form in which Habermas characterized student activities. In particular they refer to his use of derogatory designations. The suggestion that the students were suffering from infantilism, insanity, emotionalism, overactive fantasy, loss of contact with reality, or narcissistic illusions was not only insulting, but also partakes in a conservative tradition that disqualifies progressive change by branding it abnormal behavior. Klaus Dörner, for example, points out that those in power have always used such terminology to make revolutionaries into pathological subjects.[13] From the perspective of the establishment in any society it is irrational to try to overthrow the existing order, and any attempt to do so is in and of itself a violation of reason. By using such terminology Habermas has allowed his theses to be appropriated by conservative apologists for the status quo whose views he would otherwise oppose. Similarly objectionable are the caricatures of revolutionary personalities (the agitator, the mentor, the harlequin) which Habermas includes at the close of his fifth thesis. Most contributors agree that the rhetoric Habermas employs is much more acerbic than he needs to accomplish his task. A serious critique of the goals and problems of the student movement would not have to stoop to the language of the 'enemy'; that Habermas resorts to such tactics indicates a deep-seated antipathy and suggests that the epithet 'leftist Fascism' used to represent the protest movement was not coined without deliberation.

A second and related area of criticism concerned the use of socio-psychological types as shortcuts for historical and sociological analysis. At issue here are two theses in Habermas's critique. In the third thesis Habermas sought to explain the origins of the student movement as a psychological reaction to certain features of capitalist society, rather than as an economically integrated component of class conflict. Although there is wide disagreement about exactly how students and the university fit into the functioning of the capitalist system, most commentators agree that Habermas is guilty of at least oversimplification. Even if we concede that Habermas has correctly categorized the psychological constitution of the student protests, this does not mean, as Claus Offe points out,[14] that Habermas is warranted in the conclusions he draws regarding the potential for the movement. In essence Offe contends that the impact need not be restricted to general enlightenment or to a repoliticization of the public sphere. The effect depends, rather, on the correctness of the analysis made by the students and on how their demands and reactions are received by other parts of the population. As Offe points out, the issues that the new left has propagated have origins and implications well beyond any single socio-psychological profile.

In the fifth thesis, on the other hand, Habermas's psychological characterizations strongly suggest the neurotic nature of student activity. In general he contends that the sort of behavior preferred by the demonstrators is an outgrowth of protests specific to certain age groups, and that a continued adherence to such activities is evidence of infantilism. In situations of imagined crisis, however, deformed psychological types surface and become prominent. But if this were the case, Furio Cerutti argues, if the protest were really reducible to specific psychological profiles and to neurotic behavior, could the students have achieved so much success in other sectors of society?[15] Furthermore, even if we admit an element of neurosis, must we not critique the society that has produced these neuroses rather than those who have the neuroses inflicted upon them? At best Habermas is guilty of using illicit psychological shortcuts instead of political analysis. By accepting in an uncritical fashion dubious social and psychological norms for neurosis and health, he undercuts his own contributions to a critical theory of society. Even when we concede partial validity to his psychologically based analysis, he is still found wanting with regard to the social origins of that particular psychology and the implications it has for strategies and goals.

Perhaps the largest area of criticism in 'The Left Answers Jürgen Habermas' concerns the validity of the Marxist perspective he employs. Habermas had argued that the student movement adheres to outmoded notions inherited from a nineteenth-century tradition. Chief among these are a crisis theory based on the labor theory of value, a notion of class conflict as the motor of historical change, and a hypothetical identification of First World and Third World protest. Anselm Neusüss notes that the SDS rejects these propositions as a remnant of communist orthodoxy; even the most traditional Marxist faction of the student movement would not accept these assertions in such undifferentiated form.[16] Indeed, much of what Habermas argues against this purported political stance of the SDS could be taken directly from SDS publications. The thesis that direct economic dependency has become a less important factor in contemporary notions of imperialism had been propagated by the SDS in its analysis of the Vietnam war. And the displacement of class conflict from the center of revolutionary activity had been perhaps the central impulse guiding the student movement. Habermas should be well aware of this, because Herbert Marcuse, on whom he depends for his insights, had been instrumental in developing the very concepts of marginal groups that helped give the new left its legitimacy. The strategy behind almost all actions of the student movement, from the campaign against Springer to the protests against emergency laws, only makes sense if one proceeds from a view that the struggle between bourgeoisie and proletariat is no longer the central emancipatory concern.

Several of the contributors to this 'anti-Habermas' volume complain that Habermas is not differentiated enough in his comments on the student movement. Peter Brückner designates three tendencies that have contributed to the formation of the SDS: the restoration of capitalism in postwar Germany, the decreasing oppositional stance of the SPD and the anti-authoritarian rebellion of individuals.[17] He notes that the beliefs of SDS members, the actions in which they participate and their goals are not identical. Critics like Habermas have overestimated the homogeneity of an organization that is more open and contradictory than they imagine. A similar critique appears at the opening of Herbert Lederer's essay, which accuses Habermas of the uncritical appropriation of distortions found in the bourgeois press. Instead of presenting a differentiated perspective on the composition and activities of the student movement, Habermas has simply reinforced the trivial notions that have served to discredit legitimate protests. The democratic organization of the movement, its principled opposition to a sclerotic establishment, its theoretical discussions are neglected, while the emotional and provocative outbursts at demonstrations are accorded primary importance.[18]

But many critics of Habermas also note that in his lack of differentiation and in his challenge to the purported dogmatism of the SDS he himself succumbs to a number of dogmatic, or at least conventional, assumptions. Ekkehart Krippendorff, for example, imputes to Habermas a traditional understanding of politics. Only in this way can he explain why Habermas is not able to recognize the politicizing possibilities in the new techniques of demonstration, and why he reduces the potential to the liberal and pedagogical function of enlightenment. His conception of Fascism similarly suffers from a narrowness of focus, since under this rubric he can only conceive of the drastic form of National Socialism.[19] Reimut Reiche locates Habermas's deficient political analysis in his inability to credit non-rational actions with political value. Emotions, too, he claims, can have a progressive function; the fantasy and imagination of students who identify with the Vietcong or with oppressed groups in the Third World is not only beneficial, but essential to the maintenance of productive protest.[20] Several critics, including Neusüss, object to Habermas's contention that the students confuse symbols with reality. Without disputing the distinction between the two, Neusüss points out that their separation without mediating moments is as undialectical as their assumed identity.[21]

Behind all of these comments lies a contention explicitly thematized by Negt in his introduction – that Habermas remains wedded to a traditional notion of revolutionary change.[22] Although he rejects the validity of Marx's analysis for the contemporary situation, the underlying assumption in his thought is that revolution necessarily involves class conflict in a traditional sense. Students can only engage in the task of enlightenment because they are not a proper class and therefore cannot become the subject of history, a role Marx reserves for the proletariat. Either Habermas has left himself without any agent for real historical change, or he still furtively adheres to a classical notion of revolution. If the former assumption is correct, he becomes either a reformist liberal or a disillusioned socialist; if we assume the latter, then he is clinging to an obsolete stance or a utopian dream. In either case he can be accused of failing to modify his notion of revolution to meet the needs of the present.

THE RECONSTRUCTION OF HISTORICAL MATERIALISM

The unbiased observer has to have some sympathy with this last set of objections to Habermas's theses. Obviously we can find the arguments Habermas criticizes in the writings and in the speeches of some individuals prominent in the student movement. If we read Dutschke's works, for example, we often encounter the attempt to connect struggles in Germany to Third World movements, and many of the factions that were close to the so-called K-groups – the variety of communist parties that adhered to Maoist, Trotskyist or Marxist-Leninist party lines – spouted rhetoric about the imminent crisis in capitalism and the central importance of the proletariat for revolutionary movements. But on the whole, the student movement was dominated by innovative thinking that rejected the dogmas of established parties and orthodox communists. Indeed, the student protests are as indebted to non-orthodox positions developed by the Frankfurt School as they are to the works of Marx and Engels. As Negt points out in the introduction to 'The Left Answers Jürgen Habermas' and as the establishment media continually emphasized, Habermas himself must be considered one of the main intellectual sources and inspirations for the SDS. So his interventions at two crucial junctures in June 1967 and June 1968 may be seen not only as confrontations with the dogmatic aspects of the student movement but also, and perhaps more importantly, as part of an ongoing theoretical debate he had been conducting with the Marxist tradition. In particular we have to understand his comments on Marxism as both the consequence of theoretical positions he had begun to develop during the 1960s and as the basis for what he would call in the 1970s the 'reconstruction of historical materialism'.

Historical materialism needed to be reconstructed because its theoretical framework was insufficient to support its still laudable goals. The very term, although associated primarily with Marx's thought, was probably an invention of Engels. In the introduction to *Socialism: Utopian and Scientific* (1892) Engels writes that historical materialism

designates that view of the course of history which seeks the ultimate cause and the great moving power of all important historic events in the economic development of society, in the changes in the modes of production and exchange, in the consequent division of society into

99

distinct classes, and in the struggle of these classes against one another.[23]

It is thus opposed both to the doctrine of 'materialism' as such, which simply postulates the primacy of matter, and the doctrine of historical idealism, which would see historical progression driven by the realm of ideas or the human mind, for example in Hegel's philosophy. What is clear from Engels's definition is that historical materialism has a foundation in the economic realm. It is therefore materialist in so far as it considers the production and reproduction of material life to be primary in the explanation of human affairs; and it is historical to the extent that it postulates a progression among different types of economic organization of society and establishes a means by which to explain how changes in economic modes of production are brought about through the struggle between competing classes.

The *locus classicus* for historical materialism in Marx's writings occurs in the 'Preface' to *Zur Kritik der politischen Ökonomie* [*A Contribution to the Critique of Political Economy*] of 1859.[24] Here Marx sketches on a grand scale the general presuppositions of his theory. Independent of their will, human beings in any society enter into relations of production that correspond to a given stage in the development of the material forces of production. What Marx means by forces of production are material and non-material factors of production: raw materials, instruments of production and labor power, including skills and training that augments productivity. Relations of production are in effect relations of ownership or effective control by persons over the forces of production and hence over the labor power of other people. The relations and the forces of production together form the economic base of society which in turn determines the forms of consciousness of individuals in society as well as the legal and political superstructure. In this sense the material foundation of society is primary, while the superstructure and consciousness are derivative. Historical progress is defined in terms of conflicts and resolutions in the economic base. When the forces of production come into conflict with the relations of production, which act as a fetter on further development of the forces, a period of social revolution ensues. The resolution to the contradiction between the forces and relations of production ushers in a new mode of production, which continues until a new conflict arises. Only with the advent of socialism will this 'prehistory' of humankind find a final resolution.

Habermas has always had an ambivalent relationship to this sketch of historical materialism. Tom Rockmore's portrayal of a linear development in Habermas's thought according to which he becomes increasingly disenchanted with historical materialism and finally rejects it for a theory of communicative action is not totally inaccurate,[25] but it fails to capture the extent to which Habermas has always practiced a distanced identification with Marx's thought. At no time do we encounter an outright rejection of Marxist theory. Despite his dissenting views, Habermas has never located himself outside the critical tradition that begins with Marx's critique of Hegel and idealist philosophy and that finds its most sophisticated continuators in the early writings of Georg Lukács and the work of the Frankfurt School. Yet at no time does Habermas subscribe to the outlines of historical materialism as they are contained in Marx's *oeuvre*. In particular, like the first generation of Frankfurt School theorists, he rejects the notion of a determining economic base. None the less, in his collection of essays, *Zur Rekonstruktion des historischen Materialismus* (1976) ['The Reconstruction of Historical Materialism'] at the same time that he discards the cornerstone of Marx's economic theory, the labor theory of value, he also maintains that 'the change of normative structures remains dependent on evolutionary challenges posed by unresolved, economically conditioned, system problems and on learning processes that are a response to them'.[26] This ambivalence is typical of Habermas's reception of Marxist theory, and even in his later work, where Marxism plays a somewhat reduced role, he never seeks to dissociate his work from the progressive tradition initiated by Marx.

From almost the very start Habermas has viewed Marx's theory as one-sided, perhaps adequate for dealing with phenomena of nineteenth-century capitalism, but deficient for a general theory of society. This is especially clear in a book he published at the height of the student movement, *Technik und Wissenschaft als 'Ideologie'* (1968) ['Technology and Science as Ideology'].[27] In this work and in other writings from the

101

late 1960s and early 1970s Habermas advances the general claim that Marx was not abstract enough in his analysis of capitalist societies. The category of social labor, which Marx placed at the center of this work, only captures one side of human progress. As a corrective Habermas introduces the conceptual pair 'labor' and 'interaction' to describe more adequately two sides of social development. He postulates that the human species progresses along both paths, cognitively in its interaction with nature conceived as labor; and morally in the intersubjective exchange among human beings conceived under the rubric of interaction. Because Marx is merely insufficient and not erroneous in his analysis, Habermas introduces the notion of reconstruction to describe his relationship to his predecessor. In contrast to a restoration, which would designate the return to something that has developed and become corrupted, or a renaissance, which signifies a rebirth or renewal, reconstruction is defined as the redesigning of a project retaining the original goal. Like Marx, Habermas's aim is to develop an emancipatory and comprehensive theory of society, but in contrast to him, Habermas believes that this cannot be accomplished if we conceive society and the category of labor exclusively in their relationship to external nature.

Habermas's central concern in a reconstruction of historical materialism is to demonstrate that there is a developmental logic for cultural traditions and institutional change that is not solely dependent on an economic substructure. Whereas Marx conceived of progress in terms of quantitative increase in the forces of production and qualitative leaps in the relations of production, Habermas asserts that development also occurs in the sphere of interaction. An important aspect of Habermas's reconstructive project entails a critique of the category of social labor as constitutive for human affairs. For this reason he places a great deal of emphasis on anthropological studies that deal with the transition from hominids to *Homo sapiens*. From these investigations he concludes that social labor actually describes the central distinguishing feature between primates and hominids. The introduction of familial relations, that is, structures characterized by intersubjectively established social norms, marks the transition to the human species. The reproduction of human life, according to Habermas, begins with a particular type of interaction, one which is characterized by a system of norms that presupposes language.

> The rank order of the primates was one-dimensional; every individual could occupy one and only one – that is, in all functional domains the same – status. Only when the same individual could unify various status positions and different individuals could occupy the same status was a socially regulated exchange between functionally specified subsystems possible.[28]

The establishment of social roles, however, is based on the intersubjective recognition of the legitimacy of these roles. Humans begin to have normative expectations independent of personality quirks. Hence we find the rise of a 'moralization for motives of action'.[29] This brings the human being out of the primate world of individual personality and force, and into a symbolically structured world of social interaction.

The origin of the human species is so important for Habermas because it suggests to him that progress can be conceived in terms of interaction rather than labor. What Habermas is proposing is that we conceive of historical materialism as the progression of ethics or of social norms, rather than of technological progress. The question that immediately poses itself is where to look for models that adequately describe such a progression. Habermas believes he has found one answer in the discipline of developmental psychology. Relying heavily on the work of Jean Piaget, Lawrence Kohlberg and others, he sketches a flexible, yet progressive view of human history that closely parallels individual development. According to the schema he adopts, the child progresses through various stages: (a) the symbiotic, (b) the egocentric, (c) the sociocentric-objectivistic, and (d) the universalist, a development that brings the human being from a state in which there are no clear demarcations for subjectivity to a phase in which the ego is able to think reflectively about itself and about normative structures. Habermas believes that such a paradigm can be employed to describe social evolution, that there are 'homologies between ego development and the evolution of worldviews'.[30] Although he is not unaware of the problems involved in generalizing from individuals to societies, he feels that worldviews can be described analogously as a progression from mythical representations to universalist forms of intercourse (e.g. the Judeo-Christian heritage) to the reflective attitude that characterizes the modern world.

The succession of different worldviews is only one aspect of interactive development. Proceeding from an analysis of speech acts, Habermas also sketches a development of role identities, starting with neolithic societies and ending with the hypothetical identification of oneself as a citizen of the world. A similar evolutionary pattern could be established for the legal and moral spheres, areas in which there is more extensive research to rely on. Habermas contends that at the basis of all three of these historical progressions – in worldviews, ego identities and legal-moral representations – are the 'structures of linguistically established intersubjectivity'.[31] A theory of communicative action that accounts for these structures should be conceived as complementary to a theory of purposive-rational action, on which historical materialism has been grounded.[32]

Rationalization and progress occur in both spheres, but there is a significant difference between progress in the two realms of action. Rationalization in the sphere of communicative action is indubitably a positive development, whereas rationalization in the realm of purposive-rational action involves strategic and instrumental decisions. Increasing rationalization in the latter area is usually seen as contributing to the alienation and bureaucratization of the modern world. But in the sphere of communicative action, rationalization means the elimination of those aspects of communication that lead to distortion. These aspects can be either intrapsychic or societal. Progress in the sphere of communicative action is thus not measured in the same way as progress in purposive-rational action. It has to be measured 'against the intersubjectivity of understanding without force, that is, against the expansion of the domain of consensual action together with the re-establishment of undistorted communication'. Habermas even suggests that this progress is more fundamental than the evolution of purposive-rational action, calling it the 'pacemaker of social evolution'.[33]

These thoughts on social evolution were published several years after Habermas's confrontation with the student movement. It is impossible to believe, however, that he did not already have something of this sort in mind when he criticized what he perceived to be Marxist dogmatism among the most vociferous of student leaders. In both his reaction to the tactics and propaganda of the protests and his rejection of a narrowly conceived notion of historical progress, Habermas sought to go beyond traditional explanations and to clarify his position based on democratic alternatives. His critique of the students was ultimately based on his belief that they grasped the social dynamics of advanced Western societies as well as the subjugation of the Third World too mechanistically and too parochially. The role he assigned to them, as facilitators for opening up public discussion on issues of general importance, was meant to vitalize and politicize the public sphere after a period in which free and meaningful political dialogue had been abandoned. He hoped in this way to call into question the legitimacy of the government at its weakest point. The result of such activities could not have been the socialist revolution that some student leaders envisioned, but a more modest advance perhaps in the arena of social interaction. In terms of his later reflections on historical materialism we could say that Habermas correctly understood that conditions were not contradictory or desperate enough for the revolutionary leap into a new mode of production. In nations that base their ethical, legal and role identities on universalist principles, it was perhaps more appropriate to thematize and to demand that society live up to its own implicit standards.

5

Systems and society:
the debate with Niklas Luhmann

In the midst of his occupation with Gadamer's hermeneutics and shortly after his most heated confrontations with the student movement, Habermas engaged in a debate with his most formidable challenger in the field of sociology. Niklas Luhmann, a prolific, abstract and brilliant theorist whose interests, like those of Habermas, cross interdisciplinary boundaries, became during the 1960s the leading representative of systems theory, a conception of sociological theory chiefly associated with Talcott Parsons in the English-speaking world. From our perspective today it seems too simple perhaps to categorize the controversy between Habermas and Luhmann as one between a progressive, critical version of sociological theory and a conservative, legitimating theory of society. But in the atmosphere of the late 1960s it was undoubtedly conceived in roughly this fashion, even though, as Habermas notes, there was a surprising affinity for Luhmann's sociological model on the part of some activist students.[1] Indeed, Habermas himself, perceiving not only the importance of Luhmann's work, but also the implicit and explicit challenges to his own position, was eager to enter into a dialogue with him because of underlying ideological differences. It was he who evidently initiated a joint seminar in Frankfurt at which they expounded their divergent views of social theory and meaning, and he was instrumental in the publication of the long and detailed critiques he and Luhmann produced of each other's works. That the controversy was timely, as well as pointed, is evidenced by the impact of the volume that contains these critiques. *Theorie der Gesellschaft oder Sozialtechnologie: Was leistet die Systemforschung?* (1971) ['Theory of Society or Social

Technology: What Does Systems Research Accomplish?'] not only sold more than 35,000 copies, an astounding figure considering the extremely demanding and at times technical styles of both Habermas and Luhmann, but spawned three supplementary volumes of essays in which different scholars commented on the initial debate.[2]

Although Habermas initiated the direct confrontation, Luhmann was not innocent of all provocation. In his writings from the 1960s he made it obvious that his theory was meant to supplant the outmoded and ultimately unfounded claims of the Frankfurt School. His book *Soziologische Aufklärung: Aufsätze zur Theorie sozialer Systeme* (1970) ['Sociological Enlightenment: Essays Toward a Theory of Social Systems'],[3] which collected earlier writings, was widely caricatured by the new left as 'Counter-Enlightenment' (*Gegenaufklärung*) because of its attacks on the sociological positions of Critical Theory. Luhmann's contempt for the 'speculative entrepreneurs', as he referred to dialectical theorists in 1964, is matched perhaps only by his disdain for those who sought an alternative to the two methods in the positivist dispute by embracing '"commitment" and sociopolitical *engagement*'.[4] Habermas could identify with both of the groups Luhmann was rejecting. Although we have seen that he ceased to employ the Hegelian language of Adorno even in his second contribution to the positivist dispute, he has always considered himself an ally, if not a direct disciple, of Adorno, Horkheimer and Marcuse; and although some radical students might disagree, his development throughout the 1960s placed him at the center of discussions about the unity of an ethical and committed theory and practice. As in all his debates, Habermas hoped to learn from the confrontation, but he also had reason to feel that he and the tradition in which he was writing were under siege.

Habermas may also have had a special interest in Luhmann's position because of the proximity of his work to that of Talcott Parsons, with whom Luhmann studied in the 1960s. Habermas had dealt with Parsons's theories in his study *Zur Logik der Sozialwissenschaften* (1967) ['On the Logic of the Social Sciences'][5] under the rubric of functionalism. Habermas recognizes that it is possible to analyze societies as self-regulating and self-contained systems, but believes that there are problems inherent in such theories. His criticisms first center on

107

two objections that are brought to light by the work of Ernst Nagel and Carl Hempel. First, the biological model of the organism that serves as the basis for functionalist theory cannot be readily transferred to social theory. The boundaries of an organism and the condition in which it reproduces its life are easily discernible. This is not so for social systems. Moreover, we have no obvious criteria for the state of equilibrium or the notion of success of social systems. Survival and reproduction, which are normally considered the goals of biological organisms, are not adequate goals for the realm of society. Following from these criticisms Habermas states his most general objection to systems theory in terms of its methodological orientation. As long as systems theory remains tied to empirical-analytical procedures it will be inadequate as a research program. The foundation for a functionalist approach must include both a historico-hermeneutic dimension, which would reflect upon social norms and meaning, and a critical dimension, which would take into account the ideological distortions of the present and the utopian anticipations of the future. Without these dimensions, Habermas suggests, systems theory, like positivism, serves to justify the repression and oppression of the status quo.

SYSTEMS THEORY AND MEANING

Habermas would return to a discussion of Parsons in *The Theory of Communicative Action*. In the late 1960s, however, his German representative was a more immediate concern. Luhmann's use of the concept 'system' can be understood by contrasting it, as he himself does, with previous conceptions. The oldest notion of system considers it in terms of parts and whole, that is, as a purely internal and mechanical ordering without reference to an outside world or environment. Equilibrium theories of systems incorporate the notion of an environment, but conceive of it solely as a disturbance to the harmony of the self-contained system; the environment is not seen as contributing to the constitution of the system. A third concept of system views it as open to the environment and existing in an active exchange with it. These types of systems are defined by the boundaries they maintain between themselves and their environment. Finally, cybernetic theory has developed a notion of system that Luhmann eventually embraces. In this variant the relationship between the system and its environment is understood in terms of a difference in complexity. The complexity of the environment is always greater than that of the system that is situated in it. The system must bring its complexity into a relationship of correspondence with the environment; it must be able to respond to a great variety of inputs from the environment, and it accomplishes this through selectivity. There exists, therefore, a complexity gradient between system and environment that defines the boundaries between them. Luhmann's most general thesis is 'that systems serve to reduce complexity by stabilizing a difference between inner and outer' (p. 11). They function in all cases, Luhmann continues, to reduce complexity.

The difference between social systems and other types of systems (cybernetic systems, biological systems) lies in the manner in which complexity is reduced. Social systems are defined by their relationship to meaning. Luhmann's contention is that social systems (and psychic systems) reduce the complexity of their environment through recourse to meaning. So the boundaries of a social system are not defined physically, but by the border of what is meaningful and what is not. This conception of meaning has two rather unusual consequences:

1 Traditionally meaning is defined through the notion of a subject that establishes it through intentional actions or utterances. Luhmann turns this relationship on its head by asserting that meaning is constitutive of the subject rather than the other way round. The subject is thus conceived as a system that employs meaning, not as the origin of meaning.
2 Usually meaning is conceived as a positivity: something has a meaning in and of itself and this meaning is independent of other meanings. Luhmann, however, conceives of meaning in a purely relational fashion. Analogous to his depiction of the mutual dependence of system on environment, he maintains that meaning is produced only by the exclusion of other possibilities. Because it does not destroy these other possibilities, but only pushes them aside or displaces them from the center, meaning also preserves complexity.

Perhaps the most problematic aspect of Luhmann's dependence on meaning – and he himself is aware of this – is that it does not solve the question of boundaries. Unlike the physical boundaries of an organism, in both its physical and temporal aspects, the limits of meaning, i.e. what is meaningful and what is not, seem impossible to ascertain with any degree of precision.

None the less, Luhmann's version of systems theory represents an advance on Parsons's in consistency and consequentiality of the application of function. We can discern the differences in the following five areas. First, Parsons, relying on Max Weber, conceives meaning as a characteristic of action, but he does not recognize it as a principle of selectivity for social systems in general. Second, although Parsons no longer connects order with notions of hegemony, his belief that order consists of normative structures is too undifferentiated for complex societies. Luhmann contends that such a conception 'entails a considerable overestimation of the consensus that is structurally necessary today as well as the consensus that actually exists'.[6] Third, Parsons is able to treat the functioning of elements inside of a structure, but Luhmann claims he fails to comprehend the function of systems and structures in general (p. 14). In simple terms we can conceive of Parsons's theory as a structural-functionalism, whereas Luhmann develops a functional-structuralism, that is, the notion of structures and their relationship to environment are themselves subjected to functional analysis. Fourth, Luhmann claims that Parsons ignores the function of scholarly theory, specifically his own theory, as a system or part of a system. By insisting on the reflexivity of all structures, Luhmann incorporates his own activity into his functionalist model and thereby establishes a unity of theory and practice. Finally, Luhmann demands that all concepts be regarded within a functionalist framework. Even the notions of truth and value are analyzed for their functions and not as basic presuppositions.[7] These failings, Luhmann claims, do not allow Parsons to develop an adequate conception of society as the largest system from which all functional differentiation stems. Only a rigorous and self-conscious application of function can make systems theory an acceptable theory of society.

Luhmann's adherence to function, conceived always as a relation between entities, suggests that his theory has some affinities with structuralism as it was developed by Ferdinand de Saussure in linguistics and applied to various disciplines in postwar France. Indeed, in his critique of Luhmann, Habermas notes his structuralist proclivities (p. 180), and there are several rather striking parallels between a systems theory approach to sociology and the structuralist model, besides, of course, the implicit claim of each to proceed in the sole scientifically acceptable fashion. The fundamental features that Jean Piaget finds in structuralism seem applicable to Luhmann as well.[8] Piaget identifies wholeness, transformation and self-generation as the seminal ideas of the structuralist enterprise. Wholeness seems appropriate to a system in that it implies more than a relationship of the parts to a whole. In both Piaget's explanation and Luhmann's theory the structure/system is defined by its inner coherence and its obedience to an internal dynamics. Thus although the notion of an outside environment is noticeably absent from the notion of structure, both conceptions rely on internal functional relations. Transformation applies to both models in that each presupposes an active entity. Neither system nor structure is passively consigned to a rigid form or prescribed a predetermined limit. Finally both system and structure operate according to principles of self-regulation. Again the emphasis in Luhmann is slightly more toward function and the interdependent environment, but both structuralism and systems theory share the notion that internal laws and not external or transcendental forces determine change and direction.

Perhaps the more important parallels between systems theory and structuralism are located in their implications for ethics and politics. What unites these two theories is a number of objectivist and scientistic claims that theoretically eliminate values while furtively affirming the status quo. Both systems theorists and structuralists claim to be impartial observers and analyzers of objective realities. In reducing complexity, the system has no further function except the maintenance of a gradient with its environment. Since Luhmann does not allow any other principles to inform the composition or the behavior of a system, a sphere of values enters into consideration only in so far as it contributes to the goal of reducing complexity. For example, the observer has no vantage point from which to critique racist or sexist values, since these can be evaluated only as functional or dysfunctional. Similarly structures provide

111

no frame of reference for criticism because they too usurp all possible frames. Good and evil function only as a binary pairs, not as ethical alternatives.

This ethical neutrality of systems and structures also has ramifications for progress and political action. Because both entities are conceived as self-regulating, and because the principles upon which both regulate themselves are so minimal and abstract, there is no way to predict direction or, of course, to influence direction. Luhmann does have some notions of evolution, which will be discussed later, but these do not allow us to forecast alterations in systems or subsystems or to intervene so that systems and subsystems could form differently. Structures adhere to an analogous notion of internal change independent of agency and will. Ultimately, therefore, the objectivist and mechanistic models underlying systems theory and structuralism exclude precisely the features that enable ethics and politics: individual will and the ability of conscious agents to alter the structures/systems they inhabit.

The reason for this exclusion of ethics and politics stems from a similar conception of the subject and 'humanism' in general. In structuralism human agency is eliminated entirely; the subject, constituted by the structure, is determined, an effect of supra-human forces. Although one cannot derive these consequences directly from Saussure's linguistic model, which contrasts a realm of individual utterance (*parole*) with the synchronically structured language (*langue*), they assume a prominent place in Parisian structuralism during the 1960s.[9] Exemplary of this 'anti-humanist' trend is Michel Foucault, whose closing remarks in *The Order of Things* have become the *locus classicus* for theories that question the autonomy of human subjectivity. Foucault points out that 'man' is a rather recent European invention, and that the 'sciences of man', that is, those disciplines that have an anthropological center, have only developed during the past century and a half. Like all previous forms of knowledge, the human sciences too are destined for extinction.[10]

Luhmann's theory echoes these sentiments precisely. The subject in his view is not a primary fact of sociology, but something constituted by an already existing field of meaning. Individuals cannot be the origin of analysis since they are entangled in a variety of systems and subsystems that are not of their making. Like Foucault, Luhmann does not deny the historical advent of the human being as the center of certain disciplines, but he too feels that these disciplines are romantically attached to obsolete conceptions of the subject and subjectivity. He admits, of course, that we can still encounter affirmations of the autonomous subject in our society (for example in constitutions or in legal codes); but he believes that these historical fictions survive solely on the basis of their functional value. For both systems theory and structuralism the subject and anthropologically based disciplines belong to the historical past and possess no value for the analysis of contemporary society.

The parallels – and the differences – between structuralism and systems theory can be found in their respective views of identity and difference. Saussure is perhaps most celebrated for his valorization of the latter term. Prior to him most linguists had assumed that a word or a sign had a positive value that enabled it to be distinguished from other words or signs. Saussure insists that signs do not function through any intrinsic value, but only through their relative position, through their difference from other signs. 'In language', he states in a famous passage from the *Course*, 'there are only differences. Even more important: a difference generally implies positive terms between which the difference is set up; but in language there are only differences *without positive terms*.'[11] With regard to meaning Luhmann's terminology differs somewhat, but his conception shows striking similarities to Saussure's. At issue for the German sociologist is the 'primacy of negation' in the constitution of meaning (p. 35). As we have seen, only in relation to the entire range of other possible meanings and only in the exclusion of other possibilities do we arrive at meaningful determinations. Luhmann calls this differentiating process, perhaps somewhat misleadingly, 'negation', and, like Saussure, he sees it as the source of all identity.[12] Moreover, both Saussure and Luhmann recognize the arbitrary match between meaning/sign and world. Saussure's notion of arbitrariness asserts that no sign is tied naturally to a particular object, and this seems to be confirmed by the very existence of different languages. Luhmann's category of contingency has a similar function in his theory, signifying that the reduction of complexity could be accomplished otherwise. Meanings and signs are neither fixed positivities nor are they necessarily tied to a singular form or expression. The primacy of difference/negation in Saussure and Luhmann establishes a tentative relational structure that is subject to infinite and arbitrary variation.

Luhmann's functionalism, however, departs from a pure model of difference in several important respects. If we conceive of Saussure's notion of *langue* as a system in Luhmann's sense, then the regulation of signs would not be purely internal to the system. Luhmann's theory presupposes not only an interchange with a more or less fluid environment, but also the mutual interdependence of systems and subsystems. Any alteration in the constitution of one subsystem has an effect on the internal composition of other (sub)systems. Above all, meaning in Luhmann's theory is determined primarily by its function inside a given structure, and not solely by the elements of the structure itself. Luhmann's notion of negation, unlike Saussure's concept of difference, also has an affirmative and a reflexive aspect. As the strategy for the processing of experience into sense, negation simultaneously negates other possibilities and 'generalizes' them, that is, at the same time that it selects one possibility, it implies the potential actualization of all other possibilities. The processing of meaning is thus not only a reduction of complexity, but at the same time a preservation of complexity. This is most evident when we consider the reflexive dimension accorded to negation. Negation can turn upon itself, cancelling the meaningful determination and allowing other possibilities to be foregrounded. So generalization and reflexivity are processes that carry Luhmann's notion of negation beyond the more static and simplistic structuralist concept of 'difference'. Occurring together as part of a total process, they constitute a necessary dimension in the reduction and preservation of complexity in social systems.[13]

THE LOGIC OF SYSTEMS THEORY

Habermas's critique of Luhmann assumes a rather unusual form. The book that he and Luhmann published begins with two essays by Luhmann, a general essay on systems theory followed by a long piece on 'Meaning as the fundamental concept in society'. Habermas does not then initiate the conflict directly, but instead includes a preliminary essay on communicative competence, in which he outlines several central notions of his own theory: universal pragmatics, communicative action, discourse, consensus and the ideal speech situation. Only after completing this brief sketch does he turn in a longer piece to objections to Luhmann. This essay, whose title is identical to that of the volume, does not restrict itself to Luhmann's two contributions, but takes up issues that surface throughout his previously published works.[14]

Perhaps just as unusual as the composition of the volume, which closes, as we shall see, with Luhmann's lengthy critique of Habermas, is the strategy Habermas employs in analyzing the shortcomings of systems theory. From his introductory remarks the reader clearly understands that his objections to Luhmann are fundamental and political. The unarticulated background to Habermas's debate with positivist tendencies, illuminated only by Adorno, was that a methodology that radically refuses reflection is an indirect apology for the status quo. Systems theory, Habermas suggests, may be considered a successor to positivism in this regard. As an apologetic, legitimizing methodology for the social sciences, it seeks to provide justification for the decrease in democracy in modern societies and to eliminate through increased rationalization the last bastions of democracy that have persevered. It represents for him the 'highest form of technocratic consciousness' (p. 145), because it seeks to define ethical questions in technical terms and thereby further erode public and non-coercive discussion of social policy. Yet Habermas forgoes this direct political assault on Luhmann – at least until the closing pages of his critique – and concentrates instead on internal inconsistencies. 'My critique applies to the thing itself, not to a function it assumes behind its back' (p. 145). Habermas thus eschews precisely the functionalist critique that Luhmann's theory could supply and examines instead contradictions in the logical construction of systems theory.

His immanent critique commences by questioning Luhmann's fundamental assumptions and categories. As we saw above, Habermas believes that systems theory is unable to solve the problems of borders and goals. If we are going to use a system as a methodological tool in analysis of societies,

115

we have to be able to establish where it ends and where the environment begins. Similarly we have to be able to ascertain what state or condition the system is trying to achieve or maintain. For organisms this appears to be simple since spatially physical boundaries and temporally birth and death define boundaries, whereas survival and reproduction appear plausible as goals or inherent values. Luhmann, of course, is aware of this difficulty, and he proposes a solution in the radical recourse to function. Both the achievement of the system (process) in its relationship to its environment and the internal arrangement or composition of the system (structure) are viewed as functionally equivalent in the reduction of complexity. Habermas's claim is that this 'double selectivity' (internal and external) overtaxes the basic assumptions of systems theory. Luhmann must assume an initial and original world complexity that exists as a problem before the existence of all structures. But the complexity of the world can only be a problem for a system that functions to reduce complexity. 'World complexity only becomes problematic for the maintenance of systems' (p. 154). Luhmann thus wants to derive the relationship between system and environment from an assumption of world complexity that depends on the prior existence of systems and environment. This contradiction, Habermas maintains, is the logical result of the inadequate determination of system boundaries and goals.

Habermas also detects in Luhmann's writings an inconsistency or ambivalence of terminology that would make any research program in the social sciences a dubious enterprise. The reduction of complexity is employed in two ways. On the one hand, it refers to the gradient that is established between the system and the environment. In accord with a general cybernetic model the system selects out only a portion of the alternatives possible in the world external to it. But the reduction of complexity is also used to describe the selectivity that occurs inside a system. From the choices that are possible in our symbolically structured world (whose alternatives are already reduced from the plethora of possibilities that potentially exist) we elect a smaller number to guide our actions. The conflict between these two senses of 'reduction of complexity' is that they tend to work in opposite directions. There is a suggestion that the world is an arena of infinite possibilities, a contingent sphere for action in which the human being has the freedom to select between alternatives. This anthropological existentialism, which Habermas associates with Sartre, is opposed, however, to an institutional anthropology that stems from Arnold Gehlen. According to this tendency the chief problem is how to limit possibilities, how to relieve oneself of the burden of coping with an overly complex world. A process of enlightenment, in which the world is opened up to possibilities, confronts a notion of anti-enlightenment, in which dogmatically asserted truths provide security from a threatening complexity. According to Habermas, Luhmann's theory, which implies both of these options, cannot explain which tendency is most functional.

From the terminology that Habermas employs it should be evident that even in this section of his 'immanent' critique he is sensitive to political ramifications of Luhmann's argument. The notion of an anti-enlightenment tendency (*Gegenaufklärung*) or the allusion to dogmatism, as well as the attempt to bring Luhmann into the proximity of the conservative anthropologist Arnold Gehlen, suggest that Habermas recognizes a retrograde tendency at the very foundation of Luhmann's project. Indeed, Habermas thematizes this conservatism when he writes of the pragmatism of systems theory. His claim is threefold. First, systems theory does not provide us with any means to distinguish between reasons for maintaining a given system of subsystem. 'Who is to decide', Habermas asks, 'whether the interests of a ruling class or whether the interests of society as a whole are operative in the objectivity of ordinary consciousness?' (p. 167). Second, the feigned neutrality of values implies an instrumentalization that could serve causes of the right or the left. In this area Habermas detects an affinity between student activists, who seek confrontations with the establishment at all costs, and political technocrats, whose goal is the avoidance of crises and conflicts: both rely on a pragmatic functionalism that excludes a hermeneutic recourse to the discussion of values. Finally, Habermas sees the rootedness of systems theory in the life process of society as a danger, since it allows no space for a reflective level between theory and practice.

Behind the attempt to justify the reduction of world complexity as the ultimate point of reference for social-scientific functionalism is concealed an unadmitted obligation of theory to pose problems in a way that conforms to domination, to serve as an apologetic for what exists in order to maintain its existence. (p. 170)

Luhmann is therefore indicted for renewing the irrationality of the philosophical direction known as 'life-philosophy' (*Lebensphilosophie*) since the preservation of the existing order is methodologically anchored in his theoretical presuppositions.

MEANING, TRUTH AND IDEOLOGY

Habermas continues his assault on systems theory with a series of objections to Luhmann's basic preconceptions. Chief among these are his assumptions about meaning (*Sinn*). Habermas agrees with Luhmann that meaning is a basic concept for the social sciences, and he at least understands his colleague's reluctance to tie meaning to the concept of the subject. The bankruptcy of the notion of a transcendental ego, whether conceived as Kantian of Husserlian, makes comprehensible the decision to locate meaning outside of subjectivity. Habermas also understands that Luhmann wants to improve on Parsons's notion of meaning by adhering more strictly to functionalism: Luhmann therefore distinguishes carefully between the cybernetic notion of information and a more fundamental phenomenological conception of meaning (pp. 39–43). Meaning functions strictly as a rule for selection; information designates an actual content of consciousness. As a result, Luhmann explains, a message can lose its informational value when it is repeated, but never its meaning, and the same complex of meaning can produce various kinds of information, depending on the circumstances in which it is communicated. So for Luhmann meaning is a category that is situated, as it were, below the surface of the normal dialogical situation. Indeed, it is seen as a prelinguistic notion, since language functions only as an augmentation of the selectivity that belongs to the communication process.

Habermas's objections concern both the notion of meaning and its separation from a foundation in language. Two general claims inform his argument. Systems theory, he maintains, operates with monological and empirical presuppositions. Although it tries to avoid the errors of philosophies that proceed from a fixed notion of subjectivity, it remains entangled in the subjectivist snare. By deriving meaning from negation, Luhmann simply bypasses the fundamental question of how identical meanings are achieved. In Habermas's view this process involves more than the monological model of a subject negating or putting aside possible alternatives so that one can become manifest; it entails a dialogical partner as well. 'The identity of meaning does not point to negation, but to the guarantee of intersubjective validity' (p. 188). Only through dialogue in a communicative practice is meaning established. This implies, however, that meaning cannot be prelinguistic either. If it results from a dialogue, then it must be conceived as an effect of language. Habermas even suggests that intention should be defined from an intersubjective perspective since it is always other-directed. The difference between Luhmann and Habermas on meaning is thus one between a conception based in a monological experience constructed through difference (negation) and one that locates meaning in the intersubjective dialogue that establishes identity.

Because of this inadequate foundation for meaning, Habermas claims that Luhmann cannot appropriately distinguish between meaning and information. Since the distinction must be made with regard to propositional content, we must be able to conceive of a form of communication in which propositional content is not at issue, a realm in which the participants in a dialogue do not converse in order to exchange information. Habermas calls this level of intersubjective exchange 'discourse' to signify the type of communication in which interlocutors problematize the validity claims of propositions, rather than the propositions themselves. 'In discourse the participants are directed solely toward the explication of meaningful connections' (*Sinnzusammenhängen*) (p. 200). Discourse, however, because it is not an institution, but rather a counter-institution, cannot be assimilated to a system. It can function only under the condition that all compulsion be removed. As a metalevel of language it does not conform to a theory that relegates meaning to the reduction of complexity. If we conceive of meaning in Habermas's terms, as a basic concept of everyday communication informed by the level of discourse, then

119

Luhmann's theory is clearly too restricted. If it retains its limited notion of meaning, it must deny a discourse on validity claims; if it accepts discourse, it has to relinquish the exclusivity of systems explanations.

Habermas uncovers a further problem when Luhmann discusses the connection between meaning, experience and action. Luhmann postulates two ways in which complexity can be reduced in social systems. If meaning is reduced by the world itself, it is called experience (*Erleben*); if the reduction is attributed to the system, it is designated as action (*Handlung*) (p. 77). Habermas objects first to Luhmann's wavering with respect to experience. Sometimes it functions as the ground for meaning, for example when meaning is defined as the form in which we process experience; but at other points experience, as in the definition just cited, is derived from meaning. But Habermas's chief objection is that Luhmann obscures the relationship between action, communication and meaning. He argues that there is actually a double constitution to both experience and action. Experience and action with the external world of objects is sensory and instrumental, whereas intersubjective experience and action is communicative. In addition to the level of communicative action, Habermas also recalls the discursive use of language. Meaning is thus not a simple conduit for experience and action but a differential concept that should be viewed in a tripartite fashion: in connection with the constitution of an empirical world of experience and cognition, in connection with the constitution of a society through communicative action, and on the level of discourse for the founding of validity claims. Luhmann's inability to conceptualize these separate levels of meaning leads ultimately to a confounding of individual and society, and of facts and norms.

But a more serious consequence of the errors of systems theory is its inability to deal consistently with the concept of truth. Like all notions, truth is not viewed as a norm that has overarching validity, but as a function inside a system. For Luhmann truth is simply one of several media that assure the intersubjective transference of meaning among groups and individuals. It functions in the way that money, power and love do to pass on the current reduction of complexity so that every person, generation or group does not have to engage in selectivity anew. As one medium among many, truth is called upon to stabilize intersubjectivity and to guarantee a *de facto* consensus. It thereby forfeits any claim to universal validity or normativity that we associate either with a correspondence to reality or with a rational consensus. Luhmann's 'truth' is relative to the system in which it operates; it is dependent solely on the successful transmission of selectivity. But Habermas points out that one cannot hold this functionalist notion of truth without entangling oneself in a number of aporias or contradictions. He argues that the removal of normativity from the notion of truth leaves us with an unusual dilemma. If truth is purely functional, then claims made on the basis of truth are ultimately no more justifiable than claims made on the basis of any other medium. We can no longer distinguish claims that rest on criteria of criticizability from those that depend on force or authority or faith or utility.

The consequences for Luhmann's own claims involve him in a rather obvious performative contradiction. The status of his theory would seem to be undermined unless we assume some normative basis for them in truth. Habermas formulates this contradiction as follows: 'the systems theoretical interpretation of the world as a whole, which leads to a reflexive identity of theory and action, demands the functionalization of the concept of truth, but presupposes a theoretical conception of truth' (p. 229). It is important to note that Habermas does not evade the obvious question of how Critical Theory, which also postulates the unity of theory and practice, avoids this same contradiction. The difference in theoretical enterprises based on Hegel or Marx is that they conceive their systems in a self-reflexive fashion. The process of cognition of which they are a part is constructed as an enlightening of the subject about its own objective conditions of existence. Truth can therefore be consistently affirmed because the theoretical claim to truth is built into the process that is being analyzed by means of reflection. Since Luhmann postulates systemic self-maintenance not self-knowledge as the objective task of the system, his theoretical statements affirm a functional notion of truth, which is necessary if it is going to remain consistent with the general framework, while they simultaneously undercut their own status as truthful accounts by eliminating all means of establishing their own validity.

Habermas brings up these inconsistencies in systems theory

121

not to demonstrate Luhmann's sloppy reasoning or his own acumen, but to suggest that the notion of system as Luhmann has developed it cannot be successfully defended without recourse to Habermas's own theory of communicative action or some reasonable analogue. As we have seen, however, Habermas also believes that there is something politically retrograde in the methodological claim that systems theory can serve as a foundation for research in the social sciences. This political critique again becomes obvious in his discussion of ideology. Habermas argues that the deficiencies in the functionalist views of ideology follow from the insufficient notion of truth. Luhmann understands truth either as a representation of reality, a theory that Habermas believes can be correctly rejected, or in the functionalist sense as a medium for transmission of selectivity. He does not consider a third alternative that Habermas proposes: that truth is reached through the consensus of interlocutors in a discursive situation. Luhmann's reduction of truth to its function as producing certainty denies him the possibility to evaluate ideologies other than in their role of maintaining systems. There can be no critique of ideology without a criterion of truth to determine which statements represent interests that are grounded in asymmetrical relations (power, status, and so on) and which statements are the expression of a genuine, unforced consensus.

In terms of Habermas's theory one could see Luhmann's error in his refusal to distinguish between communicative and strategic action. The former orients itself on values and is pursued by means of consensus between participants; the latter involves interests and presupposes an inequality of power between participants. Because Luhmann lacks a notion of communicative action and genuine consensus, he comprehends the role of ideologies only as they function with regard to the internal works of systems. Habermas cites as an illustration Luhmann's discussion of racist ideology. Luhmann, of course, does not affirm racism, but he understands the absurdity of racist values as a confirmation of his thesis that the content of the ideology is itself unimportant as long as it serves its function 'of neutralizing undesired consequences in the area of the causal interpretation of action and of expanding the area of allowable means' (p. 258). According to Habermas this explanation misses the point entirely. Ideologies, he contends, are sets of beliefs that dissolve when they are called into question, since they are maintained only by restricting systematically free and public discourse. The functionalist view of ideology thus neglects the connection between the interdiction of communication and legitimation. It ignores the double and paradoxical function of ideological worldviews in providing fundamental justification for social norms, while at the same time prohibiting an uncoerced discourse that would expose their falsehood.

In its obfuscation of the function of ideologies, Luhmann's theory is itself ideological. Habermas recognizes that Luhmann's reasoning is not unpersuasive. His contention that systems in complex societies simply do not permit the same type of communicative input and democratic control is at least plausible:

> The key to Luhmann's arguments is that the internal complexity of developed social systems can be increasingly better managed to the degree that the centrally regulated programs of action are severed from the motivations for action of those who are affected. (p. 263)

Although Luhmann does not totally dismiss the role that practical discourse can play in legitimation, he can point to two phenomena of modern society that seem to be in accord with his analysis. One is the alarming tendency to accept institutional decisions routinely without rational justification; on the other hand, we can observe the growing need for legitimation in contemporary societies. Habermas feels that Luhmann's explanations are insufficient because they posit the demise of claims to legitimation. In Habermas's view the need for legitimation, as we saw in the previous chapter, continues to grow in advanced capitalist societies (and in bureaucratic socialist societies as well) and is still implicit in various institutional forms (elections, legal procedures, administrative processes). A theory like Luhmann's, which assimilates all systemic justification to a model of purposive-rational action, which considers only function and ignores the implicit discursive consensus underlying norms and institutions, serves 'as a justification for the systematic restriction of practically efficacious communication' (p. 267). It provides the theoretical model for an administered society devoid of genuine public discussion by presupposing that the tendency towards instrumental reason can become absolute and abolish every vestige of communicative reason.

POLITICS AND PROGRESS

Luhmann's reply to Habermas took the form of an essay of over 100 pages in which he responded to both theoretical objections and political implications. He clarifies several distinctions that Habermas criticized (meaning versus information, experience versus action), and defends ably his functionalist notion of truth as a medium of communication. He also demonstrates that discourse, if conceived as discussion, does not fall outside the boundaries of systems analysis, as Habermas had contended, but can be easily conceived as a system itself. The underlying theme of Luhmann's response is that Habermas is not wrong if we accept his terminology and his framework of communicative action, but that this terminology and framework are obsolete, idealist and irrelevant for the understanding of modern society. Habermas, for example, assumes an opposition between technical and practical knowledge in his critique of systems theory, but Luhmann points out that his notion of action disputes this very separation. Habermas's concept of technology (*Technik*) reduces its meaning to the production of objects (p. 359), an important, but severely limited, aspect of the term. Because of this simplistic dichotomization of social functions Habermas's theory of society remains hopelessly outdated.

Furthermore, Luhmann denies that communicative action, discourse, or purposive-rational action are adequate notions for coping with the problem that he feels is the central theoretical concern in social sciences: complexity. He concedes that this seminal concept has not been adequately defined by the tradition, but he insists that the terminology Habermas had adopted is too superficial to comprehend it at all. Habermas's critique misses its mark, Luhmann claims, because his would-be emancipatory theory has failed to emancipate itself from the superannuated conceptual framework of the sociological and philosophical tradition.

For this reason Luhmann rejects the political dimension of Habermas's critique as hopelessly out of touch with current political realities. Indeed, he argues that the traditional categories for viewing political affinities are no longer meaningful. Because society is changing at such a rapid pace, conservatives, defined as those who want to maintain existing social structures are compelled to change their views continually. Leftists, on the other hand, more often find themselves in the role of 'conservatives' since they are really trying to preserve values and propagate ideals that have long since been overtaken by a progress they cannot fathom. Habermas's repeated recourse to the notion of hegemony (*Herrschaft*) is a case in point for leftist conservatism. Luhmann locates the term in the historical realm of agrarian relations, when the patriarch or master was considered superior in all ways to his serfs and servants. He was the exemplar of reason, beauty, wealth, love and power, in short for all the media of complexity reduction. This notion cannot be reconciled, Luhmann contends, with contemporary society, where the reduction of complexity through the various media must be viewed in a more differentiated fashion. Hegemony is no longer an adequate reduction of complexity, as it may have been earlier, and those who evoke it today are either tied to a romantic tradition, or endeavoring to intimidate in political discussions through its connotative suggestions. Luhmann advises Habermas to stop postulating a sphere free of hegemony for his ideal of discourse and to start, instead, to employ concepts free of hegemony (pp. 399–401).

The political stakes for Habermas and Luhmann can perhaps be most readily grasped by looking briefly at their respective views on social evolution. In Luhmann's model evolution is based heavily on the notion of differentiation, which occurs in three distinct forms. Segmentation differentiates society into subsystems that have an equal status in terms of the interface of system and environment. Luhmann illustrates segmentation by referring to archaic societies in which descent or settlement or a combination of both are determinate for the systemic structures. Inequality of systems is the consequence of differing environmental conditions, and although it is not systemic in nature, it is still 'decisive for the process of evolutionary differentiation of different societal systems'.[15] Stratification divides societies into unequal subsystems. It maintains equality with regard to elements within a given system, but presupposes an inequality between systems and their environments.

The ancient Greek city state, which presumed an equality of the citizenry, but a difference between social strata, is an example of what Luhmann means by this term. Finally, functional differentiation operates 'on the basis of a functional equality within systems and a functional inequality between systems and their environments'.[16] Luhmann argues that all functions in society are interdependent, but in order to accomplish them efficiently, primacy is accorded to one or another system. For example, politics functions to provide collectively binding decisions, the economic system mediates material needs, and religion is assigned the task of explaining the incomprehensible. The functions of these three systems are unequal, but the access to the functions is equal in the sense that each is independent of other functions.

From this description of the three forms of differentiation it should come as no surprise that Luhmann describes evolution as a process of increased differentiation in which modern societies are those in which functional differentiation predominates. He emphasizes, however, that the evolutionary process is complex and that segmentation, stratification and functional differentiation do not appear in their pure forms, but as mixed forms in which one type of differentiation prevails. In the contemporary world, for example, functional differentiation is dependent on segmentation and stratification. If we examine the world political system we find that decision-making is dependent on territorial distinctions into nations, and that this segmentation is not simply a remnant of historical process, but a prerequisite for the maintenance of maximal participation. In the economic realm functional differentiation seems to presuppose the stratification associated with unequal distribution of wealth. Formerly stratification was the principal organizational form for societies, but in the exigencies of functionally differentiated societies it manifests itself in entities such as class structures. In this regard capitalist and socialist societies do not differ in the inequities of distribution (stratification), but simply in the degree to which the bureaucracies in the respective systems function to uphold and validate the inequalities. Even in societies in which functional differentiation dominates social organization (i.e. modern industrial societies), system maintenance would be impossible without segmentation and stratification.

Habermas's central criticism of Luhmann's evolutionary

126

model is that it takes into account only one aspect of social development. Although he credits him for his discovery of evolutionary universals (generalization, differentiation, reflexivity and communicatory media) as far as they relate to systems dynamics, the supra-subjective processes that inform Luhmann's scheme of evolution are only one class among many. According to Habermas we must admit three dimensions for any theory of evolution that hopes to comprehend adequately the complexity of modern society. In addition to the regulation of social systems in terms of strategic action and socio-technical planning, we also need to consider scientific-technical progress, which assumes a cumulative learning process with regard to our relationship to the external world, and 'the emancipatory change in systems of institutions', which results from learning processes in the area of ideologies (p. 276).

Relying on his own adaptation of categories from Marxist theory, Habermas suggests four terms that Luhmann's functional analysis neglects: production, interaction, everyday communication, and ideology. If these categories are included as foundational for a description of socio-cultural development, then we can account for evolution in terms of a progressive unfolding of forces of production and a critique of worldviews that legitimize hegemony, not merely in terms of the capacity of systems to regulate complexity. Habermas's point is simply that Luhmann's theory casts social evolution as a one-dimensional, socio-technical, and supra-individual process involving systems and environments. He thereby ignores the relationship between humankind and the external world, as well as conflicts and problems that are internal to systems.

Luhmann counters by asserting that his notion of evolution is situated at a higher level of abstraction and is therefore more encompassing than Habermas's. Above all Luhmann wants to distinguish his notion of evolution from obsolete evolutionary theories of the nineteenth century. Common to these previous attempts to understand social development – and Habermas's is included among them by implication – is the analogy with laws from the sphere of nature. Evolutionary theory should not be conceived as a process of organic growth and development, according to Luhmann, but as 'the theory of systemic structures and processes that produce evolution, but are themselves not evolution' (p. 362). In a sketchy summary Luhmann proposes that different mechanisms are operative in individual systems in different circumstances. Variation is seen primarily in the realm of language; mechanisms of selection are accorded to the media of communication; and stabilization is associated with the construction of systems. With this tripartite theoretical postulate Luhmann believes that he can accommodate Habermas's objections. On the one hand, the construction of systems is viewed as only one moment in an evolutionary process that includes language and communication as well. On the other hand, it allows Luhmann to retain his notion that all evolution depends on system differentiation. He can resolve this paradox because 'there is not just one single system' (p. 369); systems can constitute themselves inside other systems.

What is at stake in this game of abstract one-upmanship may not be readily apparent. Luhmann's attempt to subsume all evolution under a systems theoretical framework effectively cancels the Marxist categories that Habermas proposed as the foundation for his tripartite notion of social progress. Habermas's theory is seen as inadequate because it is obsolete, i.e. because it depends on 'an old European tradition' of organically conceived progression to higher stages (p. 372). Instead of introducing the notion of production as primary and interpreting the economic system from it, Luhmann wants to derive production from the economic system. In Luhmann's view production is not abstract enough to comprehend what occurs in the economic arena:

Economy is really not at all a 'material substrate', but rather one of the most ingenious institutions of human life. It was differentiated out as a subsystem relatively late and acquired a leading evolutionary role. Therefore I would consider temporally ordered selectivity as essential for the concept of production, and along with it the capability of organization. (p. 373)

Marx, who believed he had conceived his categories abstractly in order to comprehend all economic development, is implicitly criticized for not being abstract enough. Similarly Habermas's notion of instrumental action is viewed as a concept that has explanatory power only as a consequence of more general changes in the 'temporal horizon' of the social system (pp. 373–4).

Luhmann's insistence on the universality of systems theory and the abstract level at which he carried out his analysis of social formations also negate the force of Habermas's notion of emancipation. In Habermas's theory emancipation is conceived as an answer to hegemony. From a systems theoretical perspective emancipation cannot even be reconstructed as a category since it refers us to the superannuated view of evolution as the result of social conflicts. Luhmann believes that emancipation is a falsely conceived issue for modern societies. The consequence of increasing societal differentiation has been the rise of the individual, enlarged space for the personality and a decrease in preconceived status. The expansion of depersonalized action in the social system has thus not led to fragmentation, alienation and the loss of personal freedom, but has actually allowed the realization of personal liberties and individuality to an extent never before imagined. Emancipation, Luhmann contends with only slight exaggeration, is a problem that presents itself only after it has been solved (p. 376). From his functionalist perspective the problems that Habermas raises are vestiges of an antiquated and irrelevant type of social analysis that continues to exorcise demons where none exists. From the vantage point of a theory of communicative action, of course, Luhmann's theory is itself a manifestation of a sophisticated social conservatism that eradicates emancipatory impulses by establishing a framework within which the significant questions concerning social emancipation and domination cannot even be raised. Systems theory and communicative action not only occupy different arenas of social analysis, but also inhabit diametrically opposed political universes. Behind the abstractions and technical terminology Luhmann and Habermas carried out one of the most ideologically charged debates of the postwar era.

POSTSCRIPT: ON COMPLEXITY AND DEMOCRACY

The highly theoretical nature of Habermas's controversy with Luhmann may obscure its relationship to developments in the Federal Republic during the late 1960s. In essence Habermas engages Luhmann in debate for the same reason he engaged the radicals in the student movement. In both instances he sensed a threat to democratic values and institutions. In the case of the students this threat came from an anarchic and undifferentiated rejection of all aspects of the social order nourished by an underdeveloped and superficial theoretical position. Luhmann's threat emanates from the diametrically opposed tendency to excuse and defend the status quo and is underwritten by a sophisticated theoretical construction. That Habermas himself perceives Luhmann's work as a negation of the very democratic causes and principles he had supported is evident in the 'postscript' to the debate, included as the penultimate chapter in the volume *Legitimationsprobleme im Spätkapitalismus* (1973) [*Legitimation Crisis*]. The theme of this book, more accurately reflected in the German title, concerns the problems in legitimation in Western countries with advanced capitalist economies. The bulk of Habermas's discussion is devoted to theories of crisis as they have been articulated for economy, rationality, legitimation and motivation and to his own analysis of social forces in late capitalism. In contrast to much of the tradition, Habermas is at pains throughout to establish that social norms can be subjected to truth claims, and that these claims are dependent on democratically conceived consensus.

Luhmann is taken up as the most serious contemporary challenge to democratic social theory. Systems theory propagates a notion of the political sphere in complex societies that isolates it from democratic control. Luhmann conceives of 'comprehensive, non-participatory planning'[17] shielded from the influence of the public and political parties as the only administratively acceptable model for Western societies. Habermas deals with three flaws in this political theory. First, while not denying that one can detect an autonomous administration in advanced industrial societies, he argues that it is illegitimate to generalize from the existing situation. In systems theory, administrations are not forced to confront the limits of their own competence or capacity to solve problems. Furthermore, there is empirical evidence that such limits to administrative planning capacity 'turn up again and again in an *ad hoc* manner',[18] and this suggests a dependency of the administrative system on other realms. Second, Luhmann explains 'rationality deficits' as the result of a continued dependence of the political system on external control. The rationality of the political realm will be attained only when 'administration develops an identity independent of society and understands itself as the authority responsible for the expansion of the horizon of possibility and the collateral thematization of alternatives excluded at that time'.[19] Habermas points out that other explanations are available, even inside a systems theoretical framework. Essential here is that Luhmann opts for the most non-participatory and potentially most authoritarian alternative.

If Luhmann's approach to politics cannot be logically grounded in either theoretical assumptions, even those of systems theory, or in empirical evidence, where does its own legitimacy reside? Habermas contends that the answer to this question lies in his theory of social evolution, the third flaw in Luhmann's work. Luhmann presumes that the problems of the reduction of complexity and the expansion of system complexity are the sole determining features in societal development. As a result he concentrates exclusively on the regulatory capacity of the political system and completely negates such constitutive features as the development of worldviews or stages of morality. Ultimately this preference for steering systems is tied to his tacit assumption of a rationality that undercuts the distinction between empirical-analytical and normative-analytical modes of procedure. Habermas characterizes such theory as 'opportunistic in principle' or, more generously, as 'pragmatic' in the bad sense of the word: 'systems research itself is part of a life-process subject to the law of increasing selectivity and reducing complexity'.[20] The 'pragmatic rationality' of systems theory is opposed to Habermas's communicative alternative, which allows us to justify norms in terms of validity claims. Habermas therefore argues in the final excursus in *The Philosophical Discourse of Modernity*, in which he discusses Luhmann's work in the context of critiques of rationality, that Luhmann has merely continued the tradition of 'subject-centered reason' by substituting 'system' for 'subject'.[21] The consequence is a social theory that abandons all critical function, sacrificing democratic input and popular control of decision-making processes for an unfounded affirmation of an autonomous administrative system. So from the late 1960s through to the 1980s Habermas's repeated and continuous opposition to Luhmann, from whom he none the less learns a great deal,[22] is inextricably linked to the implications of his theory for the realization of authentic democratic institutions in modern industrial societies.

6

Modernity and postmodernity: the debate with Jean-François Lyotard

The inclusion of a discussion of Niklas Luhmann at the close of *The Philosophical Discourse of Modernity* indicates that Habermas associates systems theory closely with other theoretical tendencies in modern Western societies. At first glance this association appears far-fetched. Systems theory, conceived by Luhmann as a model for social science research, would appear to have little to do with the main subject of Habermas's book, which concentrates on philosophical critiques of modernity from Nietzsche to Derrida. Luhmann's program, although philosophically informed by the phenomenological tradition, in particular by the work of Edmund Husserl, none the less draws its inspiration most directly from a sociological tradition that extends from Emile Durkheim and Max Weber to Talcott Parsons. Its key concepts are drawn from the world of cybernetics. Its appeal is not to students of philosophy or to humanists, but to social analysts and sociological researchers. Yet Habermas does not situate the volume that summarizes Luhmann's theoretical outlook in the tradition that its title, *Soziale Systeme* (1984) ['Social Systems'], evokes, but rather in the heritage of 'consciousness philosophy' from Kant through to Husserl.[1] What Habermas deems important in Luhmann's work in 1985 is its relationship to a project that he defines as modernity. What he criticizes is Luhmann's indirect affirmation of an obsolete model of subjectivity. Thus his connection with philosophers such as Foucault and Derrida lies less in any shared poststructuralist or postmodernist proclivities than in the presuppositions underlying their analysis of the modern condition.

THE UNCOMPLETED PROJECT OF MODERNITY

The first time Habermas outlines these presuppositions and places them in a larger historical framework is in an acceptance speech for the Adorno prize in September of 1980.[2] He begins by examining the history of the word 'modernity'. The concept appears during periods of European history when the consciousness of a new epoch formed. It gained particular importance during the eighteenth and nineteenth centuries in opposition to the ancients or the classics. Most often the moderns associated themselves with the Middle Ages to underline the contrast with antiquity. During the German romantic era, romanticism (*Romantik*) was at first synonymous with the Catholic Middle Ages and opposed to pagan Greece and Rome. Eventually this notion of aesthetic modernity dissociates itself from the Middle Ages and the opposition ancient-modern becomes the more abstract and general dichotomy between anything new and the tradition. Beginning with Baudelaire in the middle of the nineteenth century we find, therefore, the use of modernity that has established itself in aesthetic discussions for the past century and a half. 'Modernity' is redefined to mean simply the 'avant-garde', and in the twentieth century we find its most self-conscious expression in the works of the Dadaists and surrealists.

> We observe the anarchistic intention of blowing up the continuum of history, and we can account for it in terms of the subversive force of this new aesthetic consciousness. Modernity revolts against the normalizing function of tradition; modernity lives on the experience of rebelling against all that is normative. (p. 5)

In his initial discussion Habermas does not appear to distinguish sharply between 'modernity' as a concept with general philosophical and historical content and 'modernism' as applied to literature and the arts. They are no doubt related in some fashion, but the purview of the former is greater and more substantial. Modernism, which we may take to be the cultural rebellion against convention that Habermas identifies with the avant-garde, would seem to have validity solely in the realm of culture. Indeed, this is the way in which Habermas employs the concept in the next part of his analysis. He observes that neo-conservatism in the United States and Western Europe has blamed cultural modernism or aesthetic modernity for the effects of modernization in postwar societies. Unable to recognize the social and economic origins of contemporary ills, the neo-conservative critique deflects attention from capitalist modernization toward those intellectuals who continue to propagate aesthetic modernity. The neo-conservative insistence on traditional community values to counter the purported divisiveness of modernism in the cultural realm misses the point. According to Habermas the erosion of traditions has to do with an incursion of purposive or goal-directed rationality into the general cultural sphere. He expresses this incursion more technically in the *Theory of Communicative Action* in terms of the 'colonization of the lifeworld by the imperatives of the system'.[3] In essence, however, Habermas is referring to the reduction of communicative rationality to instrumental rationality. The neo-conservative critique correctly detects a problem of the lifeworld in modern industrial societies, but shortsightedly identifies it with the subversive aesthetic modernity.

In order to understand the modern world, Habermas contends, we must look beyond the aesthetic modernity of the avant-garde and identify the larger 'project of modernity' of which it is a part. Following Max Weber, Habermas characterizes modernity by the separation of three spheres, which also correspond roughly to Kant's three critiques: science, morality and art. With the disintegration of a unified religious or metaphysical worldview, each sphere achieves autonomy and is assigned a particular question and domain: truth, conceived as an epistemological matter is ascribed to natural science; normative rightness, formulated in terms of justice, is relegated to morality; and the determination of authenticity or beauty is determined through judgements of taste in the realm of art. Habermas continues these tripartite divisions by identifying a specific rationality with each sphere: cognitive-instrumental for science, moral-practical for ethics and aesthetic-expressive for art. Only with the advent of modernity do we witness an immanent history for each of these three realms; only in the modern era do these spheres begin to operate under internally developed laws and imperatives.

But there are inherent dangers in this process: the increasing specialization within each sphere, which Habermas calls rationalization, fosters a culture of experts that excludes collective decision-making. What Luhmann greets as increased functional differentiation, Habermas bemoans as an impoverished lifeworld. The project of modernity, which is in Habermas's view identical with the project of the Enlightenment, is to promote the increased rationalization of each sphere, while simultaneously releasing 'the cognitive potentials of each of these domains to set them free from their esoteric forms' (p. 9). As formulated in the eighteenth century, the goals of the three spheres are objective science, universal morality and autonomous art. The Enlightenment held out the hope of employing the accumulated knowledge in each sphere for a more satisfying, enriching and rational organization of everyday life.

The development and the 'false programs' of aesthetic modernity in Habermas's conception can now be discerned more clearly. The tendency of art since the middle of the eighteenth century has been toward increased autonomy, toward a separation of aesthetic products of culture from a connection with truth (as conceived by science) or goodness (as a moral postulate). Kant's *Critique of Judgement* may not have been the inaugural document in this process, but it was certainly one of the most important.[4] With Kant the trajectory for modern art was firmly established. An aesthetic realm, based on a universal notion of taste, separates itself out from the cognitive and ethical sphere. Although in the Enlightenment philosophy of Kant a *sensus communis* still underlies our faculty of judgement, making beauty a necessarily intersubjective determination, the process of specialization soon takes hold. Art as an end in itself leads ineluctably to a severing of the connections between art and the more general public. Eventually the type of formal experimentation and elitism we associate with twentieth-century art becomes the norm: in literature and the pictorial arts representation gradually relinquishes its sway and is replaced by a foregrounding of the media themselves. Lines, color, shapes, sounds, words, or even letters themselves become aesthetic objects. Art appeals to experts, not to a larger community.

The avant-garde challenges this formal hegemony by calling into question what Peter Bürger has called the 'institution of art'.[5] Behind this challenge Habermas detects an endeavor to

136

recuperate the 'promise of happiness' that emanates from the original Enlightenment project. But the surrealist 'warfare' against autonomous art fails in two respects. First, removing the aura from art, declaring everyone to be an artist, destroying the legitimacy of aesthetic forms, as the avant-garde had done, does not necessarily lead to the desired liberation. 'When the containers of an autonomously developed cultural sphere are shattered, the contents get dispersed. Nothing remains from a desublimated meaning or a destructured form; an emancipatory effect does not follow' (p. 10). More importantly, the surrealist challenge ignored the need for communicative practices that cross all domains: cognitive, moral-practical and expressive. The rationalization of the lifeworld cannot be countered by actions against a single sphere:

A reified everyday praxis can be cured only by creating unconstrained interaction of the cognitive with the moral-practice and the aesthetic-expressive elements. Reification cannot be overcome by forcing just one of those highly stylized cultural spheres to open up and become more accessible. (p. 11)

In short, the surrealists initiated a false or one-sided negation of art that did not lead to an all-encompassing emancipation but to a reaffirmation of the very aesthetic categories it sought to efface.

Habermas counters the surrealist revolt with some cautious suggestions for how art may assist in true emancipation. He notes that bourgeois art functions in two ways when it is received by the general public. On the one hand, it is supposed to educate the public so that each individual becomes an expert. On the other hand, it relates to the life experiences of the public, establishing connections to the lifeworld of its audience. This second manner of reception, decried as naive identification, has revolutionary potential, according to Habermas. Drawing on a proposal of Albrecht Wellmer, he suggests that art can be employed to illuminate a 'life-historical situation', changing our cognitive relationship to the world (science) and our thinking about norms and values (ethics). His chief illustration of how art can accomplish this task comes from the *Ästhetick des Widerstands* ['Aesthetics of Resistance'] a novel by Peter Weiss.[6] In this book workers are able to move freely between their lifeworld and the works of high art with which they are confronted, allowing one to comment on the other. The reception of art that Weiss thematizes in his novel would serve as a model for a critique of aesthetic forms that is both critical and emancipatory. It contributes to a completion of the project of modernity by relinking in a differentiated fashion the sphere of culture to the realms of science and morality. It avoids both the conservative affirmation of an unreflected tradition and the avant-garde anarchism of aesthetic iconoclasm.

Clearly such a program of revitalization through the aesthetic realm has an idealist dimension. Political reformation through art, found prominently in the German tradition from Friedrich Schiller's *Letters on the Aesthetic Education* to Herbert Marcuse's late aesthetic reflections, is a utopian project of the Enlightenment, and Habermas is sober enough to admit that 'the chances of this today are not very good' (p. 13). Increased capitalist modernization coupled with a continued skepticism toward cultural modernism are the agenda he sees in the 1980s. The intellectual ballast for this agenda is an unusual alliance of postmodernists and premodernists that Habermas divides into three groups. The neo-conservatives affirm the hegemony of modern science in contributing to technological progress and modernization and defuse the explosive contents of cultural modernism. The results are tendencies that divorce science from the lifeworld, that sever the ties between politics and morality, or that propagate a pure aestheticism without utopian content. Habermas identifies the followers of the early Wittgenstein, Carl Schmitt and Gottfried Benn respectively with these three variants of neo-conservatism. The Old Conservatives, by contrast, approve of nothing in the modern world and resort to positions anterior to modernity. In this connection Habermas refers to neo-Aristotelianism, in particular to the works of Leo Strauss, Hans Jonas and Robert Spaemann.

The Young Conservatives are distinguished from these other two groups by their embracing of the central position of aesthetic modernity. Paradoxically they represent their modernity as anti-modernity, or more accurately as postmodernity. To counter instrumental reason they have recourse to spontaneity, the archaic, the anarchic, the emotional and the irrational.

Bataille, Foucault and Derrida are specifically mentioned as representatives of Young Conservatism. Rather than a common political program what unites the Old, New and Young Conservatives is their anti-modernity, their putative opposition to the program first articulated by the European Enlightenment.

JEAN-FRANÇOIS LYOTARD AND THE HETEROGENEITY OF LANGUAGE GAMES

Although Jean-François Lyotard was not included on Habermas's list of Young Conservatives, he apparently assumed that he belonged to this group. He had good reason for this assumption. As one of the leading intellectual figures in France, Lyotard's extensive writings on philosophy, aesthetics and psychology have been seen as a seminal contribution to poststructuralist thought. The publication in 1979 of *La Condition postmoderne* [*The Postmodern Condition* (1984)] cemented this connection between Lyotard and poststructuralism. In Germany this book was understood as a foundational text for the avant-garde direction in contemporary French theory. Manfred Frank, whose *Was ist Neostrukturalismus?* (1984) [*What is Neostructuralism?*] was the most influential and most comprehensive study of poststructuralism in Germany, deals with Lyotard's book in order to lay the groundwork for his discussions of Derrida, Foucault and Deleuze and Guattari. Frank chooses this text not only because he considers it a basic work of the poststructuralist canon, but also because Lyotard is one of the few French theorists who evinces an interest in contemporary German thought. All poststructuralists are familiar with German idealism, and the entire movement would be unthinkable without the philosophies of Nietzsche and Heidegger. But only Lyotard engages, at least peripherally, the philosophically informed social theory of Habermas and Luhmann.[7] Indeed, *The Postmodern Condition* could probably be conceived as the poststructuralist answer to both communicative action and systems theory. In dealing with language at the level of knowledge and society, Lyotard not only defines our current state in terms of postmodernity, but also critiques rival explanations.

With regard to Habermas's first discussions of modernity and postmodernity, the publication date of *The Postmodern Condition* is significant. Written in the late 1970s, it obviously did not take into account Habermas's remarks on Young Conservatism. Only in the appendix to the English translation, which contains an essay from 1982, was Lyotard aware of the Habermas essay discussed earlier. In the body of the text Lyotard is more centrally concerned with Habermas's notion of legitimation and his views on consensus. In the introduction Lyotard lays the groundwork for his criticism when he states that the connection between legitimacy and consensus found in Habermas's writings 'does violence to the heterogeneity of language games'.[8] What Lyotard means by this becomes clearer only when the reader has finished his second and third chapters. With respect to civil laws that prescribe behavior for the citizenry, 'legitimation is the process by which a legislator is authorized to promulgate such a law as a norm'. In the realm of science legitimation is defined analogously as 'the process by which a "legislator" dealing with scientific discourse is authorized to prescribe the stated conditions . . . determining whether a statement is to be included in that discourse for consideration by the scientific community' (p. 8). The two domains are linked by a logic identified with the Occident. Habermas's notion of legitimation thus differs in two regards: (1) Whereas Habermas usually refers to legitimation in contemporary societies in relation to state decisions to intervene in the economic sphere, Lyotard expands the notion to refer to the decision-making status of any authority. Lyotard's concept has a greater purview and in fact comes closer to what Habermas discusses under the heading of validity claims. (2) Habermas wants to separate the realms of natural science and ethics/politics in terms of cognition in the objective world and communication in the social world. Lyotard finds a common ground for both by evoking the Western tradition.

The second element in Lyotard's critique is language games, which are discussed in his third chapter. The term obviously stems from the later work of Wittgenstein, and Lyotard's use of it differs only in the consequences he draws from this notion. He too associates language games with pragmatics, and he initiates his discussion with illustrations of denotative, declarative and prescriptive utterances. He makes three observations about language games. First, the rules by which they are played are not inherent in them, but rather agreed upon among the players by contract. Second, the rules and the game are mutually dependent. If a rule is changed, the nature of the game or a correct move in the game is altered; if an incorrect move is played, then it does not belong to the game. Third, there is no utterance that escapes one or another language game. Lyotard's conclusion from these observations involves the literalization of the metaphor of game and move in a particular way. Conceiving of the game as a competition, he surmises that utterances are moves made by an opponent in order to succeed against an adversary: 'to speak is to fight, in the sense of playing, and speech acts fall within the domain of a general agonistics' (p. 10). Even in speech acts that apparently do not have an opponent, for example in poetry, he believes that we engage in struggle. The source of our pleasure in such language games, which may employ anything from puns to figures of speech, is derived from our conquering of language itself or its connotations. Speech (*parole*) for Lyotard is by its very nature agonistic, a struggle for advantage over an adversary.

Lyotard never refers directly to Habermas in these two chapters, but he does return to him at the very close of his book, summing up his objections in two central points. First, Lyotard claims that legitimation cannot be tied to universal consensus – the position he identifies with Habermas – because the pragmatic realm of language games is ungoverned by transcendental or pre-established rules. Only if we could determine beforehand that we were all playing by the same rules could we still entertain the possibility of agreement. Lyotard attributes to Habermas the following assumptions: 'that it is possible for all speakers to come to agreement on which rules or metaprescriptions are universally valid for language games, when it is clear that language games are heteromorphous, subject to heterogeneous sets of pragmatic rules' (p. 65). It appears that Lyotard has misunderstood Habermas's project of 'universal pragmatics'. Habermas would presumably admit that on the empirical level, where pragmatics has traditionally been located, there are innumerable 'games' played by rules that one cannot know in advance. Only from the context do we know what type of game we are playing. However, as we saw in Chapter 1, Habermas's point is that in addition to the empirical level, pragmatics has a universal or formal dimension. Accompanying every utterance are validity claims – truth,

141

appropriateness and sincerity – that are normally unstated, but always implicit. Lyotard apparently understands these validity claims as 'metaprescriptives' or rules that govern the level of actual utterances; Habermas views them as anthropologically based universals inherent in language itself.

Lyotard expresses his second objection in the form of another assumption he imputes to Habermas. He supposedly holds the view that 'the goal of dialogue is consensus'. This cannot be so, according to Lyotard, because consensus is only 'a particular state of discussion, not its end' (p. 65). The true end of dialogue is 'paralogy', a term that Lyotard relates to the paradoxes, discontinuities, and undecidabilities of utterances. Essentially Lyotard is here privileging dissension over consensus as the motivating force in linguistic encounters. As Manfred Frank has argued in his book on the Habermas-Lyotard encounter, Lyotard's position is not really as opposed to Habermas's as he believes.[9] When Habermas writes of the ideal speech situation and of discourse, he tends to emphasize the harmonizing dimension of his theory; but the only way in which an authentic consensus can be achieved is by allowing all possible dissenting viewpoints to be raised and argued. So Habermas's theory of consensus implies and encompasses the dissension to which Lyotard accords priority.

Lyotard may counter with the agonistic claim that one party wins every language game, as one player wins a contest against another. By this he could mean that the 'better argument' does not always prevail, that linguistic contests rely on force and not consensus. But Habermas would not dispute that on the empirical level arguments are most often not resolved on the basis of the universal claims inherent in language. Frequently disputes are resolved on the basis of power or coercion. These are not illustrations of genuine dialogue, however, simply because their resolution does not depend on employing language in argument, but on rhetoric, deception or threats. Dialogue as discourse occurs only when the power relations of the world, the interests of the interlocutors, are set aside. The notion that the better argument wins may be idealistic and, as Lyotard states, consensus 'is a horizon that is never reached' (p. 61). Habermas, however, is not talking about actual encounters, but about the condition of possibility for meaningful encounters to occur at all.

In both of the assumptions that he identifies with Habermas Lyotard has missed the level on which Habermas locates discourse and the ideal speech situation. His confusion of the empirical world of actual utterances with the realm of formal pragmatics that establishes minimal ground rules for these utterances in the three validity claims leads him into a performative contradiction that is typical of postmodernist thought.[10] Lyotard presents his theory as a criticism of Habermas's notion of consensus, and posits as an alternative that dissension is the trajectory of speech acts. If we assume that Lyotard is correct and that dissension is the *telos* of speech, then we are unable to account for the status of his own statement. We cannot agree with the propositional content of his statement without simultaneously denying the validity of the statement. In short, Lyotard cannot consistently maintain an argument that seeks to convince us that universally arguments do not aim at our consent. As Habermas points out, there are certain unavoidable assumptions that accompany any argument, and the propositional content of the argument cannot contradict these assumptions. In criticizing Habermas, Lyotard necessarily plays by certain rules that are inscribed in language itself. Lyotard's claim concerning dissension is thus left with two equally distasteful alternatives. Either we take the claim seriously and fall into performative contradiction, or we do not admit that Lyotard is offering an argument and therefore do not have to bother with assent or dissent.

THE NARRATIVE OF POSTMODERNITY

Behind Lyotard's objections to consensus there is an assumption that goes to the heart of his theory of postmodernity. His most general claim about Habermas's notion of consensus is that it is based on a narrative of emancipation that is no longer valid for contemporary, postmodern society. To understand why Lyotard believes this we must review briefly the narrative he establishes to demonstrate the loss of belief in narratives. Lyotard conceives of the history of knowledge as a struggle between narrative and science. At some point in the past narratives were the pre-eminent form in which knowledge was formulated and transmitted. Although we may associate narrative forms of knowledge with 'primitive' cultures, Lyotard indicates that such narratives persist in a number of important variants in more modern civilizations as well. Scientific knowledge, which appears to extend back to at least Plato (p. 28), differs from narrative knowledge in five areas:

1 Whereas narrative knowledge permitted a great variety of language games, scientific knowledge admits only denotative utterances.
2 Whereas narrative knowledge presupposed a shared social bond linking narrator and audience, scientific knowledge presumes no such bond.
3 In scientific knowledge competence is restricted to the sender of the message alone; in narrative knowledge sender, receiver and referent had competence.
4 Statements of scientific knowledge are always tentative in the sense that they are potentially falsifiable (Lyotard is following Popper here); narrative knowledge cannot be falsified.
5 The game of science establishes itself as diachronic through memory; it is concerned with cumulative knowledge and progress. Narrative knowledge establishes a temporal dimension based on rhythm.

Despite these differences Lyotard emphasizes that from the perspective of language games neither scientific nor narrative knowledge is more necessary than the other. They do differ, he claims, in the degree of tolerance that each shows for the other. While narrative knowledge can admit certain scientific statements, the opposite is not true. Science introduces, according to Lyotard, a notion of legitimacy into the arena of knowledge that makes narrative knowledge appear primitive, backward and superstitious.

The struggle between narrative and science is resolved in a number of ways. Lyotard believes that science is unable to legitimize itself on its own terms; from the very beginnings of philosophical thought, therefore, we encounter a narrative form of discourse employed to found science. Plato's dialogues are his primary illustration of a non-scientific inaugural discourse for science. In a certain sense Lyotard here only modifies a position Habermas had assumed in the positivist debate. In that controversy, we will recall, Habermas also posited that natural science is ultimately grounded in an intersubjectively established sphere of values. Lyotard, like Habermas, also suggests that this non-scientific foundation (which the early Habermas associated with technical interest) is eventually forgotten, and that at some point in the modern era the legitimacy of science is conceived as a matter internal to the scientific community. But Lyotard also suggests that narrative, which corresponds roughly to the intersubjective lifeworld in Habermas's thought, returns on another level in modernity. From the Renaissance through most of the twentieth century he finds narrative knowledge accompanying the rise and hegemony of the bourgeoisie in the socio-political sphere. 'Narrative knowledge makes a resurgence in the West as a way of solving the problem of legitimating the new authorities' (p. 30). What marks the modern era is a type of legitimation that combines the consensual scientific mode with the socio-political narrative mode.

Lyotard outlines two major versions of the narrative of legitimation. The first, identified as the 'narrative of freedom', posits humanity as its hero, equal access to science, and the necessity of primary education. Lyotard appears to associate this narrative with the French educational system that concentrates more on primary than on university education, and that intervenes in the training of the people under the pretext of ensuring progress. The second scenario is clearly German and involves a greater emphasis on the university and the idealist notion of *Bildung* or self-culturation. In contrast to the narrative of freedom, the subject of the 'narrative of speculation' is not humanity, but the spirit; a philosophical system and not a political state determines and administers knowledge. These two metanarratives have predominated during the past two centuries, and Lyotard suggests that most ideological formations can be explained as variations of them. Marxism, for example, has vacillated between these versions of legitimation. In its more orthodox forms the party, the people and dialectical materialism are substituted for the university, humanity and speculative idealism, and the metanarrative of freedom becomes the march towards a communist utopia. In the more critical Marxism of the Frankfurt School, the metanarrative is fashioned in terms of the liberation of the individual subject from alienation and oppression. The fascist ideologies of the right can also be seen as variations of these metanarratives.

145

Instead of humanity or the spirit, race becomes the operative subject in this perverted narrative.

Lyotard's notions of modernity and postmodernity are defined in relationship to the function of metadiscourses, such as the narrative of freedom and the narrative of speculation.[11] 'Modern' refers to any type of knowledge that legitimates itself by making an appeal to a grand narrative or metanarrative. In the 'Introduction' Lyotard's illustration of a modernist position would seem to be a reference to Habermas: 'The rule of consensus between the sender and addressee of a statement with truth-value is deemed acceptable if it is cast in terms of a possible unanimity between rational minds' (p. xxiii). This 'Enlightenment narrative' makes the hero an ethico-political player in a progression towards the laudable end of universal peace.

But belief in such narratives is *passé*. In the postwar era Lyotard detects a decline in narrative and a growing incredulity towards its function of providing a legitimation for knowledge. This process of delegitimation and distrust of metanarratives defines the postmodern condition. Indeed, at one point Lyotard characterizes postmodernity by the loss of nostalgia for these lost metanarratives (p. 41). The seed of their decline was inherent in the grand narratives themselves. Hegel's deprecation of positive knowledge in the natural sciences in favor of a self-contained and self-legitimizing dialectic was a sign of the problem all speculative narratives faced. Nietzsche's philosophy was the first that poignantly called our attention to the compatibility of nihilism and science. And Vienna at the turn of the century was a society which was weaned on the pessimism that stems from delegitimation. With these three reflections on the delegitimation process, Lyotard presses home his point that the struggle between positive knowledge as expressed in the natural sciences and narrative knowledge in its various manifestations has continued to inform our thought for the better part of the last 200 years.

In the metanarrative that structures Lyotard's discussion of the decline of metanarratives, Habermas's philosophy is relegated to the role of a well-meaning, but obsolete attempt to refurbish legitimacy for a discourse of emancipation. This is accomplished by subordinating science to intersubjective consensus, a position we can most readily find in Habermas's discussions of positivism. Actually Habermas is never mentioned by name in this section of the book, but it seems likely that Lyotard is here describing a theoretical position – or, as he prefers, discourse – identical to Habermas's. Lyotard identifies the distinguishing characteristic of this discourse in its grounding of 'the legitimation of science and truth in the autonomy of interlocutors involved in ethical, social and political praxis' (pp. 39–40). Implicit in such a theoretical stance is the essentially correct demotion of science to merely one discourse among others. Science has no special legitimacy, no basis outside the agreement among members of a community. Lyotard accuses this discourse, however, of establishing a false link between claims for truth and claims for justice. One cannot move between the denotative language game of truth and the prescriptive language game of ethics, since each game has 'autonomous sets of rules defining different kinds of relevance, and therefore of competence' (p. 40). The recourse to a meta-narrative of emancipation grounded in the consensus of unconstrained subjects that informs such a theoretical program is ultimately for Lyotard an attempt to recuperate an outmoded Enlightenment myth.

If Lyotard is indeed identifying Habermas with this endeavor to rescue Enlightenment values via consensus, then he leaves himself open to at least two objections. First, he ascribes to a putatively Habermasian science precisely what Habermas denies: the ability to reflect truthfully states of affairs in the world. The basis on which Lyotard asserts the incompatibility of scientific truth and ethical justice indicates that he has not grasped the type of distinction Habermas has suggested. When Lyotard writes: 'There is nothing to prove that if a statement describing a real situation is true, it follows that a prescriptive statement based upon it . . . will be just' (p. 40), he is assuming a correspondence theory of truth that Habermas explicitly denies. Habermas does not try to assimilate practical knowledge to scientific knowledge by means of a correspondence theory of truth, as Lyotard seems to assume; rather he ascribes underlying normative values to the decisions, statements and justifications of the natural sciences. Science differs from ethics in the manner in which it goes about its investigations and in its methodological self-understanding. But science cannot establish truth without reference to an intersubjective

147

realm in which statements are submitted to validity claims any more than politics or morality can. Here it is not Habermas who is adhering to an obsolete view of scientific legitimation, but Lyotard.

Lyotard's second oversight in dealing with Habermas involves his baffling conception of what a language game entails. In asserting the non-reducibility of rules from one language game to another, Lyotard separates not only the realms of ethics and science but also, within these large arenas, various subdiscourses. Thus Lyotard, in citing Wittgenstein, maintains that the social bond is woven from innumerable language games obeying different rules (p. 40). While Wittgenstein could point to chemical symbolism and the notation of infinitesimal calculus as the 'suburbs of our language',[12] Lyotard remarks that during the postwar era this list has expanded significantly to include

> machine language, the matrices of game theory, new systems of musical notation, systems of notation for nondenotative forms of logic (temporal logics, deontic logics, modal logics), the language of the genetic code, graphs of phonological structures and so on. (p. 41)

It is not entirely clear why this expansion of language should be so fascinating or so troublesome. The example from Wittgenstein, taken from paragraph 18 of the first part of his *Philosophische Untersuchungen* [*Philosophical Investigations*], is simply illustrating the point that no language is complete. Lyotard, on the other hand, uses Wittgenstein illicitly to contest the communication between various language games. He does this by writing of 'new languages' and 'old languages' where Wittgenstein is obviously referring to parts added to a larger whole. Thus Lyotard's conclusion that 'nobody speaks all those languages, they have no universal metalanguage' (p. 41) really misses the point. That no single person commands all areas of a language is certainly beyond dispute. But this does not mean that we require a universal metalanguage to move from one language game to another (or indeed from one language to another). The guarantee of communication between language games does not in fact lie in the existence of a universal metalanguage, but in the very nature of speech acts. To argue against Habermas, Lyotard consistently negates a transcendental realm outside language games that would purportedly regulate them. Habermas would not disagree with him on this point. Lyotard fails to grasp that Habermas conceives of consensus, discourse, validity claims and the ideal speech situation as notions derived from reflection on everyday language. The common denominator for Habermas does not reside in some metaphysical principle, but in normal linguistic competence.

THE AESTHETICS OF POSTMODERNITY

The main text of Lyotard's *The Postmodern Condition* does not deal with Habermas's own reflections on modernity and postmodernity as formulated in various works from the first half of the 1980s. Indeed, from the elementary errors in Lyotard's criticisms it appears that his general acquaintance with texts by Habermas was not very substantial. Several books by Habermas turn up in his footnotes, but there are no citations in the text, and it is often difficult to see how the footnoted volumes support or even relate to the points Lyotard is making. He appears to draw most of his knowledge from an unsympathetic and inaccurate reading of *Legitimation Crisis*, a work quoted twice in the footnotes. In the essay appended to the English version of *The Postmodern Condition*, however, we can be relatively certain that Lyotard is well acquainted with at least the Adorno prize speech discussed earlier, since he cites directly from this text. This does not mean that he makes an effort to understand Habermas any better in the essay than he did in the rest of the book. After correctly identifying Habermas's opposition to postmodernism as a defense of the uncompleted project of the Enlightenment, Lyotard proceeds to render the rest of his article incomprehensible:

> Jürgen Habermas . . . thinks that if modernity has failed, it is in allowing the totality of life to be splintered into independent specialties which are left to the narrow competence of experts, while the concrete individual experiences 'desublimated meaning' and 'destructured form', not as a liberation but in the mode of that immense *ennui* which Baudelaire described over a century ago. (p. 72)

First, Habermas does not decry the splintering of reality;

following Max Weber, he sees it as a necessity of the modern world. In fact he advocates the development of objective science, universal ethics and autonomous art according to the inner logic of each sphere. Second, Habermas mentions expertise only in connection with art, making two observations: that bourgeois art tries to educate its audience to expertise, and that experts deal with the inner logic of the aesthetic realm. Third, he refers to 'desublimated meaning' and 'destructured form' in connection with the failure of the surrealist revolt to revolutionize the institution of art. Baudelaire's program, by contrast, was the early modernist attempt to show the irreconcilability of the aesthetic and the social world.

Lyotard distorts Habermas's thought in order to assimilate him to a conservative paradigm of artistic realism. But his claims that Habermas seeks 'to suspend artistic experimentation' and 'to liquidate the heritage of the avant-garde' (p. 73) are again the consequence of sloppy reading and an unwillingness to understand Habermas's point. Habermas did not advocate anything about artistic production; he merely suggested that there are possible receptions of art not framed in the language of critics, and that these ways of reception may assist us in renewing our cognitive and ethical relationships with the world. The single illustration he cites, Peter Weiss's *Aesthetics of Resistance*, is not a traditional novel in the realist mode, but an experimental text with avant-garde (and political) pretensions.[13] The modest program that Habermas outlines for the reception of contemporary art is not meant to counter experimentation and the 'traditional' avant-garde, but to advance its political program, which has quite obviously been an unsuccessful revolt. Habermas's suggestions are thus trying to build on the failures of aesthetic modernism, while he accuses the Young Conservatives of adhering anarchically to an outmoded model of permanent aesthetic revolution. He does not call into question the goals of this branch of modernity; on the contrary, he theorizes a possible path for the realization of those goals. Finally, although Habermas does consider it possible for the arts to contribute to the revitalization of the lifeworld, he does not propound a 'unity of experience' (p. 72). In his zeal to associate him with a totalizing and totalitarian project, Lyotard confounds the possible role art can plan in rethinking science and politics with a conservative vision of unitariness.

In his actual views on art and on the notion of modernity and postmodernity in the aesthetic realm, Lyotard is much closer to Habermas than he probably suspects. Both theorists criticize cultural conservatives who would curtain experimentation and thereby negate the original impulses of the avant-garde. Both situate the modernist revolt as a challenge to conventions in an institutionalized aesthetics. And both view the postmodern as a 'part of the modern' (p. 79). The difference between the two views is that whereas Habermas locates art historically and socially, Lyotard conceives of it almost exclusively in terms of representation. 'I shall call modern', he writes, 'the art which devotes its "little technical expertise", as Diderot used to say, to present the fact that the unpresentable exists' (p. 78). Characterizing the modern age in terms of a nostalgic aesthetics of the sublime, Lyotard simply raises the stakes to describe the postmodern:

> The postmodern would be that which, in the modern, puts forward the unpresentable in presentation itself; that which denies itself the solace of good forms, the consensus of a taste which would make it possible to share collectively the nostalgia for the unattainable; that which searches for new presentations, not in order to enjoy them but in order to impart a stronger sense of the unpresentable. (p. 81)

Marcel Proust, who calls forth the unpresentable using the grammar and syntax of the traditional novel, is the quintessential modernist. James Joyce, who makes the materiality of language manifest, belongs to postmodernism. The formal characterists that Lyotard employs to make his definitions force him, in contrast to Habermas, to take a leap of faith into political significance. Like the surrealists whose limitations Habermas tries to overcome, Lyotard makes permanent aesthetic revolution a progressive political activity. His final call – 'Let us wage a war on totality; let us be witnesses to the unpresentable; let us activate the differences and save the honor of the name' (p. 82) – recalls and repeats the radical gesturing of the quondam avant-garde. Lyotard thus supplies an example and an affirmation for the very position of aesthetic modernism, posing as post- and anti-modernism, that Habermas labeled Young Conservative.

THE PHILOSOPHY OF MODERNITY

The debate between Habermas and Lyotard never takes place. Unlike the controversies with positivism, Gadamer, student radicals and Luhmann, there are no direct confrontations where interlocutors address mutual concerns. Lyotard's remarks about Habermas are cryptic and evince a repeated misunderstanding of what he has written. Habermas's comments on Lyotard are almost non-existent. Even in his response to an essay by Richard Rorty that thematizes Lyotard's opposition to his position on postmodernity, he fails to mention him.[14] Yet even though a debate does not occur, two fairly well defined positions of contemporary continental thought are articulated in their writings. The first, associated with Habermas and the continuators of Critical Theory in Germany (Wellmer, Apel), retains a faith in reason, progress, the Enlightenment and the project of modernity. It is not uncritical of the West and specifically rejects the exploitative nature of capitalism, but it sees no reason to attribute all the ills of the world to the undifferentiated straw man identified with metaphysics, subjectivity or logocentrism. The second group, usually labeled poststructuralist, deriving its inspiration from the German philosophical tradition of Nietzsche and Heidegger, calls into question the founding principles of Western philosophy: reason, logic and autonomous subjectivity. It virulently rejects system and totality as politically repressive, advocating instead decentered and local activity. Lyotard's championing of postmodern thought against modernity, his preference for discontinuity over consensus and progress, his insistence on myriad language games without any centralized rules, are all part of a familiar trend in French thought.

Although Habermas did not respond directly to Lyotard, he has not ignored completely these recent developments in French intellectual circles. His rather facile dismissal of Derrida and Foucault as Young Conservatives in 1980 was based on their opposition to the precepts of modernity rather than on their actual political affiliation, and in the next few years he set about defending these remarks within a philosophical framework. *The Philosophical Discourse of Modernity* of 1985 is the result of Habermas's efforts to legitimate his initial label and to defend the Enlightenment against its many detractors, particularly in France. Probably occasioned by the growing reception of French thought in West Germany after the *Tendenzwende* (conservative change of direction) of the 1980s, it has been among Habermas's most controversial volumes, particularly among humanists in the United States. His refusal to buy into the global critique of metaphysics, his advocacy of reasoned alternatives based on an affirmative reception of the Enlightenment, and his skepticism concerning the revered masters of poststructuralist thought (and the tradition from which they emanate) have earned Habermas the wrath of theorists infatuated with contemporary French thought. During the past few years in the United States, Habermas was repeatedly compared with Derrida and Foucault in lectures and classrooms, and was almost always made to appear a crypto-conservative unable to fathom the depth and significance of his opponents.

The problem is that Habermas simply views the problem of modernity and postmodernity differently to the French and their epigones. His account of the vicissitudes of modernity does not begin with the agonistic confrontation between science and narrative, as Lyotard's does, but with the initial consciousness of modernity in the late eighteenth century. Although Kant and Fichte established subjectivity as the constitutive concept of modernity, Habermas claims that Hegel was 'the first philosopher for whom modernity became a problem' (p. 43).[15] Emancipating itself from the dogmas of religion and the past, modernity sets itself the task of creating its normativity out of itself. Hegel assumes this to be the central problem for his philosophical system and it leads him to the view that the modern age is 'marked universally by a structure of self-relation that he calls subjectivity' (p. 16). Subjectivity as conceived by Hegel has connotations and implications that reach into all areas of life and thought. Perhaps most important for Habermas, it establishes the essential forms in which modern culture will develop. The natural sciences are now free to confront a disenchanted nature unconstrained by the fetters place on subjectivity by extra-scientific dogma. Morality develops according ω notions of free subjects exercising free will, resulting in individual freedom and universal rights. And modern art, labeled romantic in Hegel's aesthetic theory, becomes characterized by its absolute inwardness. The spheres

153

of science, morality, and art, based on principles of truth, justice and taste were not only separated from belief, but also encompassed under the principle of subjectivity. Hegel's philosophy, proceeding from the Kantian critiques, sets itself the task of grounding modernity in self-contained subjectivity.

According to Habermas's reading, Hegel was unable to accomplish his goal satisfactorily because he solves the problem of modernity 'too well' (p. 42). We can see the difficulty in two areas. By taking subjectivity and a philosophy of reflective self-consciousness as a starting point, Hegel propounds not only the freedom and unity of the subject, but also its objectification and alienation as object of its own subjectivity. The pernicious consequences of Hegel's solution become even more evident in his writings about the state. Habermas notes that the subject encounters itself both as universal subject embodied in the state and as individual subject or citizen of the state. In a potential conflict between the two, the concrete absolute of the state receives precedence. 'For the sphere of the ethical, the outcome of this logic is the primacy of the *higher-level subjectivity of the state* over the subjective freedom of the individual' (p. 40). The consequences of investing reason or self-conscious subjectivity with absolute authority is a deprecation of individual experience and criticism.

> Hegel's philosophy satisfies the need of modernity for self-grounding only at the cost of devaluing present-day reality and blunting critique. In the end, philosophy removes all importance from its own present age, destroys interest in it, and deprives it of the calling to self-critical renewal. (p. 42)

Hegel's awareness of the necessity for the modern age to ground itself in self-conscious subjectivity paradoxically leads him to depreciate the exigencies of his own era.

Habermas detects an alternative to the philosophy of consciousness or subjectivity in Hegel's early works in which he wrote of the Christian community. The road Hegel does not choose, that of intersubjectivity, becomes foundational for Habermas's thought. Mainstream philosophy, however, continues to try to reconcile the demands of modernity with what Hegel had established as the philosophy of modernity. In the aftermath of the Hegelian solution Habermas outlines three directions that emerge, all of which criticize a notion of reason grounded in self-conscious subjectivity. The first, associated with the Young Hegelians, turns to a philosophy of practice that seeks to liberate a rationality pent up in its bourgeois forms. This group, whose most celebrated figure was Karl Marx, remains true to the spirit of the Enlightenment, but feels that its goals can only be accomplished by turning to the material world. For Marx the concept of labor replaces subjectivity as the key to modernity. The second group affirms Hegel's notion of the state and religion as compensation for the disruptions and alienation of modern society. Originally identified with right Hegelians this group becomes the neo-conservative tendency in contemporary times. Defending institutions and traditional values against radical critique, the neoconservatives want nothing more than to allow bourgeois society to unfold according to its own dynamic.

It is the third group, however, with which Habermas is most concerned. In a grand revolutionary gesture, these post-Hegelians seek neither to further the Enlightenment nor to freeze its accomplishments, but to oppose the notion of reason itself. From the third through to the tenth chapter Habermas investigates various versions of this total critique of reason. Nietzsche's philosophy at the beginning of this movement inaugurates a branch of speculative endeavor that includes Heidegger's ontology as well as Adorno and Horkheimer's *Dialectic of Enlightenment*, and that ends in Parisian poststructuralism of the postwar era. Nietzsche's significance lies in his conception of a critique of modernity without any emancipatory content. Although his anti-Enlightenment philosophy, including its Dionysian dimension, has its roots in the romantic tradition, his was the most congenial and influential starting point for subsequent thinkers. Habermas notes the two strands of his thought that had the most impact on the 'Young Conservatives'.The first conceives of an aesthetically based critique of Western philosophy that would oppose all claims to truth by valorizing the will to power. The anthropological, psychological and historical aspects of such a subversion of reason have been examined in recent times by Bataille, Lacan and Foucault respectively. The second avenue that Nietzsche opens attempts to uncover the metaphysical roots of the philosophical tradition without relinquishing its own claims to philosophical rigor. This internal critique of metaphysics is associated with the works of Heidegger and his French disciple Derrida.

In Habermas's narrative of the philosophical tradition, fundamental ontology, negative dialectics, poststructuralism and deconstruction are simply variants of the dead end of the post-Hegelian philosophy of the subject. His point is that no matter how much these attempts to oppose enlightenment conceive of themselves as escaping the problematic of modernity, they inevitably fall back into it. The program that Hegel proposed established subjectivity as the founding principle of the modern age. Beginning with the Young Hegelians philosophy has tried in various ways to critique this notion, but always from within a philosophy of consciousness. The radical critiques of the ancestors and advocates of poststructuralism commence by accepting the terms set down by Hegel, and in this acceptance they remain trapped within a set of problems that has no possible solution. The outside, or other, or 'post' that is envisioned as an alternative is thus always just the irrational mirror image of reason conceived as self-contained subjectivity. Even the radical gesturing that accompanies these philosophical assaults on tradition is nothing new. As Habermas points out, the topos of the end of philosophy is a characteristic of the very earliest critiques of the Hegelian solution:

> Today the situation of consciousness still remains the one brought about by the Young Hegelians when they distanced themselves from Hegel and philosophy in general. And the triumphant gestures of mutually surpassing one another, in which we gladly overlook the fact that we remain contemporaries of the Young Hegelians, have also been in currency since then. Hegel inaugurated the discourse of modernity; the Young Hegelians permanently established it, that is they freed the idea of a critique nourished on the spirit of modernity from the burden of the Hegelian concept of reason. (p. 53)

Habermas views poststructuralism as just the latest of these philosophical convulsions in reaction to, but also in consonance with, Hegel's founding problematic of modernity.

This is the context within which Habermas reads the work of Derrida, the French philosopher with perhaps the largest following in the Anglo-American world. In contrast to his reception by literary theorists, Habermas is less interested in his notion of free play and undecidability than in his critique of the phenomenological tradition. The chapter he devotes to Derrida focuses almost exclusively on his early deconstruction of the Husserlian theory of meaning. Habermas is not totally unsympathetic to Derrida's critique. He agrees when Derrida takes exception to Husserl's 'Platonizing of meaning' and 'the disembodying interiorization of its linguistic expression' (p. 171), but he contends that Derrida's objections are on the level of semiotics, while his own differences with the phenomenological tradition are formulated in terms of the pragmatics of speech. In essence Husserl's problem stems from his adherence to a philosophy of subjectivity, and Derrida operates, according to Habermas, within the framework of this philosophical tradition. Derrida follows in the footsteps of his mentor Heidegger, who similarly criticizes the phenomenological project while remaining entrapped in a philosophy of consciousness.

The difference between Heidegger and Derrida is that the former critiques Western philosophy from the perspective of the history of Being, while the latter finds that even the notion of Being is part of the metaphysical heritage. In true Young Hegelian fashion Derrida ups the stakes of Heidegger's critique by positing a realm of pure difference in which proto-writing performs the function of philosophical foundation. This slight variation on a familiar theme accounts for the divergent political implications in Heidegger's and Derrida's thought. Derrida, like Heidegger, 'degrades politics and contemporary history to the status of the ontic and the foreground, so as to romp all the more freely, and with a greater wealth of associations, in the sphere of the ontological and the archewriting' (p. 181). But while Heidegger's philosophy of Being evolves 'the authoritarian admonition to bend before destiny', Derrida 'stands closer to the anarchist wish to explode the continuum of history' (p. 182).

THE DEFECTS OF POSTMODERN DISCOURSE

The ire of Derrida and his American disciples was roused less by Habermas's discussion of Derrida and Husserl or the charge of political anarchism than by his remarks in a subsequent excursus concerning the leveling of the genre distinction between philosophy and literature. Their central complaint was that Habermas never quotes directly from Derrida's works. Indeed, in Derrida's only published response to Habermas he appears more concerned that he is never cited – he mentions this half a dozen times in the space of two pages – than in the point of the objections.[16] Habermas, who makes it perfectly clear that he is going to base his discussion on Derrida's popularizers in the United States (most notably Jonathan Culler), is really more interested in a general feature of postmodern discourse than in the citation of any single theorist. What disturbs him in the postmodern text is that its authors are unable to give a satisfactory account of their own status. Common to deconstruction, negative dialectics and genealogy is their equivocal position between philosophy and literature. While they implicitly make claims about the validity of their arguments, they simultaneously deny these very claims as propositions. If we treat them as serious scholarship, they seem to resist understanding by their refusal to engage in the institutionally established vocabularies that would make them comprehensible. If we classify them as literary, that is as discourses that make no claims to validity, then their arguments forfeit all logical force:

> No matter whether Adorno paradoxically reclaims truth-validity, or Foucault refuses to draw consequences from manifest contradictions; no matter whether Heidegger and Derrida evade the obligations to provide grounds by fleeing into the esoteric or by fusing the logical with the rhetorical: There always emerges a symbiosis of incompatibles, an amalgam that resists 'normal' scientific analysis at its core.

This equivocation cancels 'institutionalized standards of fallibilism' (pp. 336–7) and thus provides an infallible defense against all objections. No matter what the argument may be, the postmodernist can always contend that the critic has misunderstood the nature of the discourse.

This performative equivocation, which is a derivative of the performative contradiction in postmodern discourse, is just one of its distinctive features. Habermas also points to a contradiction in the 'radical critique of reason' between its normative intuitions and its stated objectives. Underlying the radical rejection of enlightenment and metaphysics is a correct sentiment concerning the ills and evils of modern society:

Whether modernity is described as a constellation of life that is reified and used, or as one that is technologically manipulated, or as one that is totalitarian, rife with power, homogenized, imprisoned – the denunciations are constantly inspired by a special sensitivity for complex injuries and subtle violations. (p. 337)

Habermas identifies the intuition behind these misguided critiques with 'a picture of an undamaged subjectivity' such as those Hegel writes about in his early works and which point to his own philosophy of communicative action. But the postmodernist is unable to contend with the sources of discontent adequately. Postmodern discourse escapes into an aesthetic realm in which the counter-concepts it develops lose all force in the world. At bottom Habermas contends that the discrepancy between the textual strategies and the concealed normative sentiments is a consequence of the repudiation of subjectivity. Postmodernity rejects not only (quite correctly) the self-conscious objectified self, but also all notions of ethical subjectivity. It thus precludes from the outset a self-conscious praxis that can assist in overcoming the problems it has intuitively recognized.

A further defect of postmodern discourse is its failure to differentiate phenomena and practices that occur within modern society. Habermas accuses these theorists of a totalizing perspective that levels significant distinctions in actual life practices. It is easy to understand what he means. The grand gesture of opposing Western metaphysics and the entire history of philosophy, the contention that power and surveillance are ubiquitous, or the notion of a totally reified and administered world do not lend themselves to meaningful social analysis. By calling into question the very distinctions that make critique possible, postmodernists do not undermine the repression and oppression they seek to eliminate but only the conceptual apparatus that provides insight into the human situation. If 'enlightenment and manipulation, the conscious and the unconscious, forces of production and forces of destruction, expressive self-realization and repressive desublimation, effects that insure freedom and those that remove it, truth and ideology' are confused and homogenized, then critique will no longer be able to 'discern contrasts, shadings, and ambivalent tones within the flat and faded landscape of a totally administered, calculated, and power-laden world' (p. 338). Habermas's criticism really has a synchronic and a diachronic dimension. Synchronically postmodern discourse shows an 'insensitivity to the highly ambivalent content' of modern culture and society, ignoring distinctions that often matter most. Diachronically, in their preoccupation with sweeping denunciations of tradition, postmodernists fail to recognize the important differences – in terms of bodily labor, freedom of choice and so on – between modern and premodern life forms.

Finally, Habermas objects to the level at which postmodern discourse articulates its critique of reason. While pragmatism, phenomenology and hermeneutics (the philosophical traditions from which Habermas has drawn most extensively) have given an epistemological status to the practices of everyday life, most variants of postmodernity shun any connection with this realm. At the very beginnings of postmodernity Nietzsche set the tone for this neglect, and his twentieth-century disciples have followed him in gliding 'over the practice of everyday life as something derivative or inauthentic' (p. 339). In this connection Habermas is obviously referring primarily to Heidegger, whose ontological proclivities effectively seal his philosophy from any connection with praxis. But this criticism is also leveled at Derrida, who, as we have seen, is accused of forsaking contemporary affairs and politics for more recondite pursuits. This removal of philosophical reflection from the sphere of everyday life is doubly pernicious. In the terms of Habermas's own theory, the rational potential inherent in everyday practices is a legitimate source for normative standards with which critics of reason can correct the over-differentiation they detect in the spheres of science, morality or art. But it is also the ultimate goal for theoretical reflection. If our philosophical musings have no implications for emancipatory activity, if everyday practice is not 'the locus where the rational content of philosophy' (p. 339) is supposed to issue, then intellectual endeavor would amount to little more than the gamesmanship that some practitioners of postmodernity seem to relish.

Habermas's opposition to proponents of postmodern discourse must be seen in this context of preserving a connection between theory and practice. Indeed, as we have witnessed in connection with his other debates, it is impossible to separate cleanly his philosophical from his political concerns. In *The Philosophical Discourse of Modernity* he tends to isolate theoretical matters, but even here we encounter repeated attempts to demonstrate the practical implications of postmodernity for political action. What makes Habermas's positions on modernity and postmodernity ultimately so compelling is his willingness to think through the philosophical positions taken by the critics of reason and to see their unarticulated ramifications as a potentially emancipatory praxis. In this regard we should recall that his 'debate' with Lyotard and his critique of postmodernity are inseparable from tendencies he detects in Western democracies of the 1980s. We should take seriously, therefore, Habermas's claim that the volume *Die neue Unübersichtlichkeit* (1985) ['The New Impenetrability'], a collection of essays with explicitly political content, is a companion to the *Philosophical Discourse of Modernity*.[17] As we have seen, in the latter work he is concerned to show how the discourse that seeks to escape modernity cancels itself in performative contradiction and thereby leaves itself open to dubious political uses. In the former book he explores the terrain on which these philosophical notions buttress a conservative reaction to modernization and aesthetic modernism. In advocating as an alternative an intersubjectively based theory of communicative action, Habermas not only penetrates the impenetrability of the postmodern discourse, but also demonstrates in a practical fashion his continued adherence to a democratic process of rational consensus.

7

National Socialism and the Holocaust: the debate with the historians

BITBURG AND THE CONSERVATIVE AGENDA

Habermas's final essay in *Die neue Unübersichtlichkeit* dealt with a theme that would become a highly controversial topic among German intellectuals in the mid-1980s. At issue in the late spring of 1985, when the essay first appeared in the liberal newspaper *Die Zeit*,[1] was how the conservative leadership of the Federal Republic had staged the ceremony at Bitburg to commemorate the end of the Second World War. The handshake between retired German and American generals at a German military cemetery on May 8 was supposed to provide a symbolic representation for the final reconciliation between the two countries, and to relegate to the past the former enmity between the two allies and German responsibility for the crimes committed by the National Socialist regime. This plan backfired, however, when it was revealed that forty-nine members of the dreaded *Schutzstaffel* (SS) were also interred at Bitburg. Under the leadership of Heinrich Himmler the SS, which was established in 1929 as a personal bodyguard for Adolf Hitler, became an empire unto itself within the Nazi state, comprising over a million members by the end of the war. Included in this political organization were the Waffen SS, an elite division of shock troops responsible for mass murders in the field, the Death's Head division, which served as the administration for concentration camps, and the Secret Services, which performed internal intelligence activities. The SS members buried at Bitburg had belonged to the Waffen SS and some were evidently active in the massacre of civilians in

Oradour-sur-Glane, France, in June 1942. Others may have even served at concentration camps.

The presence of SS soldiers at Bitburg caused a worldwide controversy that temporarily ruined the conservative plans for refashioning the German past.[2] In the essay 'Entsorgung der Vergangenheit' ('Relieving concern about the past') Habermas is centrally concerned with the significance of Bitburg in connection with the change (*Wende*) or turn to the right in German politics in the 1980s. On the one hand, he sees President Reagan's appearance at Bitburg as part of a bargain; the gesture of reconciliation is compensation to the Germans for the agreement to station missiles on the soil of the Federal Republic. On the other hand, Reagan had become a pawn in the game of *Vergangenheitsbewältigung*, a word that means coming to terms with or mastering the past. He had become an unwitting accomplice to conservative attempts to establish a continuity with a dubious heritage.

These attempts pursued three strategies. The first and most familiar was to establish a connection with the German past by declaring the National Socialist experiment to be an aberration carried out by a small minority. This strategy is as false and one-sided as the collective guilt thesis, which maintained that all Germans shared responsibility simply because they were German. Each evades a differentiated confrontation with the most pernicious moments and events of German history. The second strategy sought a continuity on the level of daily life and subjective experience. Selective memory of local occurrences and personal recollections of the good old days should replace the crimes committed in the national and international arena. Finally, on a political level, continuity can be established through recourse to anti-socialist and anti-communist sentiments. In this strategy the alliance between the United States and the Federal Republic is viewed as the continuator of the main war aim of National Socialist Germany: the destruction of the Soviet Union.

Two additional factors seemed to disturb Habermas about this attempt to whitewash the German past. The first concerns the role of the state in social integration and identity formation. As we saw in Chapter 4, Habermas believes that in the most advanced industrial societies social integration and identity are grounded in universal principles, not in particularist or statist policies. The intervention of the state in fostering a nationalist continuity is an illicit attempt to abrogate a process that should occur independently of governmental influence:

> Today the tasks of social integration and self-understanding are no longer matters for the political system. There are good reasons for us not having a Kaiser or a Hindenburg any more. The public sphere should refuse to tolerate spiritual-moral leadership (*geistig-moralische Führung*) from those in high office.[3]

Although the Federal President, because he is not elected by the voters, has the opportunity to address the moral conscience of the nation, other political leaders should confine themselves to the administrative and legislative tasks for which they were chosen.

A second disturbing feature that Habermas noted was the attempt to denigrate the calls for continued preoccupation with the National Socialist past. The chief offender he cites is the neo-conservative Swiss philosopher Hermann Lübbe, whose speech in January 1983 at a conference to commemorate the National Socialist assumption of power sought to reinterpret the West German endeavor to master the past.[4] Lübbe's thesis, simply stated, is that the apparent failure to deal with National Socialism after the war was, paradoxically, the only successful way to deal with the Fascist past. The lack of public discussion, the almost total silence of politicians as well as of intellectuals was, according to Lübbe, the prerequisite for the stable and successful development of the Federal Republic.[5] His argument is predicated on the questionable assumption that National Socialism had been completely discredited after the war and that the citizenry was free from vestiges of National Socialism on a normative level; the historical record quite obviously contains a great deal of material which casts doubt on both these claims.[6] More interesting, however, is the general tendency of his argument with regard to further developments. For Lübbe the democratic impulses in the Federal Republic originate in the silence about National Socialism, while the generation maturing in the 1960s, those children of National Socialists who finally brought issues of Fascism into the open, are censored for their social, ethical and political concerns. Lübbe follows a conservative tendency in valorizing continuity and collective identity over any other concern. The repressed 1950s has thus become the golden era we should strive to emulate in the late 1980s, while we should avoid at all costs the anti-Fascist questioning of the 1960s or even the rather mild admonitions of the present-day SPD. As Habermas notes, the significance of Lübbe's speech only becomes apparent in light of the events planned for 8 May 1985.

REWRITING GERMAN FASCISM

Habermas conceives of his initial contribution to the historian's debate (*Historikerstreit*), which began in the summer of 1986, as an opposition to the same tendencies he observed in Lübbe's talk and in Kohl's thwarted reconciliation at Bitburg. In the essay that inaugurated the controversy, 'Eine Art Schadensabwicklung' ('A kind of settlement of damages'), Habermas makes this continuity clear in a preface he added for the book publication.[7] The conservative goal is here stated in its boldest terms: the Federal Republic should reacquire its self-confidence as a member of the Western alliance by means of salvaging an acceptable past. Making the past acceptable entails a leveling of those elements that hinder identification (for example Auschwitz), and the assertion of a continuity in face of the common enemy of freedom: Soviet Bolshevism. The failure of the governmental bureaucracy successfully to stage this coup at Bitburg meant that others had to be mobilized for the task of meaning production (*Erzeugung von Sinn*). With an obvious touch of irony Habermas treats recent work of select conservative historians as a second wave of ideological bombardment after the débâcle at Bitburg. The historians are called upon to accomplish what politicians could not do: supply a positive exegesis of the past that will provide political legitimation for the conservative policies of the present. Habermas obviously does not believe that the historians in question were part of a conspiratorial pact to cleanse the German past. He does indicate, however, that with the change of the political agenda in the 1980s right-wing tendencies that had been latent became part of a discourse threatening to rewrite the German view of Fascism.

It is certainly not coincidental that Habermas begins his observations on recent historiography with Michael Stürmer.

Formerly a historian at the University of Erlangen, Stürmer served for a time as a speech writer for Kohl and now directs a conservative think-tank, the Ebenhausen Foundation for Science and Policy.[8] Habermas does not deal with any of his larger historical studies, but with two essays, one that appeared in a collection on German identity in 1983 and a short article published in the *Frankfurter Allgemeine Zeitung* (*FAZ*) in April 1986. In the former piece Habermas detects a plea for leveling diversity and for forging a new national identity. Stürmer appears to advocate precisely the position that Habermas criticized in connection with Bitburg. The state should not be content simply to administer, but should, like a religion, give meaning and identity to the citizenry by means of nationalism and patriotism.

In 'History in a land void of history' Stürmer has a slightly different agenda. He begins by observing that history has enjoyed a renaissance in the Federal Republic. The significance of this reawakened interest in the past may be seen in a revitalization of historical consciousness and in the search for direction. The two actually go together, and both have implications for the politics of the present:

> The loss of orientation and the search for identity are closely related. But anyone who believes that all of this has no effect on politics and the future, is ignoring the fact that in a land without history whoever fills the memories, coins the concepts and interprets the past will win the future. (p. 36)[9]

Stürmer closes with the suggestion that a conservative historiography is 'morally legitimate and politically necessary' (p. 38). The thought that history should be conceived instrumentally as a means for controlling politics is obviously anathema to Habermas. The conclusion he is compelled to draw from Stürmer's remarks is that he countenances a conservative historiography that will work in consonance with government to construct a new national consciousness.

Habermas finds the agenda implied in Stürmer's essays fulfilled in the most recent work of Andreas Hillgruber. A historian at the University of Cologne who has worked extensively on diplomacy and foreign affairs, Hillgruber published in early 1986 two essays dealing with the Second World War in a short book entitled *Zweierlei Untergang: Die Zerschlagung des Deutschen Reiches und das Ende des europäischen Judentums* ['Two Kinds of Demise: The Shattering of the German Reich and the End of European Jewry']. For Habermas even the formulation of the title raises questions about Hillgruber's intentions. The word 'shattering', he points out, presupposes an act of aggression and an agent performing the aggressive act. An 'end', by contrast, can come about of its own accord. The contents of the two accounts, which are in no way connected by the author, seem to confirm the bias of the title. In the first essay Hillgruber is interested in explaining the reasons why the soldiers on the Eastern front fought so desperately at the end of the war. To do so he portrays the physical suffering of the civilian population at the hands of the invading Red Army and gives a detailed examination of the psychology of the German soldier fighting to enable the innocent victims of war to escape the clutches of Soviet revenge. The second essay, which is one-third the length of the first, is by contrast dry and factual; occurrences are narrated in a detached tone. There is no attempt to empathize with the fate of individual Jews. Indeed, the focus is on 'Judentum' (Jewry), a collective noun that was evidently selected to parallel 'Reich'.[10] The discrepancy in style and in sympathies appears to reinforce the infelicities of the title.

Habermas criticizes further several dubious implications of the two essays. In particular he objects to the rhetoric of anti-communism and the portrayal of Germany as the 'land of the middle', which, as Charles Maier observes, is a shibboleth of conservative historiography.[11] If Germany is viewed in a geopolitical middle position between Russia on one side and France and England on the other, then Hitler's war becomes assimilable to a familiar, understandable and almost acceptable pattern. Habermas also berates Hillgruber for his failure to comprehend issues from a social vantage point. The allied policy of disinterest in the fate of the easternmost German territories, which were taken over by Poland and the Soviet Union after the war, is attributed by Hillgruber to the clichéd view they held of Prussia and an overemphasis on the role Poland would play. Habermas suggests that an analysis of the conservative power structure in Prussia could help explain a great deal about the general constitution of the Reich. Similarly

167

he takes Hillgruber to task for his discussion of the attitude of German officials and the German population to the extermination of the Jews. Hillgruber's inability to think in terms of the social sciences leads him, according to Habermas, to explanations that rely on general and empty statements about human nature and anthropological constants. That he is particularly shocked at the participation of German academics in National Socialism is indicative of his inability to escape the very tradition of German mandarins that he fails to understand.

What disturbs Habermas most about Hillgruber's book is the perspective from which he examines the Eastern front in the first essay. To understand this we must recall that the original talk that served as the basis for the essay was delivered in the context of the discussion on how to celebrate the fortieth anniversary of the end of the war: as defeat or emancipation. Hillgruber's answer to this question is unequivocally 'defeat':

> The concept of 'liberation' implies an identification with the victors and is of course completely justified for the victims of the National Socialist regime who were freed from concentration camps and prisons. But it is inappropriate to the fate of the German nation as a whole. 'Liberation' does not describe the reality of the spring of 1945.[12]

Hillgruber is advocating a suspiciously singular perspective. He maintains that viewing the end of the war as liberation would be tantamount to identifying with the Red Army or with the victims of National Socialism incarcerated in concentration camps. For 'the German nation as a whole' such a perspective is illicit, in his opinion. The question here, of course, is what constitutes the German nation and what is its 'fate'. More progressive and earlier historians might have used these terms to refer to some ideal entity worthy of preservation. Hillgruber apparently identifies 'the German nation as a whole' with the Third Reich as it existed in 1945. What is worse, he appears to accept uncritically the war strategies and aims of 'the German nation as a whole' in these final months of the conflict. Otherwise, it is difficult to see why the military defeat of Germany could not be conceived as an emancipation – not just for the direct victims of National Socialism in the camps, but for its indirect victims, for the soldiers who were dying on all fronts and for the civilian population suffering behind the fronts.

Hillgruber continues his discussion of perspective by clarifying further his reasoning for considering 'liberation' an inapposite interpretation of the end of the war:

> If one wanted seriously to comprehend with this concept [liberation] the collapse of the Reich, then this would presuppose that the war aims of the allies in the West and in the East consisted of nothing other than the elimination of National Socialist hegemony. But this is not the case, however, even though surely many Englishmen and Americans sought the elimination of dictatorship in Germany – beyond the power politics of their government – in order to dissolve the German identification with this dictatorship and their involvement with it.[13]

This is an odd and illogical explanation. It assumes once again that the vantage point of the German military should be the perspective of the German population. Since the allies had goals other than the liberation of the German populace, the Germans cannot consider themselves liberated by allied actions. While no one will deny that the motives of the United States, England and the Soviet Union were not totally unselfish or simply directed towards crushing dictatorship and establishing democracy, there is no reason why the effect of allied actions in defeating Germany should not be classified as liberation no matter what their overt or covert goals. Hillgruber's statements here and elsewhere tend to minimize the undeniable fact that National Socialism was a regime that held much of the German population captive, that forced this population into war and that was responsible for the death and suffering of millions of Germans as well as peoples of other nationalities. That Germany could not liberate itself, that it had to be emancipated by foreign armies, is an unpleasant historical fact. But from any perspective that incorporates the most elementary rights of human beings to exist without want, fear and conflict, the military defeat of the German armies would have to be viewed, at least in part, as a liberation. Hillgruber is guilty of identifying himself not with the innocent populace, as he claims, but with those very elements of society that were at least partly responsible for the absence of these basic human rights.

Hillgruber is at best inaccurate when he states that the historian of the catastrophe in the East has only one choice: to identify himself/herself 'with the concrete fate of the German populace in the East and with the manifold desperate and self-sacrificing activities of the German army in the East and the navy in the North Sea'.[14] Identification with these two groups assumes a short-sighted and short-term perspective. The 'concrete fate of the German populace' should have included considerations of more than momentary discomfort or even death; the 'fate' of the people also involves freedom from physical and psychological constraints placed upon it by its own government, as well as prospects for the cessation of a situation in which the murder of innocent people had become one of the primary war goals. The 'perspective of liberation' is irrelevant only if these considerations are also irrelevant to the 'concrete fate of the German people'. This is what Habermas means when he criticizes Hillgruber for his narrow-minded insistence that historians must place themselves within the limited perspective of participants in the conflict.[15] Historians should not ignore this perspective – especially since it is necessary if they are going to make sense of events in the last months of the war – but they must recognize that this is only one viewpoint and that subsequent events invalidate it as a perspective from which to write history. Habermas contends that Hillgruber eschews a normal, hermeneutic perspective to avoid confronting the question of morality in a war of attrition. By evading the most significant ethical considerations of the war, Hillgruber provides an acceptable German past populated by well-meaning, courageous soldiers unfortunately fighting for an evil regime.

ERNST NOLTE AND THE SINGULARITY OF AUSCHWITZ

The third person whose recent works appear suspect to Habermas was not really a historian by training. Ernst Nolte, a student of Martin Heidegger, was educated as a philosopher, although he is known almost exclusively for his work in the history of political ideas. His phenomenological approach to political history in *Three Faces of Fascism* was well received in the 1960s,[16] and his work since then has centered on issues surrounding Germany in twentieth-century history. Perhaps more than any single writer besides Habermas, Nolte bears responsibility for the outbreak of intellectual hostilities that has been called the historians' debate. It was his article, 'Vergangenheit, die nicht vergehen will' ('The past that will not go away') in the *FAZ* on 6 June 1986, a month before Habermas's assault on conservative historians, that brought controversy into the larger public sphere, and a quotation from Nolte's piece is used by Habermas as a motto for his own essay. Nolte further assisted in igniting a conflict by stating that his essay was scheduled to be a talk at the 'Römerberg-Gesprächen' (Römerberg Conversations) in Frankfurt (a yearly forum devoted to the discussion of important issues), but that he was disinvited for unknown reasons and thus compelled to promulgate his thoughts in the newspaper. Since Habermas was a member of the board of the organization that sponsored the talks, and since Hans and Wolfgang Mommsen, both of whose views on National Socialism are more in line with Habermas's than with Nolte's, delivered talks on the topic on which Nolte was supposed to speak, there was at least some suggestion that Habermas or his not inconsiderable influence had something to do with the alleged disinvitation.[17] Habermas, who states he was privy to the correspondence between Nolte and the organizers of the 'Conversations', claims only that the talk was published in the *FAZ* under a 'hypocritical pretext'.[18]

The circumstances in which the talk appeared only in a printed version was hardly its only provocative dimension. Like many other conservative and, in recent years, even some more liberal historians, Nolte contends that the Third Reich should no longer possess a special status, that it should be integrated into the normal history of Germany. He offers three reasons for normalization. First, the preoccupation with the 'Final Solution', which is the main bone of contention for Nolte, has directed our attention away from other important matters. Not only have we not been as concerned with other aspects of National Socialist barbarity as we should have been – Nolte cites the euthanasia program and the treatment of Russian prisoners of war – but the Holocaust has deflected our attention from important contemporary issues, such as the life of the unborn or mass murders in Vietnam and Afghanistan. Second, Nolte suggests that National Socialism supplies us with black-and-white schemes that have an impact on our contemporary sensibility and hinder our confrontation with the present. Instead of criticizing the military build-up in the postwar era we refer back to Nazi Germany as a scapegoat; similarly the patriarchal attitudes of National Socialism are viewed as responsible for the oppression of women today. 'National Socialism', Nolte summarizes, 'is therefore the present enemy in the last form in which it is entirely unmistakable' (p. 40). Finally, Nolte suggests that conjuring up the evils of the Third Reich serves the interests of certain groups. He cites two specifically; the new generation in their eternal struggle against their fathers and 'the persecuted and their descendants' who seek to perpetuate a privileged status for themselves.

Although Nolte's discussion of the function of National Socialism for the present is provocative, it received almost no attention from critics. What was evidently deemed more important were the arguments diminishing the historical uniqueness of the Holocaust. This was accomplished by Nolte in a series of suggestive analogies. He opens the essay, for example, by noting that the theme he was given, 'The past that will not go away', implies that the era of National Socialism is somehow different from other epochs in history, for example the time of Napoleon Bonaparte. Later he compares President Reagan's visit to Bitburg to Konrad Adenauer's visit to the cemetery at Arlington and asks what would have occurred if Adenauer had refused to attend this ceremony because some of the soldiers buried there had perpetrated 'terrorist attacks against the civilian population of Germany' (p. 42).

His chief argument by analogy concerns other cases of mass murder or brutality in the twentieth century. In order to place the destruction of European Jewry in a historical perspective more favorable to Germany, Nolte brings up two previous illustrations. The first was the deportation and annihilation of the Armenian population of Turkey during the First World War. In this connection Nolte cites the biographer of Max Erwin von Scheubner-Richter, a German diplomat who witnessed the events in Asia Minor and who for a time was a close associate of Hitler. In 1938 the unnamed biographer recalls the

'Asiatic manner' in which the Turks dealt with the Armenians. The second example was Stalin's elimination of millions of opponents to communism during the 1930s. Combining these two 'precedents' for the Holocaust, Nolte claims that Auschwitz represents nothing new in the history of Europe; the sole difference between the destruction of European Jewry and previous horrors was 'the technical procedure of gassing' (p. 45). Indeed, he hypothesizes further that Auschwitz can be understood historically as a response to the Gulag, as an 'Asiatic deed' committed to assure that the same type of 'Asiatic deed' would not be done to Germany. In this sense Nolte even claims that there exists a 'causal connection' between the Gulag and Auschwitz.

In spite of the provocative and public aspects of this newspaper article, Habermas devotes relatively little attention to it. Instead he discusses at greater length an essay that Nolte had contributed the previous year to a collection entitled *Aspects of the Third Reich*. The editor of this volume, H. W. Koch, was obviously somewhat uncomfortable with Nolte's submission. At various points in the essay, whose title was 'Between myth and revisionism? The Third Reich in the perspective of the 1980s', Koch felt compelled to insert editorial comments to distance himself from several volatile and historically questionable assertions. In essence this essay is a more extensive treatment of the themes Nolte presented journalistically in the summer of 1986. Habermas is interested in this piece not only because it openly propagates a revision of our view of the Third Reich, but because it had been cited with approval by Klaus Hildebrand, a noted historian of Nazi foreign policy teaching at Bonn. What attracted Hildebrand to Nolte's essay was precisely the aspect that Habermas most sharply rejects: the denial of uniqueness to the destruction of European Jewry.

The stronger version of Nolte's thesis on Auschwitz and the Gulag, articulated at greater length in this essay, is that both belong to a more global historical picture that extends back into the nineteenth century. Examining statements and actions of a variety of left-wing and right-wing movements from the utopian socialists to the regime of Pol Pot, Nolte concludes that 'annihilation therapy' was a favorite cure for the ills that have arisen from the industrial revolution. The perceived solution to problems that erupted in society as the result of modernization was often the eradication of a whole group of people, whether this group was called the bourgeoisie, the Jews or some national minority. The destruction of European Jewry undertaken by National Socialism is thus merely one in a series of historically conceived 'annihilation therapies'. It is neither original nor unique, but rather 'a reaction or a distorted copy'.[19]

Nolte asserts his highly speculative thesis with an arrogant certainty. He condescendingly grants 'noble motives' to those who do not want to see Hitler's annihilation of the Jews in his grand historical context, but contends that these people simply 'falsify history'.[20] He concludes by stating three 'postulates for the history of the Third Reich' that can be deduced from his thesis. First, National Socialism has to be investigated historically in relationship to the 'changes, crises, fears, diagnoses and therapies produced by the Industrial Revolution'. Its most important precondition should be seen as the Russian Revolution; its utopian dimension should be treated in accord with other 'liberation movements'. Second, 'the instrumentalization of the Third Reich' should cease. In line with Lübbe's essay, Nolte demands that structures and hierarchies of the Federal Republic should no longer be associated with Fascism. Above all Nolte is here taking exception to the long leftist tradition that considers capitalism an indispensable foundation for Fascism. Finally, Nolte advocates a historicization of National Socialism in the manner suggested by Martin Broszat, the late liberal director of the Institute for Contemporary History. The Third Reich must be viewed as 'a part of the history of mankind which not only reproduced traits of the past in a very concentrated form, but which at the same time anticipated future developments and tangled manifest problems of the present'.[21]

Habermas has difficulties with several details of Nolte's presentation. He is obviously disturbed by the sort of leveling comparisons Nolte employs to bolster his thesis, since these tend to apologize for actions undertaken during the era of National Socialism. Habermas does not entirely believe that the history of the Third Reich has been written from the perspective of the victors. He cannot agree that the historiography of that period can be likened to a history of Israel composed by a victorious PLO, as Nolte suggests. Habermas, along with

Koch, is also dismayed at the evidence Nolte presents that 'might justify the consequential thesis that Hitler was allowed to treat the German Jews as prisoners of war and by this means to intern them'.[22] At issue is a statement made by Chaim Weizmann in a letter to Neville Chamberlain on behalf of the Jewish Agency on 29 August 1939 to the effect that the Jewish people would fight with England against Germany in the Second World War.[23] Although it is unclear whether Nolte is proposing that this is indeed a justification for German actions against its Jewish population or whether he is simply citing it in connection with David Irving's controversial exoneration of Hitler, Nolte nowhere indicates how absurd it is to use this statement as a vindication for anything, much less Germany's treatment of its Jewish citizens. Habermas is finally and justifiably angered at Nolte for his apparent carelessness in referring to 'the so-called annihilation of the Jews'.[24] Nowhere has Nolte ever indicated that he doubts the historical account of the Holocaust, but his slip in phrasing here is disturbing none the less.

Perhaps more important in the context of the conservative resurgence in the 1980s is the role Habermas assigns to Nolte. In Nolte's thesis the conservatives seem to have found the perfect answer to the two major problems that Stürmer posed for historians interested in shaping present and future German identity. The first concerned the dilemma between the production of meaning and the adherence to scholarly methods. The second refers to the problem of constructing a viable German identity in the absence of a national state. Nolte's work, Habermas states, kills two birds with one stone:

> The Nazi crimes lose their singularity by being made comprehensible as the answer to a Bolshevist threat of annihilation (that continues to exist today). Auschwitz is reduced to the format of a technical innovation and is explained as an 'Asiatic' peril by an enemy that is still standing today outside our gates.[25]

Nolte's achievement is therefore conceived in two areas. By relativizing the responsibility for the destruction of European Jewry he delivers an apology for the moral responsibility that had become an accepted part of German consciousness since the end of the Second World War. By relegating ultimate responsibility for this mass murder to the Soviet Union in its Stalinist phase, Nolte also preserves the desired connection with NATO and the conservative policies of the cold war. The memory of the murdered Jews is sacrificed for the sake of a national identity that is both purified, in the relative sense of not being any worse than other national identities, and steadfastly anti-communist.

THE IMPOVERISHED PUBLIC DEBATE

Habermas's critique of what he considered apologetic tendencies within German historiography unleashed a series of responses and defenses that lasted for two years. Since the publication of 'A kind of settlement of damages', there have appeared at least half a dozen books and scores of essays in newspapers all over Germany and the world that deal specifically with the issues he raised.[26] In much of the discussion that ensued both friend and foe concentrated on the singularity of Auschwitz. This focus represents an impoverishment of Habermas's concerns since it reduces his argument to a dispute about historical occurrences and neglects the inherent political aspect of his remarks. Relegated to secondary status are the critique of neo-conservatism, the reflections on identity and the objection to the instrumentalization of scholarship in the public domain. Another unfortunate aspect of the selective reception of Habermas's article was that the largest part of the controversy was carried out within the confines of the historians' guild. Here the various opinions about the uniqueness of Auschwitz were bandied about without any satisfactory resolution. It is easy to understand why. The manner in which the issue was formulated already contains two irreconcilable aspects. As several more astute commentators pointed out, the destruction of European Jewry is a singular event at least to the extent that every historical event is singular. Yet no occurrence is so completely unique that it does not admit comparison with others, or that it does not have precedents or causes. Habermas's argument, that the relativization of Auschwitz was being used for politically conservative purposes, was too often lost in the shuffle.

The singularity of focus helps to explain the nature of the rebuttals from the conservative camp. Joining Stürmer,

Hillgruber, Nolte and Hildebrand in their opposition to Habermas was a variety of historians with different methodological and political proclivities: Joachim Fest, the author of a major biography of Hitler and one of the editors of the *FAZ*; Imanuel Geiss, a former liberal historian who appears to have evolved towards the right, and Thomas Nipperdey, a moderate conservative known for his work in nineteenth-century history. Their most frequent complaint about Habermas's argument had little to do with his political objections; rather, they seemed most often determined to defend the integrity of historical studies against outsiders. Habermas is therefore accused of ignorance of the relevant documents and of the latest developments in the field. Hildebrand accuses him of not knowing 'the new sources, the new knowledge and the new questions that constitute the progress of scholarship' (p. 89). Geiss, who devoted an entire book to what he calls the 'Habermas Controversy', challenges his competence to make judgements in the field of history.[27] And Hillgruber, whose reaction was understandably the most vituperative in the group of rather caustic responses, disqualifies his opponent as a 'non-historian' (p. 234). All three point to Habermas's own statements about his qualifications as support for their evaluations.[28] But each misses the obvious irony in Habermas's self-disqualification. His point is that the matters these historians have promulgated are not the possession of an elite cadre of experts, but issues for public debate and discussion.

The almost total lack of insight into Habermas's purpose is most manifestly reflected in the conservative concentration on alleged errors of citation and sloppy research. Habermas is repeatedly charged with the most heinous crime for an academic historian; inaccuracy with regard to his sources. Hildebrand finds that one of the central problems of the entire debate is 'Habermas's dubious relationship to the scholarship and research' (p. 86). The alleged misuse of a passage from Hillgruber's text assumes a prominent place in his argument. Stürmer calls Habermas's article a combination of 'slipshod research and jumbled quotations' (p. 98). Fest points to his 'miserable scholarly method' in operating with fragmented citations; Habermas 'confounds things with an insensitivity which has been without precedent for a long time' (pp. 101–2). Hillgruber states flatly that he 'works with falsified quotations and manipulation of quotations' (p. 232). And Geiss devotes an entire section of his book and his entire appendix to an examination of how Habermas misuses the quotations of the historians he cites.[29] Once we examine the material, however, it is difficult to see what the fuss is about. Habermas does make use of sentence fragments and often combines ideas from various essays by the same author. But even in the case most frequently cited, in which he uses an adjectival form instead of the verbal form in the original, the resulting phrase does not stray far from the meaning of the original. The conservative historians were obviously disturbed by the implications Habermas drew from their work. But by arguing so pedantically on the level of inaccurate citations they only confirm Habermas's contention that they are evading a confrontation with the substance of his claims.

The evasiveness of their tactics appears confirmed by the frequent recurrence of *ad hominem* attacks sprinkled liberally in all of the adversaries' replies. Habermas, of course, had not treated the conservative historians with kid gloves, and several of those who leaped to his defense were less reserved in their comments than Habermas was. None the less, the conservatives could at least have saved face by keeping their arguments on a high level. Instead, several writers stoop to suggesting that Habermas's motives were egotistical, unethical or fantastic. Hildebrand, for example, contends that Habermas launched his campaign in a desperate attempt to regain the public influence he has lost. In the process, Hildebrand concludes, he sacrifices truth for sophistry (p. 291). Fest, whose methodological proclivities hardly qualify him as an innovative spirit, prefers to portray Habermas as employing hopelessly outdated categories. He is held up to ridicule as a veritable Don Quixote of the Enlightenment, 'deeply enmeshed in the spiritual struggles of yesterday and the day before', imagining a chimerical 'Wende' and a conspiracy behind it (p. 110). Hillgruber fulminates against Habermas's dogmatism. The philosopher of 'pluralism' (a label that indicates the approximate depth of Hillgruber's understanding of Habermas) supposedly seeks to curtail any discussion outside of a narrow leftist circle (p. 345). Along similar lines Stürmer tries to disqualify Habermas's essays with the epithet, 'socialist nostalgia' (p. 98).

What is most disturbing about these invectives is that they are inevitably accompanied by a total oblivion to the connection between historical scholarship and politics that Habermas thematizes. The dichotomy between *Wissenschaft* (scholarship or science) and politics or morality is a veritable leitmotif of the conservative position. Without exception Habermas's adversaries accuse him of the very charge that was leveled against them, as if he were the perpetrator of this violation of generic and disciplinary boundaries. Hildebrand wants to rescue the purity of scholarship (*Wissenschaft*) from the depravity of politics and censures Habermas for 'mixing' the two (p. 84). Fest frequently refers to the hard facts and scientific evidence of his colleagues as opposed to the imputed motives and moral opinions of Habermas. Nipperdey decisively rejects Habermas's procedure of 'measuring scholarly statements and their contribution to knowledge in terms of their asserted political "function"' (p. 216). And Hillgruber claims that Habermas's arguments are not grounded in scholarship, but are politically motivated. Perhaps the classic statement of this separation comes from the Berlin historian Hagen Schulze, who also supported the conservative cause with the following apodictic statement: 'Scholarship has to do with the world of Being (*Sein*), morality and politics with the world of Ought (*Sollen*). One cannot ground moral judgements scientifically, or scientific sentences politically. But this is precisely what Habermas continuously does' (p. 144).

HISTORY, POLITICS AND POSTCONVENTIONAL IDENTITY

Reading the various responses to his article, Habermas could justifiably have felt himself caught in a time warp. The absolute separation of fact and value, of science and morality, that the chorus of historians advocated was a central point in the positivist dispute of the early 1960s. If this had been a debate about methods, Habermas could have answered these antediluvian objections simply by referring them to this older controversy. His point here, however, was not to give a lesson in the logic of the social sciences, but to demonstrate with empirical evidence how the supposedly scientific procedures of contemporary historiography in the Federal Republic are informed by values (in this case conservative presuppositions) and are themselves instrumentalized for overt political causes:

> The pompous outrage over an alleged mixing of politics and science shunts the issue onto a completely wrong track. Nipperdey and Hildebrand either get the wrong message from the wrong pigeon-hole or they get the address wrong. They obviously live in an ideologically self-contained milieu that is no longer accessible from the real world. It is not an issue of Popper versus Adorno, it is not a question of disputes about scientific theory, it is not about questions of value-free analysis – it is about the public use of history. (pp. 251–2)

Habermas's critique had to do with the conservative attempt to manipulate the consciousness of history through the establishment of historical museums, through political indoctrination and through guidelines for history classes. Methodological disputes and quarrels within the discipline were of secondary importance. He himself states that he would never have written his inflammatory article if the historians had confined themselves to their scholarly journals. If we wanted to sum up the conservative misunderstanding in one thought, we could say that his opponents fail to understand that Habermas has viewed their foray into the public sphere from the perspective of Bitburg.

The historians' debate remained an aborted controversy largely because the conservatives never took up what really matters in Habermas's arguments. Habermas was eventually forced to defend himself against the ludicrous charge that he distorted his adversaries' arguments through his shoddy use of citations and scholarship.[30] But his central concerns, outlined in the final section of his initial essay, in his first rejoinder ('Concerning the public use of history') and in an address in Denmark during May 1987 ('Historical consciousness and posttraditional identity: the Western orientation of the Federal Republic'), were virtually ignored by friend and foe alike. On the narrower topic of historiography Habermas's objective is a defense of pluralism, not the affirmation of a particular view, as his adversaries claimed. The dream of historicism in the early nineteenth century was – as embodied for example in the work of Gervinus – the creation of a unified and progressive national consciousness, and the successors to this tradition continued to propogate a nationalist ideology, but purged it of its liberal moments. The postwar breakdown of the nationalist monopoly on historiography is for Habermas a fortunate occurrence. The very diversity of perspectives and outlooks that have informed the writing of history since 1945 has provided the opportunity to understand the historical heritage in all its multiplicity. The discussion that results is reflective and critical of the tradition and contrasts with the conventional type of identity propagated by a one-dimensional historiography allied with state power. What Habermas fears above all in the varied remarks of Stürmer, Hillgruber and Nolte is the attempt to level German history in order to pave the way for a conventional, nationalist identity.

The precise connection between nationalism and identity is a topic Habermas takes up in more detail in his speech in Denmark. In essence nationalism is 'a specifically modern form of collective identity'[31] that has three characteristics. First, at least in its European manifestations, it is opposed to older religious identities; its profane origins and its propagation by the new social sciences explain its conscious appeal to many strata of society. Second, nationalism combines a common cultural heritage, usually conceived in terms of language, literature and history, with a governmental form of state hegemony. And third, national consciousness evidences a tension between two tendencies: the orientation toward universal values such as democracy and freedom, and the particularism that necessarily accompanies any attempt to distinguish one national state from another. This third characteristic of nationalism is particularly important to Habermas. During most of the nineteenth and early years of the twentieth century the balance between universalist and particularist tendencies was maintained by various sorts of compromises. Only with the advent of the 'integral nationalism' of Mussolini and Hitler were the universalist and democratic origins of nationalism completely supplanted by particularist elements. The defeat of the Axis powers in the Second World War has given Germany an opportunity to develop a nationalism in keeping with universalist principles. In Habermas's scheme the understanding of Auschwitz as an outgrowth of a one-sided national identity represents an opportunity for the Federal Republic to realize a nationalism of universal values.

Jürgen Habermas

On the level of political history, therefore, the conservative historians, by relativizing the Holocaust rather than recognizing the progressive lessons to be learned from it, are advocating a regression to a nationalism and a concomitant national identity from a bygone era.

Habermas's thoughts on nationalism and national identity account for his almost allergic reaction to the neo-conservative portrayal of Germany as a land caught in the middle. In his view the rhetoric of 'middle Europe' harkens back to a political attitude that sought to reject precisely the democratic orientation of Germany towards its Western neighbors. Accompanying the notion of Germany as a country caught between East and West is a rejection of the values of the Enlightenment that has been a common thread for conservative ideology from the romantics to Heidegger. During the era of National Socialism this repudiation of 'civilization' acquired a social Darwinist interpretation, and this mentality, Habermas claims, helps to explain how Auschwitz could occur. Indeed, the chief lesson that can be learned from the Holocaust in terms of political orientation is that Germany should not pursue a special path (*Sonderweg*) that separates its destiny from the heritage of its Western neighbors, but should firmly embed itself in the traditions originating in the Enlightenment. These remarks on Germany's political past help to shed light on Habermas's dispute with postmodernism as well. One of the strongest criticisms that has been leveled at reason and enlightenment by the critics of reason is that it is implicated in the most horrific crimes that humanity has ever committed. Habermas countered philosophically by asserting the existence of two kinds of reason, rational-purposive and communicative. On the political level his response would seem to be that the deviation from Western enlightenment values as manifested in the middle European alternative, not the logical consequences of reason, explains the darkest side of Germany's history.

For Habermas the postwar era in the Federal Republic represents a decisive rejection of the limited nationalism and anti-Western traditions that contributed to National Socialism and its barbarous actions. He alluded to this turn towards a different type of nationalism in his initial article in the historians' debate when he wrote of a 'constitutional patriotism' as 'the only patriotism that does not alienate us from the West'.[32] In the Denmark speech he qualifies this thought by speaking of 'the readiness to identify oneself with the political order and the principles of the Basic Law'.[33] Indeed, what separates contemporary patriotism from its early forms is that it is no longer grounded in the continuities of a national tradition. Formerly continuity was secured largely by means of military victories, and national identity was therefore tied to an uncritical nationalist fervor. After 1945 for the first time nations possess the potential to establish identities based on the 'ambivalence of every heritage', on the 'chain of irreparable violations', on 'the barbaric dark side of all previous cultural accomplishments'.[34]

Habermas attributes the erosion of particularism to many and varied factors. As examples from different spheres of modern existence he names the diminishing importance of military service as an element of nationalism, the relativization of life forms made apparent by the gross injustices of internment and concentration camps, the dramatic progress in mass communication and mass tourism that has acquainted us with the heterogeneity of cultures, and the international integration of scientific and scholarly research. For all these reasons it is senseless for the Federal Republic to conceive its ties to the West solely in terms of NATO strategies, as the conservatives implicitly suggested. Rather, the German bond to its closest allies should be framed in terms of a commitment to the universal values found in the 'political culture of the West'. This affirmation of democracy and enlightenment, not the convenience of an anti-communist military alliance, is for Habermas 'the greatest intellectual achievement of our postwar period.'[35]

This intellectual achievement is inseparable from the moral commitment articulated in the same heritage. For this reason Habermas cites Karl Jaspers' *Schuldfrage [Question of Guilt]* prominently in response to his conservative critics.[36] Jaspers' work was the most important philosophical response to National Socialism among German intellectuals in the period immediately after the war. Published in 1946, it attempted to differentiate levels of responsibility for the crimes perpetrated in the name of the German people. Besides criminal guilt, which merits punishment before a court of law, Jaspers describes a political, moral and metaphysical guilt, each of which has varying consequences and is under the jurisdiction of different authorities. As Habermas notes, Jaspers' problem at the end of the war was to distinguish between the personal guilt of actual criminals and the collective transgression of those who allowed crimes to be committed. The nature of the question changes in the 1980s simply because of demographic factors. The vast majority of those currently living in Germany have neither direct nor indirect responsibility for the actions of National Socialism. Yet Habermas contends, much to the dismay of conservatives in West Germany, that Germans cannot simply appeal to the good fortune of being born late enough to avoid all complicity with Fascism.[37] 'Even those born later', he maintains, 'have grown up in a life form (*Lebensform*) in which *those things* were possible'.[38] Contemporary life in Germany and the circumstances in which Auschwitz occurred are 'internally linked' by a complex mesh of familial, local, political and intellectual traditions. In short, Habermas concludes that Germans are what they are today as a result of a historical process that includes Auschwitz.

Jaspers' work established the moral agenda for the Federal Republic for the first forty years of its existence, and Habermas believes that his country has two reasons to adhere to this notion of responsibility. The first is the obligation of Germany towards the direct and indirect victims of the National Socialist regime. The dead, as well as the descendants of the dead and victimized, have a right to expect that the memory of suffering and violence will not be obliterated. Second, Habermas cites political implications for foreign policy, particularly with regard to Israel. The historians' debate, however, is less concerned with how the Germans appear to others than with how they relate to their own tradition. Habermas's view is that Jaspers's work provides an acceptable way for Germany to accept its tradition, and that the symbolic representatives of the Federal Republic – Heinemann, Heuss and Weizsäcker – have adhered to the implicit self-understanding articulated in the late 1940s. After Auschwitz there is no longer the possibility of finding an unbroken relationship to German history. Instead Germany has to seek connections with the democratic and enlightened portion of a heritage that must be appropriated in a critical and differentiated fashion. Habermas's objection to the implicit project of the conservative historians is that they sought to abrogate this moral continuity and substitute an identification with a dubious part of the past. Instead of viewing the Nazi period as an obstacle that has to be overcome, Habermas advocates that Germans conceive it as a filter through which we can evaluate the very substance of an ambivalent tradition.

The central issue of the debate for Habermas is not the singularity of Auschwitz but the way in which historiography aids in the constitution of a national identity. The conservative historians are not significant in and of themselves, but only in so far as they participate in a cultural climate that has been established since the assumption of power by the Christian Democratic Union and that endeavors to form a national consensus on 'conventional' identity. The terms 'conventional'/'traditional' and 'postconventional'/'posttraditional', which, in association with 'identity' or 'morality', Habermas employs to distinguish the conservative position from his own, are part of a scheme he has adopted from studies by Lawrence Kohlberg. In his study of moral development Kohlberg distinguishes a preconventional, a conventional and a postconventional consciousness. At the preconventional level one can distinguish right and wrong, but these values are interpreted only as they affect the individual directly and physically. At the conventional level, family, group or nation are conceived as valuable in their own right; actions are undertaken in conformity with pre-established goals for the purpose of maintaining the larger entity. Postconventional morality entails the ability to arrive at decisions independent of group sanctions. At this highest level individuals are able to reflect upon actions and separate themselves from the authority of the larger body.[39]

As we saw in Chapter 4, Habermas adopts Kohlberg's views for his reconstruction of historical materialism, and in the *Theory of Communicative Action* he also has recourse to his psychological theories.[40] Although there are obvious problems in the transition from subject to society, in essence individual development in Kohlberg is translated into social evolution by Habermas. The objection to conservative historiography can thus be formulated in terms of the morality, consciousness or identity that it seeks to foster. National identity in its simplest form is conventional in that it propagates adherence to the group and does not allow for reflection based on universal principles. Habermas's charge is that what Stürmer desires and what Hillgruber and Nolte promote is a non-reflective

185

consciousness that affirms Germanness while excluding perspectives critical of nationhood. The implication is that a conservative political program can survive best when it does not have to undergo the scrutiny of a critique based on universal values. The perceived attempt to reinstitute a conventional morality strikes at the very core of Habermas's political thought and explains the caustic and vehement nature of his intervention. For a democracy to function on a more than formal basis, it is necessary for its citizenry to reflect critically on the policies and directions of its government. Any endeavor to curtail such reflection undermines the fundamental structures on which democratic institutions are built. 'Constitutional patriotism' and 'postconventional identity' are therefore not murky concepts that hide socialism, as Fest charges (p. 91), but on the contrary the cornerstones of any political system that thrives on free and unhindered utterance.

EPILOGUE TO THE DEBATE

The initial evaluation of the historians' debate was that Habermas and the group of liberal historians that supported his position had prevailed. The reason for this judgement was quite simply that the conservative attempt to relativize the Holocaust was deemed unacceptable by the vast majority of historians who sought to comment on the controversy. The contributions by eminent voices like Hans Mommsen, Jürgen Kocka, Dan Diner, Saul Friedländer and Hans Ulrich Wehler have been both more numerous and, for most West German intellectuals, more persuasive. But the determination of victor and loser in a dispute of this sort is not necessarily made by the public response of a certain stratum of society. What the conservatives accomplished should not be measured by how much overt support they garnered but by how they managed to determine the public agenda that was discussed. As Habermas has pointed out, an implicit consensus on the ethical and historical role of Auschwitz in German history was established after the war. This consensus existed as a public position sanctioned by the government and its officials. This does not mean, however, that all citizens agreed with the stance that Germany was compelled to adopt. We can imagine that an immediate conversion to democratic values and universalist morality did not take place in large segments of the population, and even the celebrated philosopher, Martin Heidegger, whose association with the National Socialists in 1933 was well known, displayed a remarkable lack of remorse and a penchant towards relativizing Nazi atrocities in letters from the late 1940s.[41] Until the 1980s such sentiments were confined largely to the private sphere or to the propaganda of the outer fringes of the right wing. The significance of the historians' debate is therefore not that the conservatives won the day with their arguments. The success of their cause must rather be seen in their ability to bring the debate into the public sphere and on to terrain that has hitherto been considered the exclusive property of the far right.

Subsequent events have also cast doubt on the purported liberal victory in the historians' debate. The sudden and unexpected dismantling of the Berlin wall in November of 1989 and the rapid movement toward German unity have brought with them a surprising recrudescence of nationalism. In the German Democratic Republic the drive for unification appears to be fueled in part by the prospects of acquiring economic security, while in the Federal Republic the conservatives, sensing the culmination of their nationalist policies, have been relentless in pushing the process toward completion. In both cases one can interpret these events as a sacrifice of universalist values, as embodied in socialism or in the founding ethics of the West, for a more conventional nationalist identity. That the same sort of regression to traditional consciousness has dominated the aftermath of the communist regimes throughout Eastern Europe is no solace for those concerned about the renaissance of German nationalism. Habermas's contribution to the process has been a plea for accomplishing unification on the basis of universalist principles. The conservatives in both parts of Germany want to use paragraph 23 of the Basic Law and have the East simply absorbed into the Federal Republic. Habermas, by contrast, advocates the application of paragraph 146, according to which a new constitution would be written and approved in a nationwide referendum. To defend this view he has used arguments that recall his position in the historians' debate:

With that enormous break in its continuity [Auschwitz]

187

Jürgen Habermas

the Germans have forfeited the possibility to ground their
political identity in any other way except on universalist
principles, in light of which its national tradition must
not be appropriated unthinkingly, but only in a critical
and self-critical fashion.[42]

Unfortunately this battle appears to have been lost before the
public debate even began; the conservatives in government
have controlled not only the tempo but also the terms of the
unification process. If we reread the historians' debate through
the filter of German unification, the hastily declared victory
for Habermas's position would have to be reversed.

In a much more important sense, however, the very fact
that the historians' debate took place signals a victory of sorts
for Habermas's general theoretical perspective, if not for the
particular positions he advocated. As we have seen in previous
chapters, Habermas has consistently argued for argument. In
contrast to many of his most recent adversaries, his theory is
marked by performative consistency: he explicitly defends the
very action in which he is engaged. His writings validate his
own efforts to engage an adversarial position, to articulate
critique and objections and to try to persuade both his
opponents and observers of the merits of his own views.
Although the historians' debate was much more public and
strident in controversy than many of the academic disputes of
the 1960s and 1970s, it exemplifies Habermas's approach to
intellectual matters. But his intervention in the business of
German historiography is also typical in another important
way. From the objections to Heidegger's republication of the
unaltered lecture *An Introduction to Metaphysics* in the early
1950s, through the methodologically informed conflicts with
positivism, hermeneutics and systems theory, to the more vis-
ible controversies with radical students in the 1960s and neo-
conservatives in the 1980s, Habermas has always reflected
upon the political dimensions and implications of theory.
Staunchly defending the achievements of Western democracies
against both left- and right-wing detractors, he has nevertheless recognized that the promises implicit in their founding
documents have yet to be fulfilled for all citizens. For the past
three decades, as critic in the public sphere, Habermas has

188

sought through both theory and practice to keep these promises alive and to assist in their realization.

Notes

PREFACE

1 Thomas McCarthy, *The Critical Theory of Jürgen Habermas* (MIT Press, Cambridge, Mass., 1978); David Ingram, *Habermas and the Dialectic of Reason* (Yale University Press, New Haven, 1987); Stephen White, *The Recent Work of Jürgen Habermas: Reason, Justice and Modernity* (Cambridge University Press, Cambridge, 1988).

2 Tom Rockmore, *Habermas on Historical Materialism* (Indiana University Press, Bloomington, 1989); Raymond Guess, *The Idea of a Critical Theory: Habermas and the Frankfurt School* (Cambridge University Press, Cambridge 1981); Rick Roderick, *Habermas and the Foundations of Critical Theory* (Macmillan, Basingstoke, 1986); Richard J. Bernstein (ed.), *Habermas and Modernity* (MIT Press, Cambridge, Mass., 1985). See also David Held, *Introduction to Critical Theory: Horkheimer to Habermas* (University of California Press, Berkeley, 1980); Russell Keat, *The Politics of Social Theory: Habermas, Freud, and the Critique of Positivism* (University of Chicago Press, Chicago, 1981); John B. Thompson and David Held (eds) *Habermas: Critical Debates* (MIT Press, Cambridge, Mass., 1982), and David M. Rassmussen, *Reading Habermas* (Basil Blackwell, Oxford, 1990).

The standard bibliography on Habermas, compiled by René Görtzen under the title *Jürgen Habermas: Eine Bibliographie seiner Schriften und der Sekundärliteratur 1952–1981* (Suhrkamp, Frankfurt, 1982) contained over 900 publications on Habermas. A revised version with over 3000 titles is scheduled for publication soon. Joan Nordquist's, *Jürgen Habermas: A Bibliography*, Social Theory: A Bibliographic Series, vol. 1 (Santa Cruz, Reference and Research Services, 1986) is also an excellent research tool, particularly for English sources and editions.

1 INTERVENTION IN THE PUBLIC SPHERE

1 Jürgen Habermas, *Strukturwandel der Öffentlichkeit: Untersuchung zu einer Kategorie der bürgerlichen Gesellschaft* (Luchterhand, Neuwied, 1962); *The Structural Transformation of the Public Sphere: An Inquiry*

into a Category of Bourgeois Society, trans. Thomas Burger with the assistance of Frederick Lawrence (MIT Press, Cambridge, Mass., 1989).

2 Jürgen Habermas, 'Volkssouveränität als Verfahren: Ein normativer Begriff von Öffentlichkeit', *Merkur* 43, no. 6 (1989): 465–77.

3 Quoted in Habermas, *Structural Transformation*, p. 106.

4 ibid., p. 119.

5 Karl Marx, *Grundrisse der Kritik der politischen Ökonomie* (Dietz Verlag, Berlin, 1953), pp. 21–9.

6 Habermas, *Structural Transformation*, p. 88.

7 Habermas, *Erkenntnis und Interesse* (Suhrkamp, Frankfurt, 1968), p. 411.

8 In the 1973 afterword to *Erkenntnis und Interesse* Habermas mentions that he hopes to present such a theory soon. It appeared in two volumes eight years later: *Theorie des kommunikativen Handelns* (Suhrkamp, Frankfurt, 1981); trans. by Thomas McCarthy as *The Theory of Communicative Action* (Beacon Press, Boston, 1984, 1989).

9 Jürgen Habermas, 'What is universal pragmatics?' in Thomas McCarthy (trans.) *Communication and the Evolution of Society* (Beacon Press, Boston, 1979), pp. 1–68; here p. 9.

10 ibid.

11 ibid., p. 26.

12 J. L. Austin, *How To Do Things With Words* (Harvard University Press, Cambridge, Mass., 1962), pp. 94–108. See also John R. Searle, *Speech Acts: An Essay in the Philosophy of Language* (Cambridge University Press, Cambridge, 1969), pp. 54–71.

13 Habermas, 'Universal pragmatics', p. 50.

14 ibid., p. 54.

15 The table is taken from 'Universal pragmatics', p. 58.

16 ibid., p. 60.

17 Habermas's review article is most easily accessible in his *Philosophisch-politische Profile* (Suhrkamp, Frankfurt, 1987), pp. 65–72; here p. 70.

18 Christian E. Lewalter, 'Wie liest man 1953 Sätze von 1935: Zu einem politischen Streit um Heideggers Metaphysik', *Die Zeit* 13 August 1953: 6.

19 Martin Heidegger, 'Heidegger on Heidegger', *Die Zeit* 24 September 1953: 10.

20 Martin Heidegger,' "Nur noch ein Gott kann uns retten": Spiegel-Gespräch mit Martin Heidegger am 23. September 1966', *Der Spiegel* 30 (31 May 1976): 193–219.

21 Paris, Lagrasse.

22 Jürgen Habermas, 'Heidegger – Werk und Weltanschauung', foreword to Victor Farias, *Heidegger und der Nationalsozialismus*, trans. Klaus Laermann (Fischer, Frankfurt, 1989), pp. 11–37; esp. pp. 30–2.

2 METHODOLOGY IN THE SOCIAL SCIENCES: THE POSITIVIST DEBATE

1 Karl Popper, *Unended Quest: An Intellectual Autobiography* (Open Court, La Salle, Ill., 1974), pp. 87–90.

2 Theodor W. Adorno *et al.*, *The Positivist Dispute in German Sociology*, trans. Glyn Adey and David Frisby (Heinemann, London, 1976), pp. 298–300. This book, from which I will quote parenthetically in this chapter, is essentially a translation of Theodor W. Adorno *et al.*, *Der Positivismusstreit in der deutschen Soziologie* (Luchterhand, Darmstadt, 1969). The English version contains two additional entries: a fine and informative introduction by David Frisby (pp. ix-xliv) and the short commentary by Popper (pp. 288–300).

3 Max Horkheimer, 'Traditional and critical theory', in Paul Connerton (ed.) *Critical Sociology* (Penguin, Harmondsworth, 1976), pp. 206–24; here, p. 222.

4 Found in Karl Popper, *Conjectures and Refutations: The Growth of Scientific Knowledge* (Routledge, London, 1963), pp. 312–35.

5 For a good discussion of the contributions by Popper and Adorno, see David Frisby, 'The Popper-Adorno controversy: the methodological dispute in German sociology', *Philosophy of the Social Sciences* 2 (1972): 105–19. For Frisby's observations on the entire debate, see his introduction to *The Positivist Dispute* and 'The Frankfurt School: Critical Theory and positivism', in John Rex (ed.) *Approaches to Sociology: An Introduction to Major Trends in British Sociology* (Routledge, London, 1974), pp. 205–29.

6 Max Horkheimer (ed.) *Zeugnisse: Theodor W. Adorno zum sechzigsten Geburtstag* (Europäische Verlagsanstalt, Frankfurt, 1963), pp. 473–501.

7 Karl Popper, *The Open Society and its Enemies* (Princeton University Press, Princeton, 1962), vol. 2, p. 193.

8 Max Horkheimer and Theodor W. Adorno, *Dialektik der Aufklärung* (Amsterdam, 1947); *The Dialectic of Enlightenment*, trans. John Cumming (Seabury Press, New York, 1972).

9 ibid., pp. 230–1.

10 Karl Popper, *The Logic of Scientific Discovery* (Basic Books, New York, 1959).

11 Jürgen Habermas, *Erkenntnis und Interesse* (Suhrkamp, Frankfurt, 1968), p. 9.

12 Another way to look at this problem would involve the notion of truth. Habermas criticizes Popper for his adherence to a 'correspondence theory of truth'. According to such a theory facts exist in themselves, independent of theory or interpretation. Habermas claims that his adherence to such a theory is simply inconsistent with his correct critique of positivism. Habermas's most extensive examination of theories of truth and his own defense of a consensus theory may be found in the essay 'Wahrheitstheorien', in *Vorstudien und Ergänzungen zur Theorie des kommunikativen Handelns* (Suhrkamp, Frankfurt, 1984), pp. 127–83.

13 See Agnes Heller, 'The positivism dispute as a turning point in German post-war theory', *New German Critique* 15 (1978): 49–56.
14 In his later work Habermas often relies on Popper's three-world theory mentioned briefly in Chapter 1.
15 Hans Albert, 'Behind positivism's back: a critical illumination of dialectical digressions', in Theodor W. Adorno *et al.*, *The Positivist Dispute in German Sociology*, trans. Glyn Adey and David Frisby (Heinemann, London, 1976), pp. 226–57.

3 ON IDEOLOGY AND INTERPRETATION: THE DEBATE WITH HANS-GEORG GADAMER

1 Jürgen Habermas, *Theorie des kommunikativen Handelns* (2 vols, Suhrkamp, Frankfurt, 1981); trans. by Thomas McCarthy as *The Theory of Communicative Action* (Beacon Press, Boston, 1984, 1989).
2 The confrontation between Gadamer and Habermas has occasioned extensive comment. The following are among the most important discussions of this debate in English: Josef Bleicher, *Contemporary Hermeneutics: Hermeneutics as Method, Philosophy and Critique* (Routledge & Kegan Paul, London, 1980), pp. 153–64, 175–80; John Brenkmann, *Culture and Domination* (Cornell University Press, Ithaca, 1987), pp. 26–56; Rudiger Bubner, 'Theory and practice in light of the hermeneutic-criticist controversy', *Cultural Hermeneutics* 2 (1975): 337–52 (this essay is followed by commentary by Thomas Blakeley, Thomas McCarthy, and Gadamer and a panel discussion [pp. 353–77]); David J. Depew, 'The Habermas-Gadamer debate in Hegelian perspective', *Philosophy and Social Criticism* 8 (1981): 426–46; Anthony Giddens, *Studies in Social and Political Theory* (Hutchinson, London, 1977), pp. 135–64; Alan R. How, 'Dialogue as productive limitation in social theory: the Habermas-Gadamer debate', *Journal of the British Society for Phenomenology* 11 (1980): 131–43; David Couzens Hoy, *The Critical Circle: Literature, History and Philosophical Hermeneutics* (University of California Press, Berkeley, 1978), pp. 117–30; David Ingram, 'The historical genesis of the Gadamer-Habermas controversy', *Auslegung* 10 (1983): 86–151; Martin Jay, 'Should intellectual history take a linguistic turn? Reflections on the Habermas-Gadamer debate', in Dominick LaCapra and Steven L. Kaplan (eds) *Modern European Intellectual History: Reappraisals and New Perspectives* (Cornell University Press, Ithaca, 1982), pp. 86–110; Thomas McCarthy, *The Critical Theory of Jürgen Habermas* (MIT Press, Cambridge, Mass., 1978), pp. 169–93; Jack Mendelson, 'The Habermas-Gadamer debate', *New German Critique* 18 (Fall 1979): 44–73; Dieter Misgeld, 'Discourse and conversation: the theory of communicative competence and hermeneutics in the light of the debate between Habermas and Gadamer', *Cultural Hermeneutics* 4 (1977): 321–44; Paul Ricoeur, 'Ethics and culture: Habermas and Gadamer in dialogue', *Philosophy Today* 17 (1973): 153–65, and 'Hermeneutics and the critique of ideology', in John B. Thompson (ed. and trans.) *Hermeneutics*

Jürgen Habermas

and the Human Sciences (Cambridge University Press, Cambridge, 1981), pp. 63–100; John B. Thompson, *Critical Hermeneutics: A Study in the Thought of Paul Ricoeur and Jürgen Habermas* (Cambridge University Press, Cambridge, 1981), pp. 66–8, 118–20, 163–70; and Albrecht Wellmer, *Critical Theory of Society* (Seabury, New York, 1974), pp. 31–51.

3 Martin Heidegger, *Sein und Zeit* (Klostermann, Frankfurt, 1927); *Being and Time*, trans. John Macquarrie and Edward Robinson (Basic Books, New York, 1962).

4 Immanuel Kant, *Critique of Pure Reason*, trans. Norman Kemp Smith (Macmillan, London, 1933).

5 'Das Sein selber ist Zeit.' Hans-Georg Gadamer, *Wahrheit und Methode: Grundzüge einer philosophischen Hermeneutik*, 4th edn (Mohr, Tübingen, 1972), p. 243; *Truth and Method*, trans. Garrett Barden and John Cumming (Continuum, New York, 1975), p. 228.

6 For an excellent recent study of Gadamer's *Truth and Method*, see Joel C. Weinsheimer, *Gadamer's Hermeneutics: A Reading of Truth and Method* (Yale University Press, New Haven, 1985). The most recent treatment of general themes of Gadamer to appear in English is Georgia Warnke's *Gadamer: Hermeneutics, Tradition and Reason* (Stanford University Press, Stanford, 1987). For the history of hermeneutics see two English readers on the subject: Kurt Müller-Vollmer (ed.) *The Hermeneutics Reader* (Continuum, New York, 1988); and Gayle L. Ormiston and Alan D. Schrift (eds) *The Hermeneutic Tradition: From Ast to Ricoeur* (SUNY Press, Albany, 1989), which collects for the first time all the major English-language texts in the Gadamer-Habermas debate.

7 'Sinn ist das durch Vorhabe, Vorsicht und Vorgriff strukturierte Woraufhin des Entwurfs, aus dem her etwas als etwas verständlich wird.' Heidegger, *Sein und Zeit*, p. 151; *Being and Time*, p. 193.

8 Gadamer's use of 'prejudice' raises more serious problems than those arising from a reflex reaction to his infelicitous, albeit deliberate, choice of words. A central difficulty, which Habermas raises in a slightly different context, is how to distinguish legitimate from illegitimate prejudices or false prejudices from the true variety. Gadamer indicates at various points that false and illegitimate prejudices cause misunderstanding. By conceding this point, however, it is difficult to see what separates Gadamer's requirement for the elimination of false prejudices from the ideal propagated by the Enlightenment, against which he argues so strongly. Gadamer confounds the issue of prejudice by refusing to differentiate between its various types, or to distinguish between various levels. He should separate 'prejudice' as an ontological prestructuring that belongs to existence as such from 'prejudice' as a pyschological predisposition or 'prejudice' as an epistemological precondition for cognition. But this distinction is never clearly maintained. Instead he suggests at various points that individual prejudices can be separated from those belonging to an epoch, and that only the latter are valid or admissible in that they are a *sine qua non*

for understanding. At another point he makes a similar distinction between prejudices that become conscious during interpretation and those that do not. 'Productive prejudices' enable understanding while prejudices that hinder understanding lead to misunderstanding. This somewhat circular manner of arguing weakens the original Heideggerian notions, which remain more consistently ontological. The reason why Gadamer does not make an effort to draw his distinctions more sharply is not difficult to understand. To do so he would need a metatheory of interpretation. He would either fall into the same enlightenment snare that he tries to avoid in proposing an objective science for evaluating prejudices, or have to embrace the absurdly relativist position that all prejudices, as part of our finite existence, are equally valid.

Finally, the very notion that the Enlightenment ideal of eliminating prejudice is a prejudice is itself subject to a similar claim from anyone who takes Gadamer seriously. If we accept the contention concerning the historicity of *Dasein*, then Gadamer too is bound and 'prejudiced' in his dealing with Enlightenment. There is no absolute or objective vantage point from which he can make a judgment about the prejudiced nature of the Enlightenment's ideals. Gadamer is aware of this contradition. He recognizes the performative contradiction in his position, namely that his theory cannot be subject to the very premises it propounds. He cannot postulate relativity without conceding the relativity of his own statements. His defense against critics who would turn his hermeneutics back upon itself is that formal refutation does not necessarily destroy the truth value of an argument. This may be true, but in denying formal logic, Gadamer gives his reader no method to check the validity of his claims. We are compelled either to reject his theory or accept it on trust.

9 See Hans Robert Jauss, *Toward an Aesthetic of Reception*, Theory and History of Literature, vol. 2 (University of Minnesota Press, Minneapolis, 1982).

10 Gadamer, *Truth and Method*, p. 269.

11 ibid., p. 271.

12 ibid.

13 See Roman Ingarden, *Das literarische Kunstwerk* (Niemeyer, Tübingen, 1930); *The Literary Work of Art*, trans. George G. Grabowicz (Northwestern University Press, Evanston, 1973); and *Vom Erkennen des literarischen Kunstwerks* (Niemeyer, Tübingen, 1968); *The Cognition of the Literary Work of Art*, trans. Ruth Ann Crowly and Kenneth R. Olson (Northwestern University Press, Evanston, 1973).

14 Jürgen Habermas, *Zur Logik der Sozialwissenschaften* (Suhrkamp, Frankfurt, 1970). In 1982 Suhrkamp published an expanded edition that included several additional essays, among them Habermas's essay on Niklas Luhmann discussed in Chapter 5. The course of the debate is now somewhat easier to follow because the major contributions are collected in *Hermeneutic und Ideologiekritik* (Suhr-

kamp, Frankfurt, 1971) and in *The Hermeneutic Tradition: From Ast to Ricoeur*. Habermas's review of Gadamer's *Wahrheit und Methode* in his *Zur Logik der Sozialwissenschaften* (Suhrkamp, Frankfurt, 1970) occasioned a reply by Gadamer entitled *Rhetorik, Hermeneutik und Ideologiekritik*, which appeared in the first volume of his *Kleine Schriften* (Mohr, Tübingen) in 1967. Habermas's answer, 'Die Universalitätsanspruch der Hermeneutik', which actually dealt with more than just Gadamer's response, appeared in *Hermeneutik und Dialektik*, a Festschrift for Gadamer edited by Rüdiger Bubner, Konrad Cramer and Reiner Wiehl (Mohr, Tübingen, 1970). Gadamer's reply to this and other criticisms of his work appeared at the close of *Hermeneutik and Ideologiekritik* and in the *Nachwort* to the third and subsequent editions of *Wahrheit und Methode*. Habermas did not participate in the debate after 1970, but did comment on Gadamer again in his *Theorie des kommunikativen Handelns*, 2 vols (Suhrkamp, Frankfurt, 1981), as discussed on pp. 74–5.

15 Jürgen Habermas, 'A review of Gadamer's *Truth and Method*', in Fred R. Dallmayr and Thomas A. McCarthy (eds), *Understanding and Social Inquiry* (University of Notre Dame Press, Notre Dame, 1977), pp. 335–63; here, p. 339. Subsequent page references to this review will be noted parenthetically.

16 This position is more fully developed by Apel in *Transformation der Philosophie*, vol. 1 (Suhrkamp, Frankfurt, 1973).

17 Hans-Georg Gadamer, 'On the scope and function of hermeneutical reflection', in David E. Linge (trans.) *Philosophical Hermeneutics* (University of California Press, Berkeley, 1976), pp. 18–43; here, p. 35. A good deal of this essay is a reply to Habermas's critique.

18 Or, as Gadamer puts it, reality does not happen behind the back of language, but rather *within* language ('Scope and function', p. 35).

19 ibid., p. 33.

20 ibid., p. 34. I have altered the translation slightly to avoid inaccuracies.

21 The German text 'Die Universalitätsanspruch der Hermeneutik', in *Hermeneutik und Ideologiekritik*, pp. 120–59, appears in *The Hermeneutic Tradition: From Ast to Ricoeur*, pp. 245–72 and in Josef Bleicher, *Contemporary Hermeneutics: Hermeneutics as Method, Philosophy and Critique* (Routledge & Kegan Paul, London, 1980), pp. 181–211. Parenthetical citations refer to the latter English version.

22 The sections of the German text that relate to issues Habermas brought up appear as 'Reply to my critics', in *The Hermeneutic Tradition: From Ast to Ricoeur*, pp. 273–97.

23 ibid., p. 288.

24 Jürgen Habermas, *The Theory of Communicative Action* vol. 1, *Reason and the Rationalization of Society*, trans. Thomas McCarthy (Beacon Press, Boston, 1984), p. 134.

25 ibid., pp. 135–6.

26 Ricoeur has commented at length on the Gadamer-Habermas dispute in an essay, 'Hermeneutics and the critique of ideology',

most readily available in *The Hermeneutic Tradition: From Ast to Ricoeur*, pp. 298–334; originally 'Herméneutique et critique des idéologies', in Enrico Castelli (ed.) *Démythisation et idéologie* (Aubier Montaigne, Paris, 1973), pp. 25–64.

27 Paul Ricoeur, *Freud and Philosophy: An Essay on Interpretation*, trans. Denis Savage (Yale University Press, New Haven, 1970), pp. 28–30.

28 ibid., pp. 32–6.

29 See Ricoeur, 'Hermeneutics and the critique of ideology', pp. 321–33.

4 DEMOCRACY AND THE STUDENT MOVEMENT: THE DEBATE WITH THE LEFT

1 *Zur Logik der Sozialwissenschaften* originally appeared as Beiheft 5 in the *Philosophischer Rundschau* in February 1967; it was republished as a separate volume by Suhrkamp in 1970. Habermas's 'Die Universalitätsanspruch der Hermeneutik' appeared in Rüdiger Bubner, Konrad Cramer, and Reiner Wiehl (eds), *Hermeneutik und Dialektik* (Mohr, Tübingen, 1970), pp. 73–104.

2 For an introduction to the student movement, see Gerhard Bauß, *Die Studentenbewegungen der sechziger Jahre in der Bundesrepublik und Westberlin* (Pahl-Rugenstein, Cologne, 1977); Margareth Kukuck, *Student und Klassenkampf: Studentenbewegung in der BRD seit 1967* (Verlag Association, Hamburg, 1977); Karl-Heinz Lehnardt and Ludger Volmer, *Politik zwischen Kopf und Bauch: Zur Relevanz der Persönlichkeitsbildung in den politischen Konzepten der Studentenbewegung in der BRD* (Druckladen Verlag, Bochum, 1979); and Frank Wolff and Eberhard Windaus (eds) *Studentenbewegung 1967–69: Protokolle und Materialien* (Verlag Roter Stern, Frankfurt, 1977).

3 Peter Dews (ed.) *Habermas: Autonomy and Solidarity: Interviews with Jürgen Habermas* (Verso, London, 1986), p. 80.

4 ibid., p. 78.

5 See the first essays in *Protestbewegung und Hochschulreform* (Suhrkamp, Frankfurt, 1969). All of Habermas's major statements on the university and on the student movement are collected here. Parenthetical references in this chapter will refer to this text.

6 See Bauß, *Studentenbewegungen*, pp. 44–68; and Uwe Bergmann *et al. Rebellion der Studenten oder Die neue Opposition* (Rowohlt, Hamburg, 1968), pp. 7–32.

7 Rudi Dutschke, *Geschichte ist machbar: Texte über das herrschende Falsche und die Radikalität des Friedens* (Wagenbach, Berlin, 1980), p. 76. This volume collects various political speeches and writings by Dutschke from the 1960s and 1970s.

8 For a more lengthy view of Dutschke's views on the student movement and war, see his contributions to the Bergmann collection, *Rebellion der Studenten*, pp. 33–93. In six months this volume went through eight printings and sold over 150,000 copies.

9 Dews, *Autonomy and Solidarity*, p. 80.

10 In his theses Habermas refers to 'Studenten und Schüler'. In German this clearly designates students in high schools as well as those studying at universities.

11 *The Structural Transformation of the Public Sphere: An Inquiry into a Category of Bourgeois Society*, trans. Thomas Burger with the assistance of Frederick Lawrence (MIT Press, Cambridge, Mass., 1989). Jürgen Habermas, *Legitimation Crisis*, trans. Thomas McCarthy (Beacon, Boston, 1975), p. 134.

12 Oskar Negt, 'Einleitung', in *Die Linke antwortet Jürgen Habermas* (Europäische Verlagsanstalt, Frankfurt, 1968), p. 32.

13 Klaus Dörner, 'Über den Gebrauch klinischer Begriffe in der politischen Diskussion', in *Die Linke*, pp. 59–69.

14 Claus Offe, 'Kapitalismus – Analyse als Selbsteinschüchterung', in *Die Linke*, pp. 108–9.

15 Furio Cerutti, 'Ein Brief an Jürgen Habermas', in *Die Linke*, p. 44.

16 Anselm Neusüss, 'Praxis und Theorie', in *Die Linke*, pp. 49–50.

17 Peter Brückner, 'Die Geburt der Kritik aus dem Geist des Gerüchts', in *Die Linke*, pp. 72–4.

18 Herbert Lederer, 'Revolutionäre Strategie und liberales Maklertum', in *Die Linke*, p. 114.

19 Ekkehart Krippendorff, 'Zum Verhältnis zwischen Inhalt und Form von Demonstrationstechniken', in *Die Linke*, pp. 164, 169.

20 Reimut Reiche, 'Verteidigung der "neuen Sensibilität" ', in *Die Linke*, pp. 102–3.

21 Neusüss, 'Praxis', pp. 54–5.

22 Negt, 'Einleitung', pp. 17–32.

23 Karl Marx and Friedrich Engels, *Marx Engels Werke* (Dietz Verlag, Berlin, 1972), vol. 22, p. 298.

24 ibid., vol. 13, pp. 7–11.

25 Tom Rockmore, *Habermas on Historical Materialism* (Indiana University Press, Bloomington, 1989).

26 Quoted in Jürgen Habermas, *Communication and the Evolution of Society*, trans. Thomas McCarthy, (Beacon Press, Boston, 1979), p. 98. Chapters 2–5 contain four of the key essays found in *Zur Rekonstruktion des Historischen Materialismus* (Suhrkamp, Frankfurt, 1976.)

27 Jürgen Habermas, *Technik und Wissenschaft als 'Ideologie'* (Suhrkamp, Frankfurt, 1968).

28 *Communication and the Evolution of Society*, p. 136.

29 ibid.

30 ibid., p. 102.

31 ibid., p. 116.

32 In the essay 'Moral development and ego identity' (pp. 69–94 of *Communication and the Evolution of Society*) Habermas describes a scheme of ego development and its relationship to his theory of communicative action in more detail. This essay also relies heavily on the work of Lawrence Kohlberg.

33 *Communication and the Evolution of Society*, p. 120.

5 SYSTEMS AND SOCIETY: THE DEBATE WITH NIKLAS LUHMANN

1 Jürgen Habermas and Niklas Luhmann, *Theorie der Gesellschaft oder Sozialtechnologie* (Suhrkamp, Frankfurt, 1971), p. 169. This volume contains the central essays in the Habermas-Luhmann exchange and will be cited parenthetically in this chapter.

2 Franz Maciejewski (ed.) *Theorie der Gesellschaft oder Sozialtechnologie: Beiträge zur Habermas-Luhmann-Diskussion* (Suhrkamp, Frankfurt, 1973); Franz Maciejewski (ed.) *Theorie der Gesellschaft oder Sozialtechnologie: Neue Beiträge zur Habermas-Luhmann-Diskussion* (Suhrkamp, Frankfurt, 1974); Hans Joachem Giegel, *Theorie der Gesellschaft oder Sozialtechnologie: Beitrag zur Habermas-Luhmann-Diskussion: System und Krise* (Suhrkamp, Frankfurt, 1975).

3 Niklas Luhmann, *Soziologische Aufklärung: Aufsätze zur Theorie sozialer Systeme* (Westdeutscher Verlag, Cologne, 1970). Subsequently three other volumes of Luhmann's work have appeared under this generic title.

4 Niklas Luhmann, 'Interaction, organization, and society', in Stephen Holmes and Charles Larmore (trans.) *The Differentiation of Society* (Columbia University Press, New York, 1982), p. 70.

5 Jürgen Habermas, *Zur Logik der Sozialwissenschaften* (Suhrkamp, Frankfurt, 1970).

6 ibid., p. 74.

7 See John McCarthy, *The Critical Theory of Jürgen Habermas* (MIT Press, Cambridge, Mass., 1978), p. 223.

8 Jean Piaget, *Structuralism*, trans. Chaninah Maschler (Routledge, London, 1971), pp. 5–16.

9 Some statements by Saussure with regard to *langue* might make him appear a precursor of 'anti-humanism'. Saussure writes, for example, in his *Course in General Linguistics*, trans. Wade Baskin (McGraw-Hill, New York, 1966): 'Language is not a function of the speaker; it is a product that is passively assimilated by the individual.' The passivity of the subject in the face of language, however, is complemented in the next paragraph by the following assertion: 'Speaking, on the contrary, is an individual act. It is willful and intellectual' (p. 14). Only the one-sided Parisian appropriation of Saussure has been able to ignore his affirmation of individuality and the (partial) autonomy of the subject.

10 Foucault, *The Order of Things* (Random House, New York, 1970), pp. 386–7.

11 Saussure, *Course*, p. 120.

12 'All identity constitutes itself through negation' (p. 60).

13 For a brief introduction in English to Luhmann's general terminology, see Peter Beyer's introduction to Luhmann's *Religious Dogmatics and the Evolution of Societies* (Edwin Mellen Press, New York, 1984), pp. v-liii; and the translators' introduction to *The Differentiation of Society*, pp. xiii-xxxvii.

14 Despite its popularity, the Habermas-Luhmann debate has not

attracted a great deal of attention in the English-speaking world. Useful commentary in English is provided by Peter H. Merkl, 'Trends in German political science: a review essay', *American Political Science Review* 71 (1977): 1097–108, esp. pp. 1100–3; and Friedrich W. Sixel, 'The problem of sense: Habermas v. Luhmann', in John O'Neill (ed.) *On Critical Theory* (Seabury Press, New York, 1976), pp. 184–204.

15 Niklas Luhmann, 'The differentiation of society', *Canadian Journal of Sociology* 2 (1977) 29–53; here p. 33.

16 Luhmann, *The Differentiation of Society*, p. 263.

17 Jürgen Habermas, *Legitimation Crisis*, trans. Thomas McCarthy (Beacon Press, Boston, 1975), p. 134.

18 ibid., p. 135.

19 ibid., p. 136.

20 ibid., p. 140.

21 Jürgen Habermas, *Philosophical Discourse of Modernity*, trans. Frederick Lawrence (MIT Press, Cambridge, Mass., 1987), p. 385.

22 How much Habermas depends on systems theory can be best seen in *The Theory of Communicative Action*, where the critical discussion of Parsons and Luhmann by no means detracts from their usefulness for a social theory. Habermas opposes the universalization of the systems theoretical approach, but adopts much of this theory to analyze economic and political administration.

6 MODERNITY AND POSTMODERNITY: THE DEBATE WITH JEAN-FRANÇOIS LYOTARD

1 Jürgen Habermas, *Philosophical Discourse of Modernity*, trans. Frederick Lawrence (MIT Press, Cambridge, Mass., 1987), p. 368. Niklas Luhmann, *Soziale Systeme: Grundriss einer allgemeinen Theorie* (Suhrkamp, Frankfurt, 1984).

2 The German text of this speech with the title 'Die Moderne – ein unvollendetes Projekt' (Modernity – an incompleted project) was first published in the newspaper *Die Zeit* on 19 September 1980. A slightly modified version appeared in *Kleine Politische Schriften I–IV* (Suhrkamp, Frankfurt, 1981), pp. 444–64; an English translation with the more confrontational title 'Modernity versus postmodernity' appeared in *New German Critique* 22 (1981): 3–14. In this section parenthetical citations refer to the English text.

3 See Jürgen Habermas, *The Theory of Communicative Action* vol. 2, *Lifeworld and System: A Critique of Functionalist Reason*, trans. Thomas McCarthy (Beacon Press, Boston, 1989), pp. 332–73.

4 Immanuel Kant, *Critique of Judgement*, trans. James Creed Meredith (Clarendon Press, Oxford, 1952).

5 Peter Bürger, *Theory of the Avant-Garde* (University of Minnesota Press, Minneapolis, 1984).

6 Peter Weiss, *Ästhetik des Widerstands* (3 vols, Suhrkamp, Frankfurt, 1975–81).

7 Manfred Frank, *Was ist Neostruktutalismus?* (Suhrkamp, Frankfurt, 1984), pp. 104–15.

8 Jean-François Lyotard, *The Postmodern Condition: A Report on Knowledge*, trans. Geoff Bennington and Brian Massumi (University of Minnesota Press, Minneapolis, 1984), p. xxv. Parenthetical references in this section and the next two sections are from this book.

9 Manfred Frank, *Die Grenzen der Verständigung: Ein Geistergespräch zwischen Lyotard und Habermas* (Suhrkamp, Frankfurt, 1988), esp. pp. 63–4.

10 In *Die Grenzen der Verständigung*, Frank develops the notion of performative contradiction in Lyotard in his discussion of his book *Le Différend* (1983); *The Different: Phrases in Dispute*, (University of Minnesota Press, Minneapolis, 1988).

11 These are obviously not the only two metanarratives. In the introduction Lyotard mentions the hermeneutics of meaning and the accumulation of wealth as 'grand narratives' as well (p. xxiii).

12 Ludwig Wittgenstein, *Werkausgabe* (Suhrkamp, Frankfurt, 1984), vol. 1, p. 245.

13 The reception of art by workers in the novel, which is seen as exemplary by Habermas, includes several works of modernist, experimental art.

14 Rorty's essay, 'Habermas and Lyotard on postmodernity' (pp. 161–75), and Habermas's response, 'Questions and counterquestions' (pp. 192–216) can be found in Richard J. Bernstein (ed.) *Habermas and Modernity* (MIT Press, Cambridge, Mass., 1985).

15 Parenthetical citations in this and the following section are taken from *The Philosophical Discourse of Modernity*, trans. Frederick Lawrence (MIT Press, Cambridge, Mass., 1987).

16 See Jacques Derrida, *Limited Inc* (Northwestern University Press, Evanston, 1988), pp. 156–8.

17 Jürgen Habermas, *Die neue Unübersichtlichkeit* (Suhrkamp, Frankfurt, 1985).

7 NATIONAL SOCIALISM AND THE HOLOCAUST: THE DEBATE WITH THE HISTORIANS

1 Jürgen Habermas, 'Entsorgung der Vergangenheit', *Die Zeit*, 17 May 1985.

2 See Geoffrey Hartman (ed.) *Bitburg in Moral and Political Perspective* (Indiana University Press, Bloomington, 1986).

3 Jürgen Habermas, *Die neue Unübersichtlichkeit* (Suhrkamp, Frankfurt, 1985), p. 267.

4 See Hermann Lübbe, 'Der Nationalsozialismus im deutschen Nachkriegsbewusstsein', *Historische Zeitschrift* 236 (1983): 579–99.

5 Lübbe's thesis is thus critical of the psychological interpretation – stated most elegantly by the Mitscherlichs in *Die Unfähigkeit zu trauern* (1967; *The Inability to Mourn*) – that claims the Germans repressed their guilt after the war and devoted their energies to rebuilding their country. Margarete Mitscherlich-Nielsen defends

this thesis by pointing out that what was repressed were not the facts of National Socialism, but feelings, ideals, deeds, and mechanisms of accommodation. See Alexander Mitscherlich and Margarete Mitscherlich, *Die Unfähigkeit zu trauern: Grundlagen kollektiven Verhaltens* (Piper, Munich, 1967); and Margarete Mitscherlich-Nielsen, *Reden über das eigene Land: Deutschland 3* (Bertelsmann, Munich, 1985), pp. 59–77.

6 Among the more recent volumes on this subject is Jörg Friedrich, *Die Kalte Amnestie: NS-Täter in der Bundesrepublik* (Fischer, Frankfurt, 1985). The involvement of former National Socialists in the affairs of state in the Federal Republic is a topic that has been discussed by writers from various countries since the 1950s.

7 Jürgen Habermas, *Eine Art Schadensabwicklung* (Suhrkamp, Frankfurt, 1987), pp. 120–36.

8 See Charles Maier, *The Unmasterable Past* (Harvard University Press, Cambridge, Mass., 1988), pp. 43–6.

9 The major texts in the historians' debate have been collected in *'Historikerstreit': Die Dokumentation der Kontroverse um die Einzigartigkeit der nationalsozialistischen Judenvernichtung* (Piper, Munich, 1987), and for convenience parenthetical citations will refer to this collection.

10 See Maier, *The Unmasterable Past*, p. 23.

11 ibid., p. 24.

12 Andreas Hillgruber, *Zweierlei Untergang: Die Zerschlagung des Deutschen Reiches und das Ende des europäischen Judentums* (Seidler, Berlin, 1986), p. 24. Hillgruber has slightly altered the phrasing of his original talk, which was published separately as *Der Zusammenbruch im Osten 1944/45 als Problem der deutschen Nationalgeschichte und der europäischen Geschichte* (Westdeutscher Verlag, Opladen, 1985). In the original passage (p. 11) he takes a swipe at the GDR and at those writers in the Federal Republic who advocate seeing the end of the war as a 'liberation'.

13 Hillgruber, *Zweierlei Untergang*, p. 24. Again Hillgruber reworked this passage slightly for publication in 1986.

14 ibid.

15 Habermas, *Eine Art Schadensabwicklung*, pp. 124–5.

16 Ernst Nolte, *Three Faces of Fascism*, trans. Leila Vennewitz (Weidenfeld & Nicolson, London, 1965).

17 Nolte suggests this in a letter to *Die Zeit* of 1 August 1986, reprinted in *'Historikerstreit'*, pp. 93–4.

18 Habermas, *Eine Art Schadensabwicklung*, p. 131.

19 Ernst Nolte, 'Between myth and revisionism? The Third Reich in the perspective of the 1980s', in H. W. Koch (ed.) *Aspects of the Third Reich* (Macmillan, London, 1985), pp. 19–38.

20 ibid., p. 35.

21 ibid., pp. 36–7.

22 ibid., p. 28.

23 Jürgen Kocka cleared up the inaccuracies in Nolte's hasty account in 'Hitler sollte nicht durch Stalin und Pol Pot verdrängt werden',

an article that originally appeared in the liberal *Frankfurter Rundschau*, and is reprinted in '*Historikerstreit*', pp. 132–42. Weizmann
was President of the World Zionist Organization, 1929–31 and
1935–46. The Jewish Agency represented the World Zionist Organization for Palestine, which was under British authority at the
time. As Kocka points out, the offer to fight alongside the British,
and in fact the entire letter, has to be seen in the context of
the relationship of the Jewish Agency and the British governing
authorities in Palestine.

24 Nolte, 'Between myth', p. 36.
25 Habermas, *Eine Art Schadensabwicklung*, p. 131.
26 Besides the volume '*Historikerstreit*', the most important essays and
discussions of the 'historians' debate' are contained in the following volumes: Dan Diner (ed.) *Ist der Nationalsozialismus Geschichte?:
Zu Historisierung und Historikerstreit* (Fischer, Frankfurt, 1987); Rein-
hard Kuehnl (ed.) *Vergangenheit die nicht vergeht: Die Historiker-
Debatte: Dokumentation, Darstellung und Kritik* (Rugenstein, Cologne,
1987); Hilmar Hoffmann (ed.) *Gegen den Versuch, Vergangenheit zu
verbiegen* (Athenäum, Frankfurt, 1987); Imanuel Geiss, *Die Habermas-Kontroverse* (Seidler, Berlin, 1988); and Eike Henning, *Zum
Historikerstreit: Was heißt und zu welchem Ende studiert man Faschismus*
(Athenäum, Frankfurt, 1988). These issues are treated admirably
in English by Charles Maier. The best discussion of Habermas's
position in the debate is John Torpey's 'Introduction: Habermas
and the historians', *New German Critique* 15, no. 44 (1988): 5–24.
In the same issue of *New German Critique*, which is devoted to the
historian's debate, Habermas's first two contributions to the debate
appear in English translation: 'A kind of settlement of damages'
(pp. 25–39) and 'Concerning the public use of history' (pp. 40–50).
I have consulted these translations throughout this chapter.
27 Geiss, *Die Habermas-Kontroverse*, pp. 49–52.
28 Habermas, *Eine Art Schadensabwicklung*, p. 124. The passage in
question precedes Habermas's remarks about Hillgruber: 'As
someone without specialist qualifications, I only dare to approach
the recent work of this celebrated modern historian because the
study entitled *Zweierlei Untergang*, which appeared in a bibliophile
edition in the lists of Wolf Jobst Siedler, is obviously aimed at the
layman.' Only a complete lack of acquaintance with Habermas's
theories or the blindness of rage can explain how these historians
could miss the irony and take such a statement at face value.
29 Geiss, *Die Habermas-Kontroverse*, pp. 48–85, 190–3.
30 He did this at the end of the volume '*Historikerstreit*' (pp. 383–6)
and in a short piece entitled 'Nachspiel' included in *Eine Art
Schadensabwicklung* (pp. 149–58).
31 Habermas, *Eine Art Schadensabwicklung*, p. 165.
32 ibid., p. 135.
33 ibid., p. 168.
34 ibid., pp. 168–9.
35 ibid., p. 135.

36 Karl Jaspers, *Die Schuldfrage: Ein Beitrag zur deutschen Frage* (Artemis, Zurich, 1946); *The Question of German Guilt*, trans. E. B. Ashton (Capricorn Books, New York, 1947).

37 Kohl's phrase for this was the 'Gnade der späten Geburt' (the grace of late birth). Habermas has consistently claimed that Kohl and other leading members of the conservative coalition have sought to exonerate Germany illicitly from responsibility for National Socialism.

38 Habermas, *Eine Art Schadensabwicklung*, p. 140.

39 See 'Moral development and ego identity', in Jürgen Habermas, *Communication and the Evolution of Society*, trans. Thomas McCarthy (Beacon Press, Boston, 1979), pp. 69–94; esp. pp. 78–80.

40 See *The Theory of Communicative Action* vol. 2, *Lifeworld and System: A Critique of Functionalist Reason*, trans. Thomas McCarthy (Beacon Press, Boston, 1989), p. 174.

41 See Herbert Marcuse, 'Gegen die Aufrechnung des Leidens' (letters to Martin Heidegger of 28 August 1947 and 13 May 1948), *Pflasterstrand* 209 (4–17 May 1985): 43–4.

42 Jürgen Habermas, 'Der DM-Nationalismus: Weshalb es richtig ist, die deutsche Einheit nach Artikel 146 zu vollziehen, also einen Volksentscheid über eine neue Verfassung anzustreben', *Die Zeit* (30 March 1990), p. 63.

Index

Adenauer, Konrad 16, 172
Adorno, Theodor W. 8, 16, 20–2,
  25–30, 33, 38, 40, 42, 46, 47, 49,
  87, 107, 115, 158, 180; *Dialektik
  der Aufklärung* [*Dialectic of
  Enlightenment*] 7–8, 33–4, 80,
  155
Albert, Hans 10, 18, 20, 22, 30,
  38–40, 41, 46, 47–8, 73
Apel, Karl-Otto 10, 64, 74, 152
application (*Anwendung*) 59–60,
  63–4, 75
Aspects of the Third Reich (Koch)
  173
Ast, Friedrich 50
Ästhetik des Widerstands
  ['Aesthetics of Resistance']
  (Weiss) 137–8, 150
Austin, J. L. 13–14
authority 60, 65, 68–9

Bataille, Georges 139, 155
Baudelaire, Charles 134, 150
Benn, Gottfried 138
Bildzeitung 80
Bitburg 162–3, 165, 166, 172, 180
Bormann, Claus von 74
Brecht, Bert(olt) 89
Broszat, Martin 174
Brückner, Peter 97
Bubner, Rüdiger 74
Bultmann, Rudolf 75–6
Bürger, Peter 136
Burke, Edmund 65

Carnap, Rudolf 34
Cerutti, Furio 96
Chamberlain, Neville 175
Christian Democratic Union
  (CDU) 79, 185
communicative action 8, 10, 15,
  104, 122, 124, 129, 139, 161
Communist Manifesto (Marx and
  Engels) 84–5
Comte, Auguste 20
La Condition postmoderne [*The
  Postmodern Condition*]
  (Lyotard) 139–51
critique of ideology
  (*Ideologiekritik*) 66, 67, 70, 72, 74,
  76, 77
Culler, Jonathan 158

dadaism 134
Dahrendorf, Ralf 22
deconstruction 156–8
Deleuze, Gilles 139
depth hermeneutics 71–2, 76
Derrida, Jacques 133, 139, 152,
  153, 156–8, 160
Descartes, René 26, 54, 76
Dialektik der Aufklärung [*Dialectic
  of Enlightenment*] (Adorno and
  Horkheimer) 7–8, 33–4, 80, 155
Diderot, Denis 151
Dilthey, Wilhelm 12, 26, 31, 49,
  51, 52, 54, 55–6, 63
Diner, Dan 186
Dörner, Klaus 95

Droysen, Johann Gustav 55
Durkheim, Emile 133
Dutschke, Rudi 83–5, 86, 88, 89, 92, 99

economic miracle
(Wirtschaftswunder) 78
effective history
(Wirkungsgeschichte) 58, 62–3
Engels, Friedrich 99; Communist
Manifesto 84–5; Socialism:
Utopian and Scientific 99–100
Enlightenment 4, 5, 8, 57, 60, 65,
66, 136–9, 146–7, 149, 152, 153,
155–6, 159, 178, 182
Erkenntnis und Interesse
[Knowledge and Human
Interests] (Habermas) 8–10, 12,
29, 36, 37, 45
extra-parliamentary opposition
(APO) 79

falsification 23, 36, 43
Farias, Victor: Heidegger et le
nazisme 17
Fascism 8, 34, 93, 98, 145, 171,
174; see also National Socialism
Fest, Joachim 177, 179
Feyerabend, Paul 54
Fichte, Johann Gottlieb 153
Foucault, Michel 133, 139, 152,
153, 155, 158; The Order of
Things 112–13
Fourier, Charles 85
Frank, Manfred 142; Was ist
Neostrukturalismus? [What is
Neostructuralism?] 139
Frankfurt School 7, 8, 25, 26–7,
29, 42, 46, 73, 99, 101, 121, 145,
152
Frankfurter Allgemeine Zeitung
(FAZ) 16, 166, 177
Frankfurter Rundschau 87
French Revolution 5
Freud, Sigmund 9, 71, 75, 76
Fried, Erich 86
Friedländer, Saul 186
functionalism 107–8, 114, 123

Gadamer, Hans-Georg 10, 51,
61–77, 78, 106, 152; Wahrheit
und Methode [Truth and Method]
49–50, 53–60
Galileo, Galilei 37
Gehlen, Arnold 34, 46, 117
Geiss, Imanuel 177, 178
Gervinus, Georg Gottfried 180
Giegel, Hans-Joachim 74
Grossner, C. 85
Grundrisse (Marx) 7, 76
Guattari, Félix 139

Habermas, Jürgen: debating
practices 1–2, 15–19, 188–9;
Erkenntnis und Interesse
[Knowledge and Human
Interests] 8–10, 12, 29, 36, 37,
45; on hermeneutics 60–77, 78;
and the historians' debate
165–87; Legitimationsprobleme im
Spätkapitalismus [Legitimation
Crisis] 87, 130–2, 149; Die neue
Unübersichtlichkeit ['The New
Impenetrability'] 161, 162; and
politics 1–2, 15, 17–18, 46–7, 48,
65–6, 73–7, 81–94, 115, 122–9,
130–2, 157, 160–1, 188–9; Der
philosophische Diskurs der
Moderne [The Philosophical
Discourse of Modernity] 131,
133, 152–61; and the positivist
debate 20–2, 29–38, 39, 40,
41–5, 46–8; and postmodernity
139–61; Strukturwandel der
Öffentlichkeit [Structural
Transformation of the Public
Sphere] 2–8, 9, 79, 87; and the
student movement 78–98,
104–5; on systems theory
106–32; Technik und Wissenschaft
als Ideologie ['Technology and
Science as Ideology'] 101;
Theorie des kommunikativen
Handelns [The Theory of
Communicative Action] 48, 49,
74, 108, 135, 185; Zur Logik der
Sozialwissenschaften ['On the
Logic of the Social Sciences']

29, 60, 107–8; *Zur Rekonstruktion des historischen Materialismus* ['The Reconstruction of Historical Materialism'] 101
Habermas on Historical Materialism (Rockmore) 101
Hegel, Georg Friedrich Wilhelm 4, 25, 40, 42, 59, 100, 101, 121, 146, 153–5, 156; *Phänomenologie des Geistes* [*Phenomenology of the Spirit*] 5, 35
Heidegger, Martin 16–18, 46, 51, 54, 55, 57, 66, 139, 152, 156, 157, 158, 160, 170, 187, 188; *Sein und Zeit* [*Being and Time*], 52–3, 56, 77
Heidegger et le nazisme (Farias) 17
Heinemann, Gustav 184
Heller, Agnes 46
Hempel, Carl 108
Herder, Johann Gottfried 26, 51
hermeneutics 18, 29, 31, 32, 39, 40, 43, 45, 47, 48, 49–77, 108, 160, 188; ontological 51–3, 54, 65, 69, 73–4, 76–7; of the sacred 75–6; of suspicion 76
Hermeneutik und Ideologiekritik ['Hermeneutics and the Critique of Ideology'] 74
Heuss, Theodor 184
Hildebrand, Klaus 173, 177, 178, 179, 180
Hillgruber, Andreas 166, 167, 177, 178, 179, 181, 186; *Zweierlei Untergang* ['Two Kinds of Demise'] 167–70;
Himmler, Heinrich 162
historians' debate (*Historikerstreit*) 18
historical materialism 98–105, 185
Hitler, Adolf 162, 174, 175
Hochhuth, Rolf: *Der Stellvertreter* [*The Deputy*] 78
Holocaust 165, 167, 171–6, 181–2, 184, 186
horizon 58–9
Horkheimer, Max 26–7, 42, 46, 87, 107; *Dialektik der Aufklärung*

[*Dialectic of Enlightenment*] 7–8, 33–4, 80, 155
Husserl, Edmund 26, 35, 42, 52, 53, 56, 118, 133, 157

identity: 163–4; conventional 181, 185; national 182–3; postconventional 180, 185–6
Ingarden, Roman 59
Irving, David 175

Jaspers, Karl: *Die Schuldfrage* ['The Question of Guilt'] 183–4
Jauss, Hans Robert 58
Jonas, Hans 138
Joyce, James 151

Kant, Immanuel 4, 9, 26, 27, 42, 118, 133, 135, 153; *Kritik der reinen Vernunft* [*Critique of Pure Reason*] 54–5; *Kritik der Urteilskraft* [*Critique of Judgement*] 136
Das Kapital [*Capital*] (Marx) 90–1
Koch, H. W. 175; *Aspects of the Third Reich* 173
Kocka, Jürgen 186
Kohl, Helmut 165, 166
Kohlberg, Lawrence 103, 185
König, René 21
Krippendorff, Ekkehart 98
Kritik der reinen Vernunft [*Critique of Pure Reason*] (Kant) 54–5
Kritik der Urteilskraft [*Critique of Judgement*] (Kant) 136
Kuhn, Thomas S. 54

Lacan, Jacques 155
Lakatos, Imre 54
Lamumba, Patrice 81
Lederer, Herbert 97
'leftist Fascism' 84–6, 95
legitimation 87–8, 130–2, 140–1, 144, 146–7
Legitimationsprobleme im Sptkapitalismus [*Legitimation Crisis*] (Habermas) 87, 130–2, 149

Index

Letters on the Aesthetic Education (Schiller) 138
Lewalter, Christian E. 16–17
Die Linke antwortet Jürgen Habermas ['The Left Answers Jürgen Habermas] 94–8, 99
Logic of Scientific Discovery (Popper) 34–5
logical positivism 20–1, 34, 41, 42
Lorenzer, Alfred 71
Lübbe, Hermann 164–5, 174
Luhmann, Niklas 10, 18, 106–32, 133, 136, 139, 152; *Soziale Systeme* ['Social Systems'] 133; *Soziologische Aufklärung* ['Sociological Enlightenment'] 107
Lukács, Georg 101
Lyotard, Jean-François 152, 161; *La Condition postmoderne* [*The Postmodern Condition*] 139–51

Maier, Charles 167
Marcuse, Herbert 46, 87, 97, 107, 138
Marx, Karl 5–6, 9, 40, 98, 99, 101, 102, 121, 155; *Communist Manifesto* 84–5; *Grundrisse* 7, 76; *Das Kapital* [*Capital*] 90–1; *Zur Kritik der politischen Ökonomie* [*A Contribution to the Critique of Political Economy*] 100–1
modernity 133, 134–9, 143–6, 149–51, 152–61
Mommsen, Hans 186

Nagel, Ernst 108
Napoleon I (Bonaparte) 172
National Socialism 16–8, 78, 80, 81, 98, 162–6, 168–70, 171–6, 182, 184–5; *see also* Fascism
nationalism 164, 166, 181–3, 185–6, 187–8
Nationalist Party of Germany (NPD) 83
NATO 176, 183
Negt, Oskar 94, 99
neo-conservatism 18, 135, 138, 164, 165, 182

Neurath, Otto 34
Neusüss, Anselm 96, 98
Newton, Sir Isaac 37
Nietzsche, Friedrich 76, 133, 139, 146, 152, 155, 160
Nipperdey, Thomas 177, 179, 180
Nolte, Ernst 170–6, 177, 181, 186; *Three Faces of Fascism* 171

Ohnesorg, Benno 81
Offe, Claus 93–4
The Open Society and its Enemies (Popper) 32, 40
The Order of Things (Foucault) 112–13
Owen, Robert 85

Parsons, Talcott 106, 107–8, 110, 118, 133
Peirce, Charles Sanders 35, 42
Phänomenologie des Geistes [*Phenomenology of the Spirit*] (Hegel) 5, 35
phenomenology 26, 35, 42, 49, 52, 53, 56, 58, 62, 75, 133, 157, 160, 170–1
Der philosophische Diskurs der Moderne [*The Philosophical Discourse of Modernity*] (Habermas) 131, 133, 152–61
Philosophische Rundschau, 78
Philosophische Untersuchungen [*Philosophical Investigations*] (Wittgenstein) 148
Piaget, Jean 69, 103, 111
Plato 144
Pol Pot 173
Popper, Karl 12–13, 20–5, 26–9, 33–4, 36–40, 41–4, 46, 54, 73, 144, 180; *Logic of Scientific Discovery* 34–5; *The Open Society and its Enemies* 31–2, 40
positivism 20–1, 22, 25, 27, 36, 37, 41–3, 48, 51, 62, 63, 64, 73, 82, 108, 152
positivist dispute 9, 18, 20–48, 49, 61, 73, 107, 115, 179, 188
postmodernity 133, 138, 143–7, 151–3, 158–61, 182

poststructuralism 18, 133, 139, 155, 156
prejudice (*Vorurteil*) 56–7, 65
Proust, Marcel 151
psychoanalysis 70–2, 74
public sphere 3–8, 16, 87, 164, 180, 188

Ranke, Leopold von 55
Reagan, Ronald 163, 172
Reiche, Reimut 98
rhetoric 69, 142
Rickert, Heinrich 26
Ricoeur, Paul 75–6
Rockmore, Tom: *Habermas on Historical Materialism* 101
romanticism 65, 134
Rorty, Richard 152

Saint-Simon, Claude Henri de Rouvroy, Comte de 85
Sartre, Jean-Paul 33, 117
Saussure, Ferdinand de 10, 110–14
Schelling, Friedrich 4
Scheubner-Richter, Max Erwin von 172
Schiller, Friedrich: *Letters on the Aesthetic Education* 138
Schleiermacher, Friedrich 50–1, 55, 63
Schmitt, Carl 34, 138
Die Schuldfrage ['The Question of Guilt'] (Jaspers) 183–4
Schulze, Hagen 179
Schütz, Alfred 49
Searle, John 13–14
Sein und Zeit [*Being and Time*], (Heidegger) 52–3, 56, 77
Shah of Iran 81
Social Democratic Party of Germany (*SPD*) 79, 97
Socialism: Utopian and Scientific (Engels) 99–100
Socialist German Students (SDS) 79, 96–7, 99
Socrates 9
Soziale Systeme ['Social Systems'] (Luhmann) 133

Soziologische Aufklärung ['Sociological Enlightenment'] (Luhmann) 107
Spaemann, Robert 138
speech act theory 13–14, 141, 143
Der Spiegel 17, 18
Springer publishing house 80, 88, 97
Stalin, Joseph 173
Der Stellvertreter [*The Deputy*] (Hochhuth)
Strauss, Leo 138
structuralism 110–14
Strukturwandel der Öffentlichkeit [*Structural Transformation of the Public Sphere*] (Habermas) 2–8, 9, 79, 87
student movement 18, 78–98, 104–5, 106, 117, 130, 152, 164–5, 188
Stürmer, Michael 165–6, 175, 176, 178, 181, 185–6
surrealism 134, 137
systems theory 18, 106–32, 133, 188; and meaning 108–10, 118–20; and social evolution 125–9; and truth 120–1

Technik und Wissenschaft als Ideologie ['Technology and Science as Ideology'] (Habermas) 101
Theorie der Gesellschaft oder Sozialtechnologie ['Theory of Society or Social Technology'] (Habermas and Luhmann) 106–29
Theorie des kommunikativen Handelns [*The Theory of Communicative Action*] (Habermas) 48, 49, 74, 108, 135, 185
Three Faces of Fascism (Nolte) 171
Tshombé, Moïse 81

unification of Germany 187–8
universal pragmatics 10–15, 141–2

value-freedom 23, 24–5, 28–9, 33–8, 40, 44
Vico, Giambattista 12, 26, 31, 49, 51
Vienna School 20–1
Vietnam War 81, 83, 92, 97

Wahrheit und Methode [*Truth and Method*] (Gadamer) 49–50, 53–60
Was ist Neostrukturalismus? [*What is Neostructuralism?*] (Frank) 139
Weber, Max 110, 133, 135, 150
Wehler, Hans-Ulrich 186
Weiss, Peter: *Ästhetik des Widerstands* ['Aesthetics of Resistance'] 137–8, 150
Weizmann, Chaim 175
Weizsäcker, Richard von 184
Wellmer, Albrecht 137, 152
Wittgenstein, Ludwig 13, 61–2, 66, 138, 140, 148; *Philosophische Untersuchungen* [*Philosophical Investigations*] 148
World War II 162, 166–70, 175

Young Hegelians 155–7

Die Zeit 16–17, 18, 162
Zur Kritik der politischen Ökonomie [*A Contribution to the Critique of Political Economy*] (Marx) 100–1
Zur Logik der Sozialwissenschaften ['On the Logic of the Social Sciences'] (Habermas) 29, 60, 107–8
Zur Rekonstruktion des historischen Materialismus ['The Reconstruction of Historical Materialism'] (Habermas) 101
Zweierlei Untergang ['Two Kinds of Demise'] (Hillgruber) 167–70